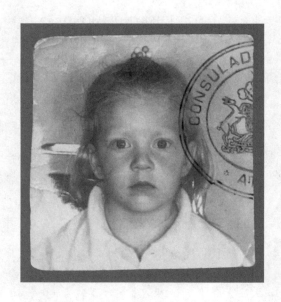

ALSO BY CHERYL DIAMOND

Naked Rome
Model, a Memoir

NOWHERE GIRL

A Memoir of a
Fugitive Childhood

CHERYL DIAMOND

ALGONQUIN BOOKS OF CHAPEL HILL 2021

Published by
Algonquin Books of Chapel Hill
Post Office Box 2225
Chapel Hill, North Carolina 27515-2225

a division of
Workman Publishing
225 Varick Street
New York, New York 10014

Grateful acknowledgment is made for permission to quote from "Gold," © Reformation
Publishing Co. Ltd, thanks to Gary Kemp/Reformation Publishing Co Ltd.

From the song "Little Boxes." Words and music by Malvina Reynolds. Copyright 1962
Schroder Music Co. (ASCAP); Renewed 1990 Used by permission. All rights reserved.

Design by Steve Godwin.

This is a work of nonfiction. Some names have been changed, and the author
has reconstructed dialogue and the time line to the best of her ability. Some minor
scenes have been compressed in the interest of space.

Library of Congress Cataloging-in-Publication Data
Names: Diamond, Cheryl, author.
Title: Nowhere girl : a memoir of a fugitive childhood / Cheryl Diamond.
Description: First edition. | Chapel Hill, North Carolina : Algonquin Books of
Chapel Hill, 2021. | Summary: "In this memoir that spans dozens of countries
worldwide, a young girl and her family adopt one new identity after another and run
from both the law and the secrets that will eventually catch up to all of them"—
Provided by publisher.
Identifiers: LCCN 2021002159 | ISBN 9781616208202 (hardcover) |
ISBN 9781643751689 (ebook)
Subjects: LCSH: Diamond, Cheryl. | Fugitives from justice—Biography. | Missing
persons—Biography. | Exiles—Biography. | Impersonation. | Family secrets.
Classification: LCC HV6762.A3 D5185 2021 | DDC 362.87092 [B]—dc23
LC record available at https://lccn.loc.gov/2021002159

10 9 8 7 6 5 4 3 2 1
First Edition

This is for the misfits.

CONTENTS

NOWHERE GIRL

PROLOGUE: Kashmir, India, age 4

MY FIRST NEAR-DEATH experience occurs at the age of four, when the brakes fail, with my dad at the wheel, sending us hurtling down the Himalayas.

I'm reclining comfortably in the backseat, high above the clouds, examining the shiny buttons on my light red dungarees. Overalls are massively underappreciated in my opinion. Depending on your mood, you don't even need an undershirt. Just pull them on, hook 'em up, and you're ready to go light up the world.

Glancing outside our car, I notice the scenery speeding by at a remarkably fast rate. To my left is my sister, Chiara, mouth agape, and beyond her, through the open window, the steep wall of dark, forbidding rock. On my right, past my brother Frank's clenched jaw, is nothing but blue sky where the narrow roadside plunges away from the mountain into nothingness.

In front sit our progenitors.

I lean forward to assess their expressions and determine how worried I should be. Mom has actually put on her seatbelt, and my father's knuckles on the wheel are showing white through his deep tan. An ancient car going in the opposite direction blasts its horn as Dad swerves close to the precipice, barely avoiding a collision.

A blind curve looms ahead, I hear the brakes being pumped and a frightening grating sound coming from the undercarriage of our car. I'm flung over sideways onto Chiara, who presses me tightly against her lap while Frank grabs for my flailing limbs and catches an ankle. For a moment there is traction and we begin to slow. I can feel Chiara's muscles relaxing, then suddenly the car lurches forward, brakes going dead, and once again we fly downward, gaining a terrifying momentum.

"There! It's flat there!" Mom yells. This must be serious; she never gives directions when Dad's driving. We careen off the paved road, bouncing uncontrollably over rocky ground, as Frank hurls his body over mine. With a metallic shriek our car abruptly fishtails, hits a hole, and comes to a shuddering, blessed stop.

Chiara relaxes her viselike hold and I sit up, coughing from the dust swirling through the open windows. We've driven directly into the center of a small village, nearly bulldozing lines of clothes hung out to dry. Surrounding us now are a few wood shacks, light brown earth, and chickens *bawk bawking* from the shock of our arrival. I can smell them from here. A goat tied to its post outside a building with a crooked red-and-white Coca-Cola sign blinks rapidly, just as surprised as we are.

The peeling sign, encouraging us to DRINK!, is the landscape's only spot of color. Like us, it looks so out of place, here on the top of the world.

Assuring Mom that we are still alive, we pile out of the offending vehicle, gulping lungfuls of thin, sweet air. From one of the houses, a boy of about sixteen—Chiara's age—approaches us, barefoot over the gravelly ground. An older man follows close behind.

I straighten my rumpled overalls; in life, it's important to make a good first impression.

The first thing I notice about the two, who appear to be father and son, is that, like so many people in Kashmir, their eyes are startlingly luminous and clear-brown. Mom says that it is because they don't play video games or watch TV. We aren't allowed these either, with the exception of checking the fluctuating price of gold on CNN. I've heard there are things called cartoons, but have never seen any hard evidence of their existence.

Through hand motions, it seems like father and son are trying to convey that the boy can fix cars, and sure enough he ducks into the hut, returning with tools and a coil of wire.

"Is that chicken wire he has?" Mom asks nervously. We all look between the chicken coop, whose occupants are still flapping their wings, and the coil on the roadside.

"Yes . . ." my father says. "Yes, it is."

The kid maneuvers his slender body under our car and within an hour has it running again. They're offended at the idea of payment, but Dad manages to slip a wad of bills into the open tool kit before gunning our free-range engine to life. To be sure the brakes will hold on the downhill slope, the boy rides behind us on his battered moped for a few kilometers, tools and chicken wire bouncing in the rear basket, just in case. We reach the next plateau without incident, and he stops his moped, bare feet on either side, his perfect smile growing smaller in the rear window as we wave exuberantly at each other.

"Now, that's customer service." Dad nods with satisfaction.

Lower down the mountain, we stop on the roadside to unwrap chapatis and bananas and celebrate still being among the living. These have become our two main food groups. As strict vegetarians, health-foodies, and constant travelers, we know there is nothing quite as magnificent as the noble banana. Us kids, sprinkled with freckles, sit on the dusty trunk of the car, our long hair wild and uncut. We are Sikhs, have been long before I was born, and never cutting our hair is part of the sacred tradition. Automatically, we recite the short prayer in Punjabi we always say before eating. Frank and I rush a little and Chiara purses her lips at us.

We are staring each other down when a rusty gray car, listing to one side from the extra men clinging to the roof, speeds past us, and all the faces turn to stare. Westerners are never seen in this region, and we must make quite a confusing picture. Parents in the front seat, doors flung wide, three kids sitting on the back. Just an average family of Sikhs. Except the father is a broad-shouldered six-foot Viking, face deeply tanned, with a head of untamed red-blond hair and a beard that touches his chest; alongside him, sharing a cup of tea from their thermos, is my mother, with her beautifully delicate profile, wide blue eyes, and slender legs crossed in form-fitting black slacks. Perched on the car are two dark-haired teenagers—Frank, startlingly handsome; Chiara, frowning as if she knows that in the eyes of the world she is obscured by his light; and then, as a much younger curveball, me. Four years old and smiling in light red dungarees, the little blonde twin of her father, and named Harbhajan Khalsa Nanak, to boot.

Personally, I quite enjoy the notoriety.

"Harbhajan, are you going to finish that?" Frank says as he reaches for the rest of my chapati. I've been savoring the bread, my face tilted up to the deep orange late-afternoon sun. There is a beautiful stillness in the soft air, the kind that only exists far from cities and civilization. Lightning fast, I curl protectively around my chapati, clutching it to my chest.

"Let her eat." Chiara shoves his shoulder with the authority of someone two years older.

"Oh shuddup." He shrugs her off, disappearing half a banana. Ever since he turned fourteen, he eats everything he can get his hands on and only grows vertically. In this, like so much else, they are opposites. And Frank reminds her of it with just a look.

Me and my chapati slide off the trunk and head toward Dad. He is standing in front of the car now, hood open, considering the engine.

"Bhajan! Excellent! Come here, I'll show you how the engine works." Leaning down, he lifts me to his chest, the ends of his beard tickling my cheek. I am assailed by twin emotions: of happiness at being held snugly in his big arms and of the dreaded realization this is going to be a long lesson. "You remember what I told you about the carburetor last time?"

My mind searches frantically but comes up blank.

"Now let's look at the pistons. Pistons compress a mixture of gas and air . . ." He pauses to put me down and retrieve the tea thermos as a prop, his enthusiasm building. I try to retain as many of his words as possible, since I know there will be pop quizzes in the future. They can be conducted any time: after a morning family Kundalini yoga session, while we are buying ghee in a market, or before our weekly half-hour silent meditation. Us three kids are homeschooled, since Dad considers all educational institutions breeding grounds for government propaganda and square-thinking bureaucrats. So we learn things on the fly. . . .

"Geography!" he'd boomed this morning, just before dawn. We had all been standing on a misty plateau, woozy from the altitude, wishing he would take us on these unexplained odysseys at a normal hour. My shoulders sagged sleepily and I stared at what looked like a bunch of clouds.

The sun rose slowly, warming my bare arms. As the mist evaporated, suddenly the sky began to open up all around us. A rare, perfect view of the Himalayas appeared, towering and powerful, as the day came to life. "There's Pakistan, and there's China." Dad pointed to the horizon beneath us, where the two countries border Kashmir. He knelt, while I gazed in awe. "That's the Earth, Harbhajan." His voice whispered against my ear, "It's yours."

Standing beside him then, I felt I could reach across the clear morning and touch the world.

"Now, WHAT DO pistons do?" Cradled against his chest, I finish my chapati and snap back to reality.

"Squish air and gas," I recite.

"Correct! Let's go." The car coughs, splutters, then wheezes back into motion, and we're on the way to Srinagar.

As night gathers around us, an open-backed army jeep swerves past, revealing two rows of solemn-faced soldiers holding guns in the rear. Kashmir has only recently been reopened to foreigners after years of bloody conflict between India and Pakistan, with troops exchanging fire at the border.

Mom is looking apprehensive and talking about turning back, but Dad points out that we're already in the soup. We can either settle by the roadside for the rest of our lives and raise chickens—with the little wire we have—or forge onward. "So what will it be, troops?"

"Onward!" the three of us chorus from the back.

Windows open to the warm, earthy air, we drive through the night. The motion of the car lulls me into my usual comalike sleep, legs thrown across Frank's lap, as we cover ground toward Kashmir's summer capital.

I wake with a start; someone is digging their fingernails into my arm. The harsh sound of voices speaking a local dialect makes me sit up, disoriented. "What's goin'—" Chiara and Frank silence me with a *shhhh*, and then both hit my shoulder for further emphasis. We aren't moving, and I become aware of two men closing in on the car, our headlights illuminating the long guns in their hands. Another appears out of the dark, leaning down to talk to Dad through the open driver's-side window. The road is deserted. My heart thumps as fat raindrops begin to fall, splattering the dust on our windshield.

The sharp beam of a flashlight makes me squint as it sweeps the back-seat, settling on each of our faces. Two soldiers, very young up close and wearing identical khaki uniforms, lift their guns, pointing them at our heads. The man talking to Dad raises his voice, as if that will help us under-stand Kashmiri, and motions for him to get out of the car. Dad makes no move toward the handle. It's part of our code to never get separated. To always, always stick together.

The soldier becomes more insistent. One of the others strides around to Mom's side, his rifle pointing at her as he walks. My stomach starts to tense, fingers digging into the cracked leather of the seat. The soldier near Dad is yelling now, reaching for the door handle. I hear Mom gasp.

Quietly, and so the soldiers don't notice, Dad changes gears.

What is he doing?

Slowly, we roll forward. The soldier screams something and Dad nods and smiles as if agreeing. Dad gives a cheerful touristy wave out the window, calls out "Thanks!" and shifts gears again. There is a moment of silent confusion behind us as our car rapidly picks up speed. I heave myself up and peek out the back window, rain hammering like bullets all around.

"Get her down," Dad yells. I'm shoved to the floor as Chiara and Frank shield me with their bodies. A knee digs into my ribs, and I try to elbow them back, shuddering with the car as it accelerates. Faster, faster . . . and we're away.

Finally I'm allowed up. We all keep glancing nervously through the rear window, expecting a gunshot or a jeep full of angry soldiers to scream after us. But the road behind us stays empty. "Holy smokes, that was a close call." Dad's voice is just above a whisper.

LUCKILY, WE'VE SLOWED down a bit by the time we hit the guy on the bike.

He appears suddenly in our headlights, pedaling across the unlit road directly in front of our car. There is a moment where the world seems to pause. The man turns to us in shock.

Once again, I'm bodily restrained from flying forward as Dad slams the brakes. There is a dull *thunk* as our car hits the back wheel of the bike and the cyclist flies forward in a long arc onto the road. I let out a panicked moan as Dad brings the car to a stop. Behind us the cyclist is lying flat, arms flung out at his sides.

We stare back in horrified silence.

But wait . . . He's moving! Gingerly he sits up, rubbing his leg. He is staggering to his feet, just straightening his body, when our car starts moving forward, the man diminishing in size.

"Wait! We can't—" Mom begins to protest.

"I don't know if those soldiers are after us," Dad yells, the veins of his neck standing out dangerously. "This isn't a game!"

In the back, I sink low, making myself an even smaller target.

So, ANYWAY. SRINAGAR is pretty much deserted when we drive through an empty marketplace in the gray early dawn light, looking for a hotel. I'm sulking, arms crossed, having been told to shut up by the big kids for inquiring repeatedly into the health and future prospects of the cyclist.

As we cruise by the opening to a narrow roadway, a large, surprisingly elegant hotel winks into view, partially obscured by trees. None of us says anything when Dad drives past, not seeing it. He is in the type of mood that, magnified by exhaustion, could transform at the slightest provocation into a screaming bout. We remain silent as Dad circles back through town. The second time he misses the hotel, Frank shoots me a look to stay silent. On the third round, he and Chiara look at me pleadingly, and I know the score.

"Daddy!" I point cheerfully. "What's that big building there?"

Up close, the place has the neglected, overgrown appearance of something left behind after all the humans have perished. "I don't think anyone's here," Dad observes as we get out of the car, stretching our legs in the ghostly silence.

From the fog, two men and a plump, pretty woman materialize, and we are hurriedly escorted into a lobby, stripped bare of furniture, with white marble floors and high ceilings. Some windows are barricaded with wood, and a few soldiers with guns mill about, large, broad-chested men. Everyone stares—I bet the last thing they expected to drive in from a war-zone is our half-blond gang of five.

I hear Dad register under a different name than the one we used at our last stop. His favorites include Cash, Sterling, and Gold. It can never match the name in our blue passports, the five of which Dad keeps on him at all times. I know it's all because we must not leave a trail, although why that's so important is not clear to me. It's so ingrained that I never question it. The same way I know to be silent at all times when around immigration officials, border security, or anyone even vaguely resembling a cop. I know my father's laws by heart, because it is what we all believe: Always be loyal to our family—for we will never betray each other. Trust no one—they are outsiders. And be a criminal—but be a noble one.

These are the rules we live by. An unbreakable outlaw code.

THERE ISN'T MUCH to do as we while away the rest of the week in Srinagar so Dad can recover by the empty pool, but that has never deterred us. In a pack of three, Frank, Chiara, and I go to the market when it opens in the morning and buy bananas in bulk to share with our new pals, the soldiers. We squat on the hot concrete surrounding the sun-bleached pool, playing cards with two of them. They don't speak English, but that is totally irrelevant in the game of Snap. I am in third place, because they are worried about hurting my small hand if we snap down on matching cards at the same time. Frank and Chiara have no such qualms. In a wide-brimmed sun hat, looking lovely and tan, Mom comes out to check on us, sighs, and then goes back inside. She is always concerned when we spend so much time with militia, ne'er-do-wells, or the Japanese mafia. But who else are we supposed to hang out with?

Chiara points up to a colorful bird, and we watch it, circling in the shimmering heat, before picking up our cards again. Something seems wrong . . . my stack is shorter now. I stop playing and frown, Frank glances suspiciously at the soldiers. But they're looking at Chiara.

"Did you take Bhajan's cards?" Frank's voice is disbelieving.

Chiara fidgets nervously. No one moves. One of the older men picks up a portion of his cards and hands them quietly back to me.

"You gave Bhajan's cards to him?" Frank's face flushes.

I stare at my sister, uncomprehending. Most people would lie to win, but she's just cheated me for no reason at all.

"Bhajan, I'm sorry, I . . . I was just trying to show you that you can't always be the best."

The bird glides over our heads, its shadow dark on the concrete, but this time no one is watching.

In the evening, Frank finds a little sewing kit in our heaps of luggage and summons me so he can sew the heels of our feet together. I am unsure as to the advisability of this project but he says "Trust me," and surprisingly the needle piercing my hardened skin doesn't hurt a bit. A red thread is visible just under the surface, weaving back and forth between my right foot and his left.

"Oh, great." Chiara surfaces from her book, "Now you two really are conjoined."

"Dork over there is jealous." Frank smirks, and we lie giggling on the carpet.

"You think you're cool just because people like you." Chiara's voice takes on the jeering tone that she saves for Frank. He locks eyes with her and I feel the familiar vibration of one of their fights building. She rises from the bed. "But inside you're just a little girl, Frank. A weak little girl."

He cuts the strings between our feet with ferocious speed and stands. He may be two years younger than her, but he's already a head taller. I scurry out of their way. It takes on a life of its own, like all their arguments, the words hurled like knives. "You want to hit me? C'mon Frank! I bet you can't even do it."

I climb onto the windowsill as my brother clenches his fists, his large brown eyes normally so warm, darkening. Chiara backs toward the wall, a glint in her pale eyes. They are so different, even in the way they stand. Him, upright and rooted to the spot, her weaving, never quite still. She scans his handsome face, the strong cheekbones and immovable chin, measuring him. . . .

Chiara steps forward, away from the wall, and in that instant her plain features turn ugly. "Little bitch." She hurls the taunt like a challenge.

"I hate you!" he growls through clenched teeth and lunges toward her, fist drawing back for a punch. The second she marks it, she drops to the floor, and unable to stop, Frank punches straight through the wall. There is a moment of sickening silence, with Chiara on the floor, me on the window, and Frank with half his arm sunk inside the plaster. "Ahhh!" He wrenches his hand out, covered with blood, dripping onto the dark carpet.

It has always been like this, for as long as anyone remembers. I've known Chiara my entire life and shared a room with her for most of it, but I'm not sure I know who she really is. Her personality is like quicksilver, constantly shifting, adapting to different environments and surroundings, yet never taking a true form. I've learned she even tried to push Frank off a fifth-floor balcony when he was three, and slapped him in the face the day he was born. The two will stay locked in a power struggle, an intractable battle, for years.

Frank is still bleeding onto the carpet when Mom bursts in from the adjoining room. She takes in the scene, the gaping hole in the wall, Chiara's elaborately innocent expression, and turns ashen. "What happened?"

Frank screams, "She's trying to drive me crazy!" His free hand clutches his wrist, attempting to stanch the flow.

"You're a jerk," I yell accusingly at Chiara. "You called him weak." In our family, there is no greater insult.

"Why are you on the windowsill?! *Zut!*" Mom grabs my arm, pulling me down.

Luckily, by the time Dad returns, we've retreated to our respective corners. Scrubbed and pajama-clad, we appear above suspicion, having just finished rehanging one of the framed pictures over the hole. Dad frowns at the bandage on Frank's hand—reminding us nothing gets past him.

WHEN THE MORNING breeze filters in, soft and warm, I do my usual stretching and conditioning session. Frank has been coaching me daily since shortly after I was born, in preparation for my career as a master athlete, which he has chosen for me. I run through the splits, backbends, sit-ups, push-ups, and handstands against the wall. Then it's time for a couple hours of school with Mom.

Today we start with math. I love my abacus, the glossy finish, the dark wooden beads that are larger for easy handling, the way it clacks and gives you the answers to such complicated math problems with a few flicks. Frank and Chiara took intensive courses during our months in Japan and are experts, their fingers moving in a blur of speed over the exercise book. They don't even need the abacus anymore and can solve even complex multiplication and division problems by simply closing their eyes and moving their fingers while visualizing the beads. We sit in a row, with me in the middle, cross-legged on the swirls of hotel carpet, Mom's sweet French-accented voice guiding us. I labor through simple additions and subtractions for twenty minutes, until I wilt on the couch for my break.

It is a great anxiety of mine that I will not end up as smart as everyone else in the family. Sure, they are much older than me, but they seem impossible to catch up to.

AFTER SEVEN DAYS of rest, Dad rises from the rickety chaise longue, notices me tossing sticks into the empty pool, and declares, "Let's go to Amritsar."

I nod agreeably. "Okay."

He considers the barren surroundings and then motions for me to sit beside him.

"Harbhajan, do you know why we're here?" We sit side by side, a big man and his miniature copy.

I shake my head.

". . . This place saved my life."

"The pool?"

His rumble of a laugh shakes our chair. "This country. Before I even came here for the first time, it saved me. When I was younger, I was trying to figure out how to live, how to be at peace . . ." he trails off.

"Was this before I was born?" I ask understandingly.

"Yes." His beard lifts. "Dark days Bhajan, dark days. . . . So, now we're going to the holiest of cities and a temple of gold. You in?"

I refuse to leave before we can find our favorite soldier so I can give him a bag full of bananas. But Frank lifts me by the back of my dungarees, strides to the car, and places me, protesting, in my spot on the middle of the backseat. This lack of respect is another reason I can't wait to grow up. Can't he see I'm not a child, but simply a short adult?

On the road to Amritsar, under a sky of endless stars, our hair tangling in the wind, we sing our family theme song.

Little boxes made of ticky tacky, little boxes all the same . . .

From backseat center, I move my arms grandly, like a conductor. Frank's teenage voice breaks a little on the high notes and I giggle, earning a warning look from the front seat.

And the children go to school,
and then to the University,
where they are put in boxes
And they come out all the saaaaame!

"Wake up, squirt." Frank squeezes my bare foot, which has somehow become wedged behind his back. "We're here."

I open my eyes and realize they have changed into traditional Sikh attire, long white silk tunics slit at the side, with Frank and Dad in turbans.

"Here, I'll help you." Chiara unhooks my dungarees and pulls my specially made matching tunic over my rumpled undershirt.

I stumble out of the car into the darkness, trying to remember where we're supposed to be. We walk along a quiet street, past some tall men in turbans, toward a large open gate that looms ahead. I'm still yawning and occasionally scratching my tummy, my habit when returning to consciousness. The moon is full and pale yellow, hanging low in the night sky, as our sandals slap lightly on the street.

I like it best when we walk like this, in unison. All of us in white. Fastened around their hips, Dad and Frank wear the kirpan, a short, curved sword, the male symbol of defending those in peril. People appear around us, dressed identically, turbans high and proud, the women's beautiful long hair hanging in thick braids down their backs. Many turn to stare, faces friendly, surprised to see any Westerner, let alone a whole family.

At the gate, a man takes our sandals and we wash our feet under taps before walking through a shallow pool. Bare feet slick on the marble, I almost slide through the archway. In the inky night, a glowing palace seems suspended in the center of a large lake, reflecting its light across the rippling water. Large and ethereal, it is all I see, all I feel.

The Golden Temple.

We step out onto a slender walkway, water lapping against the sides, forming an otherworldly path to the sanctuary. The peppery scent of incense carries in the velvet night air. Even if I am just a squirt now, with banana-sticky hands and undone pigtails, I know. I know I will never forget this moment as long as I live.

Inside, the temple's high walls rise up to a gold-plated dome covered with vibrantly colored mosaics and lavish floral patterns. I stand absolutely still, trying to absorb the sensory overload. Tall people press all around as their excitement builds, mixing with the haunting pulse of Nagara drums. Frank reaches for my hand. "C'mon Bhajan." He grins. "Let's go get closer to God."

We climb to an inner balcony running along the first floor. Smiling people, already seated, make space for us, and I settle on Mom's crossed legs.

Frank and Chiara sit as far away from each other as possible. It's quieter up here, and the tall arched windows are free of glass, allowing a whisper of wind to flow though. I rest my head against Mom's beating heart, waiting for the Greet the Dawn service to begin.

From outside, the sound of voices chanting draws closer, and I glimpse a shower of pink and white rose petals as the Guru Granth Sahib, the Sikh holy book, is carried reverently into the temple. Under a jeweled canopy, the priest takes a breath and opens the book. His long beard dips toward the pages, and the sound of his strong, deep voice fills the temple. Men around him join the chant, and the prayer builds in power, making my skin tingle.

"Ek ong kar, sat nám, kartá purak, hnirbhau nirvair, jap, ád sac, jugád sac, hai bhí sac, nának hosí bhí sac." I learned the prayers a year ago, and sing along as everyone joins. *There is but one God, Truth is His Name. Maker of all things, Free of fear and hate . . .*

My head bowed, I chant the words of Guru Nanak, the founder of this religion based on Truth, and one of my namesakes. Of course, my family did not give me just one name to live up to, they gave me three.

Harbhajan Khalsa Nanak.

Song of God.

Pure.

Truth.

It's not just a name, it's everything I know we stand for. Honor our principles, search for truth, and love each other no matter what may come.

Outside, the first light of dawn colors the sky.

PART ONE

1: The Chase

IT's THE SIMPLE mistakes that get you caught. Not the epic dramas we imagine—a high-speed car chase or a helicopter spotlight pinning you in the darkness. Instead, it's the fingerprint on the edge of a letter, a call to your mother on her birthday, or a surreptitious visit home. Some of the cleverest fugitives in the world were captured because they thought it was safe to let their guard down, to breathe, for just a moment.

I learned all this in my years on the road with my family, decades of moving without warning from city to city, country to country, continent to continent. I memorized the mantra of Sikh prayers, how to add and subtract on an abacus, and how an internal combustion engine works. But my hardest lesson was something very different. I had to learn our rules:

- Always have a back story. Rehearse it until it is your real story, until it comes without thinking.

- Never give outsiders the phone number of where you live. Never. Instead, set up an answering service in a different town, where people can leave a message after the beep. Always check these messages from pay phones.

- Make sure all mail goes to a P.O. box. Before picking it up, take abrupt turns, circuitous routes, with eyes trained on the rearview mirror, making sure there isn't a tail.

- Pay for everything in cash. Never own a credit card.

- And, most important, when you leave a place—no matter how much you love it, no matter how many friends you've made—you can never, ever go back. You cannot contact people you used to know. Relationships have to go up in smoke along with old documents.

It sounds simple, but few people can do it continuously over many years. They get tired and careless, or start to miss those they've left behind. And then, as Dad likes to remind us, you're as good as dead.

That hallucinatory feeling of early dawn at the Golden Temple, the words of Guru Nanak chanting gently from my lips, is as smooth as a dream in my memory but also as real as yesterday. Those moments in India, my father's warm hand on my shoulder as dawn broke over the Himalayas, were the first beliefs I developed and stored permanently in my heart. It was all somehow perfect, even the young soldiers armed with big guns, even my brother's fist going through the wall. Everything Dad promised seemed easily within our reach. There was so much more I didn't understand—not then, hurtling down a mountain, or later, when Frank and Chiara turned into people I could never imagine, nor on the last day I saw my brother. Not even today.

But why did we run so fast and for so long? Why did we risk it all?

That answer is simple.

We were being hunted.

And yet, my family sang on, in a little car held together with faith and chicken wire, even as the seeds of our dissolution—my father's temper, Frank and Chiara's battle of wills—began to take hold. In the years that follow, those moments of beauty will become more and more fleeting. By then we'll have mingled with the Yakuza in Japan, witnessed apartheid at its turbulent end, seen the Pyramids, and eaten hot cheese deep in the wilds of Romania. By the age of nine, I will have lived in more than a dozen countries, on five continents, under six assumed identities. I'll know how a document is forged, how to withstand an interrogation, and most important, how to disappear.

And the money? It's never clear where that comes from. I'm taught to shoplift, but that's just to build character. The cash seems to appear without anyone exerting visible effort. Sometimes Dad says it's the interest on an investment, and sometimes he'll let out a whoop while watching the gold prices spike on CNN, but there never seems to be anything like work involved. As long as I can remember, there has always been another bank account. Always there, just a wire transfer away. Ready to buy us freedom.

Watching my father as he drives across borders, the sharp angles of his Viking profile so like mine, I came to see that in our life of inconsistencies, there is one enduring thing: He believes in me. They all do.

This feeling has nothing to do with the beautiful places they take me to, the temples, ancient ruins, and untouched beaches. It's because even when I'm so tiny that Dad jokingly makes restaurant reservations for four-and-a-half people, they always treat me as a full member of the team. Of course there is a huge amount expected of me in return. I know that I must be the best, the fastest, the bravest. As a gymnast I will push myself all the way to a podium at the Junior Olympics, and standing there, I'll know it's only a step in the right direction. Yet, I see the pride in their eyes, even if I am their overly sensitive, idealistic, stubborn, impossible fireball. They know I will fight to the death for them.

I don't care how many cops are on our trail, I don't care about Interpol. They are my world. Maybe not a perfect one, but I see all the best in them. It makes me want to fly higher and higher so they will always look at me like this; like they don't want me to be a girl who sits quietly and lets the world go by, but one who chases it, bursting with life. Their partner in crime.

Back then it all seemed so right. I could not imagine that my future had already been written in the stamp of a fake passport before I was even conceived. That my fate would be a harsh one—meant to be impossible to overcome or escape.

Some people believe life is a chess match, where each move you make affects your destiny, and you decide the strategy. But what if everything was already decided?

What if you were born on the run?

2: Amritsar, India, age 4

WE ACQUIRE SOMETHING I've never experienced before—a routine.

Each dawn is ushered in under a golden dome and every afternoon we head back to the temple complex, to help at the Langar—the free kitchen in Amritsar, where volunteers feed thousands every day, working almost around the clock. Following my family at a jog, I weave through the streets as the sun beats down, surrounded by women in vibrant tunics and men in multihued turbans.

There's noise, a haze of incense, careening mopeds, and color, color everywhere. The rest of the world seems to live in black and white compared to India. We halt only briefly, so Dad can carry a tiny turtle across the road to safety. He is committed to saving various creatures through rescue protocols and strict vegetarianism. The fate of the cyclist is a hiccup along this path that we would, honestly, rather not discuss.

Our gang steps into the complex—white buildings with stately columns—stretching in front of us. Today, I'm determined to help make chapati, despite Frank telling me confidentially that people under four feet tall with blonde hair aren't allowed to help. The dining space is cavernous, filled with the clatter of bowls as long lines of people sit cross-legged on the floor, eating.

Mom manages to get me into the open kitchen, near the giant cauldrons cooking dahl lentils and the rich scents of curry, where I settle between Frank and Chiara. There is much winking and conspiratorial smiling between Mom and the woman in charge. I give them a look of great dignity, intending to blow their minds with my efficiency. Frank and Chiara mold the dough and I slap it in the center a few times before it's flipped onto a huge searing plate. Dad doesn't actually help—manual labor is not his thing. Instead, he talks to people, discussing philosophy and religion.

Once someone starts speaking with my father, they seem to become mesmerized, hardly moving from the spot. I have seen it many times before, the instant power of that smile, of his unshakable presence. It makes me sit straighter, because out of everyone, he's ours.

Glancing around the rest of the dining area, I begin to notice a disturbing trend. Some of the people we serve are hungry. Not the type of famished I get after a day of not finding safe food to eat while we travel, but hungry with the worried, inward-looking stare of someone who is all alone.

Very late that night, I tiptoe into my parents' dark bedroom and poke my father's shoulder. His eyes open and focus immediately. Dad is good at waking up alert and ready for anything. "Hi," I say. "It's me."

He grins. "I can see that. Come on up." He helps me climb over him, all elbows and knees, and I begin to divide his wiry Viking beard into three parts so I can braid it.

Mom stirs, sleepily touching my arm. "Did you have a bad dream, Bhajan?"

I look at them both. "Why are there poor people?" My parents pause, and then rally, explaining how there are so many people and there isn't always enough to go around. "But why isn't there a law that rich people have to give them something?" I feel myself becoming teary.

"That's communism, sweetheart," Dad says. "It can be a slippery slope. . . . Although, some people like to be other-directed. They just want someone to tell them what to do."

"But *why*?"

"Ah, that's the secret of how governments control millions. You tell people they'll be taken care of, if they do what they're told. It's comforting not to have to think for yourself."

"I don't want to be other-directed!" I burst out, my voice louder than I expected.

Mom's soothing, cool hand strokes my forehead, and Dad looks at me in that way he sometimes does— as if he dearly wants to share everything he knows, as if I will desperately need it to survive. "If you want to be in charge of your destiny you have to be constantly aware, Bhajan. Constantly. Otherwise someone will lead you, and you'll be just another slave."

My hand is on the rise and fall of his chest and I can feel his heartbeat quicken. I stay silent in thought. He often talks this way, in extremes, with triumph or disaster the only two possible outcomes. If there is such a thing as doing all right, or muddling through, it's an entirely foreign concept to me.

"I'll never be other-directed." I promise. My words are soft in the dark, but I mean every one.

He touches my cheek and lifts the blanket so I can fit snugly between them. All the worries and questions begin to lose their shape, and I feel my eyes closing. Because there is no better place than this. Tucked between them, where no nightmares, monsters, or fear can touch me. The safest place in the world.

TWO DAYS BEFORE we are due to leave for Delhi to continue our pilgrimage of discovery, Chiara gets a marriage proposal. Apparently, another dad approached our dad at the temple. The family is well-known, and has quite a bit of money, so they were shocked to hear that our father thought sixteen was too young for Chiara to be entering into holy matrimony. Like the traffic, major life decisions seem to move fast here. I don't think Chiara is even interested in this boy and has never chatted with him. Of course Dad would never have allowed us to talk alone with someone, especially of the opposite sex, unless expressly approved by him. That's something other people do. People who don't think of their futures.

I stroll toward the hotel with Mom and Chiara, along the white temple path for the last time, smiling at the people we know.

"Wait!!" Frank is sprinting after us, with the long-legged stride of an athlete, dark ponytail flying.

He skids to a stop, barefoot. "Mom, Mom, I just heard! Dad told me. This is perfect, it's so perfect . . . We could leave Chiara here!"

"Frank." Mom rolls her eyes.

"No, no, please just *listen*," he implores, actually dropping to his knees on the pathway. "This family will take care of her, they will! And let's face it; she may never get another proposal. We could be free!"

Chiara stares down at him angrily. Mom takes a deep breath, releases it, and then continues walking, Frank still entreating her.

Back in our hotel room, Frank's tall body collapses on his bed, a defeated arm thrown over his eyes. I climb up and sit cross-legged on his chest to comfort him.

"Oh Bhajan," he says sadly. "We were so *close*."

I BRACE A leg against the back of Mom's seat as our car fights its way into Delhi, trying to steady the world. On all sides we're besieged by vehicles: tiny cars, lumbering buses with people hanging out the windows and clinging to the sides, rickshaws, bikes, and motorized scooters, all driven by people who clearly have no regard for the sanctity of life. I'm feeling oddly weak, my head lolling against the seat.

On nearly every concrete island, between honking traffic lanes, are makeshift shelters built from junk and tied together with twine or rags. I see skinny, big-eyed children in torn T-shirts standing barefoot on the blistering concrete while cars scream by. Outside the more modern buildings, child beggars sit, some missing an arm or with a mutilated eye barely healed into a jagged scar.

We veer into a tight roundabout, seemingly endless because no one lets anyone change lanes, and I start to feel my stomach heave. Crumpling forward, I moan.

"Shh, don't cry," Mom reaches back to rub my knee.

"It's good for you to see this, Bhajan." Dad tells me sternly, still stuck in the left lane, going into his sixth round. "Don't ever forget how lucky you are—"

"I need the bathroom!" I sob as pain shoots through my belly. Dad's whole expression changes in the rearview mirror as he focuses on my face.

"Don't throw up on me!" Frank frantically rolls down his window and maneuvers me toward it. I squeeze my eyes shut as Dad leans on the horn and fights his way into the next circle of hell. We screech to a stop in front of a café with taxi drivers drinking chai and swatting at flies outside. My legs don't seem to be working properly, so I'm half-dragged, half-carried to the bathroom. The stomach cramps are so violent that I scream out in pain while Mom grips my hands.

"What's wrong with her?" Dad asks anxiously when I emerge, slumped against Mom's leg.

"She must have caught a strong virus. We have to get her to a hotel. Now."

Frank is tilting a water bottle to my lips, but I turn away. All I want is to crawl into a quiet corner and sleep. When they haul me out of the car at a big hotel with a revolving glass door and uniformed parking attendants, I'm delirious with fever, blabbering—and then my world fades to black.

I'm not sure how much time has passed when I wake to the sound of frantic calls for a children's doctor, any doctor. Faces swirl above me, my mother with her cool hands and soft kisses. "Say something, Bhajan. Bhajan, look at me." I can't move my mouth, I'm just too tired, so I close my eyes. It feels like I'm drifting peacefully, a raft being pulled farther and farther from the shore

It's nighttime. Another voice. A cold instrument presses over my heart, and through barely open lids I see an Indian woman leaning over me, a doctor's bag on the bed. The longer I look into her kohl-rimmed eyes, the deeper they seem, like moving amber. She turns away abruptly and speaks to my parents.

"She's going to die soon. Unless you can find a way to get a lot of fluids into her."

Her words rob the room of all sound, and then everyone starts talking frantically. They're arguing about a hospital and whether I will just catch something worse if I go. The terror-sharpened voices fade away, away, until . . .

. . . Something hard is clicking against my teeth and I crack open an eye to see Frank and Chiara on the bed, sitting on either side of me, with little glass droppers in their hands.

"It's just water, sweetie. You have to have some, okay?" Chiara is using her perky voice, which I can't stand, but even that doesn't bother me now. Dad is yelling at someone on the phone about airplane seats, but that's nothing unusual. Mom's focus is on changing the cool cloths on my forehead, squeezing my hand, and heaving suitcases out of the closet. Why don't they all just go to sleep, for God's sake and let me be? I turn away.

"Bhajan, Bhajan." Frank rubs my shoulder. "Let me give you this water!" Up close, I can see he's trying not to cry. "It's *me*, Bhajan, will you do it for me? C'mon."

I feel the dropper click against my teeth and, for him, I try. The first drops of water burn down my throat. Then suddenly I am in Mom's arms, draped over her shoulder, boneless. "Move! Move!" Now Dad is issuing orders. We rush through the deserted lobby and out into the gray early-morning light.

"Open the trunk." Dad snaps at the sleepy taxi driver and together they start shoving our bags into the back.

That's when I see her. She's among the raggedy kids who are sleeping against the wall of the hotel. Except she's awake. Her body is small and delicate, the torn clothes she's wearing barely cover her emaciated limbs. She must be four or five, like me, with the same large, almond-shaped eyes, dark brown instead of blue. She doesn't move. Time stops, and we watch each other as everyone else loads the car. I notice her arms tremble, like the just-played string of a sitar. They are crossed, as if trying to hold herself together.

"All right, get in!"

I feel Mom move forward, hugging me tightly, as if to press her strength into my body.

It's so clear to me in that last moment, before I slip into unconsciousness: This little girl is not going to make it. There are just three meters of space separating us, but she is being left to die. I'm being saved. And we both know it.

3: Sydney, Australia, age 5

I TURN ON the TV and fall in love.

"I'm the Bush Tucker man!" A weathered ex-military operative in his thirties holds a squirming worm aloft as he crouches in the wilderness. "You may think this is just a worm," he addresses the camera in his thick Aussie accent, "but really, it's also protein."

This is the first manifestation of my attraction to competence above all else when it comes to men. Can he survive in an apocalypse? That's my question. My experiences, combined with listening to my father, have led me to believe that an apocalypse is not only likely, but something that should be taken into account while making everyday decisions. I'm not panicked necessarily—just alert.

It's four months since we left India, and with a steady diet of avocados, flax seed oil, Bush Tucker man, and illegally obtained raw goat's milk, I've made a remarkable recovery. The allowed hour of TV during my convalescence was a shock at first, but Dad approves of my program choice—I'm picking up survival skills in case of a military takeover.

Having successfully learned today's lesson—which roots are edible, and which will kill ya' dead—I run across the apartment in my new favorite outfit, a poofy floor-length white dress that I got for my fifth birthday. Climbing to my favorite perch on the windowsill of our massive apartment, I can see clear across the harbor to the white curves of the Sydney Opera House. To me, the view looks like the sails of some magnificent ship against the achingly blue sky. It's beginning to feel like home. And that is when I notice the change in him.

As I sit on the windowsill, Dad plants a kiss on my now rosy cheek and starts to pace, looking preoccupied. I watch him, so restless, his body silhouetted against the sky, eyes searching the horizon. It unsettles me and maybe that's why, two days later, I make a mistake.

My gymnastic team and I line up on the track field. "Ryyyyyight, kids," Coach Anita announces, stretching out the vowels, Aussie-style, "We're going to have a number of races today to see where we're at." She directs us to our positions twenty-five meters from the finish line.

The shrill whistle pierces the air and we're off. I sprint ahead, fists pumping, suddenly in the lead and feeling the joy of being so alive. Of being strong again. Halfway through I realize the other girls aren't even trying to win. It's probably the smart choice; today is blistering hot and I already sense how exhausted I'm going to be. But where is the fun in running slow?

Coach Anita takes me aside after the second sprint. "Now, Harbhajan, don't you think it would be *nice* for you to even things out and let the others win from now on?"

Has the woman lost her mind? I consider informing her that this sounds dangerously like communism, which can be a slippery slope.

By the time we're done, I'm sweaty, exhausted, and limping slightly. "Well done!" booms one of the other girls' fathers, smiling heartily at me. I've seen him around a few times, looking very Australian with his broad shoulders, ruddy complexion, and open face. "So how are you liking it here, or do you miss all those street cars?"

Panic comes at me fast. *Backstory, what's our backstory?* I try to jog my memory, but we've been in Australia a while and, besides, I think I have heatstroke.

"I was there in '82," he hollers. "Smashing place, what area did you live in?"

Oh God, I've been briefed on this, but can't remember. With each new country, Dad not only changes our last name, but also builds a different history, a different place we're from. He drills me in mock interrogations when I least expect it. I've asked him if we could just schedule a time for this, so it doesn't occur when I'm relaxing on the couch planning my future with the Bush Tucker man. But apparently, real interrogations happen when you aren't feeling like it.

The correct response to each question is always deflection, suggesting the interrogator should ask my mom or dad. I used to break down sometimes and cry in these rehearsals, at the confusion of telling my dad to ask my dad, but I'm five now and I think I've got it down. Why there are so many people chasing us, though, is a mystery to me. I know one of them is called Interpol, because I've heard my parents talking about its alerts and searches. But they aren't the only ones after us. In my mind it's like a many-tentacled beast. Waiting for us to make the slightest slipup, or let down our guard for a moment . . .

. . . The broad-shouldered, ruddy-faced dad is still staring at me, morphing from a chatty well-meaning Aussie into one of the shadowy people I fear. "Well?" he asks, looking confused.

Am I going to mess everything up? Destroy us all? Is he with the authorities? My head pounds. "Ask my Mom," I blurt out, and half-run, half-limp to the car.

DAD DECIDES WE'RE going to leave the country a few days later. I know I'm probably not the reason—it's something about visas and moving targets being harder to find—but I still feel guilty. Grabbing our Monopoly set, I find Frank sprawled on the floor of his room, reading. "Oh God," he groans. "Why do you have to wear that thing?"

I look down at my poofy dress. "It's elegant."

"It's ridiculous. And I'm not going to play with you."

"Pleeeease."

"No."

"Yes!"

He picks me up, deposits me outside his room, and slams the door.

An hour later I'm lying on my bed, like a beached starfish in my party dress, when my door clicks open. "Move over." Frank tosses *Asterix and Cleopatra* onto the duvet and we lie on our bellies, side by side, as he reads to me. His long, square-tipped finger traces the words I need to learn. Apologies are unnecessary.

Frank and I spend the majority of our time together since he can't stand Chiara, and given that we move so often, the thought of putting effort into maintaining outside friendships is exhausting. Other kids don't really get us and can be frighteningly persistent in their questioning. Even Mom has become strangely silent and withdrawn; I can tell she doesn't want to leave Australia. But she never complains, and so I decide it's time to take action on her behalf.

When everyone except Dad has turned in, I climb out of bed. Tiptoeing from my room, I join him on the sofa of the darkened living room. His arm warm around my shoulders, we crack open pistachios and watch the stock prices on CNN while he explains how to buy long and sell short. "Does Mom want to stay here and have a house?" I ask tentatively.

"You don't miss a lot." He smiles at me.

"So are we gonna settle down?" I hear a bit of hope creep into my voice; I like the Aussies.

"Bhajan, that's exactly the kind of weak thinking that leads to disaster."

I chew thoughtfully, watching the numbers scroll across the bottom of the screen, as a woman with immobile blonde hair talks.

"Staying in one place looks safe, but that's how they find you. Always remember—you should never operate from a position of uncertainty or fear. Never."

I imagine them coming, men with guns breaking down our door in the night, the screams of my family. He must feel me tense, because his voice softens. "Bhajan you don't have worry. I'll always take care of you."

IT'S ACTUALLY A relief to wake to the sound of packing tape being unrolled and stretched across cardboard storage boxes. Mom works seamlessly, deciding what we have to haul across the world and what can be turned over to the storage gods. I keep a sharp eye out, making sure none of my treasured stuffed animals or dolls get put into the wrong box. Storage is, in my experience, a black hole from which things rarely reemerge. We have stuff stashed all over the place, spanning continents, and Dad often forgets to pay the bills. Our possessions are forever getting auctioned off or incinerated.

Tomorrow we'll be gone—but I have no idea where we're headed. As the youngest, I'm usually left in the dark so I can't accidentally spill the beans. We've told people we're moving to France, so I know for sure we won't set foot there. Dad glides in through the front door, looking sharp in a loose white shirt and linen slacks, and leans a strong hand on the windowpane. "It's looking nebulous," he observes, almost to himself, then glances over at me and winks. "Time to follow the sun."

4: Cape Town, South Africa, age 5

WE FIND FRED inside a joke shop in downtown Johannesburg. Outside, the movement to end apartheid is coming to a boil. Police stand with batons in hand, guns on hips, watching passersby suspiciously. I'm used to pressurized situations, but the mood on the streets of Joburg is actually making the hair on my arms stand up. Everywhere we've been in this country, white and black people remain markedly separate, and tension ripples like heat waves across the cracked pavement. But Dad has always wanted us to experience living in beautiful South Africa, and he isn't about to let a little thing like the possibility of armed conflict stand in our way.

In the window display of the joke shop, I examine a fake eyeball while the rest of the gang browse the aisles nearby. Outside, a young black man, probably a teenager, strides by on the sidewalk. His face is serious, older than it should be. My attention is drawn to his bright white T-shirt, to where it's marred with a smear of red. His nose is still bleeding but he walks tall.

I put back the eyeball.

"Now this is just the thing!" Dad booms suddenly from across the store, holding a severed arm aloft. It's wearing the sleeve of a crisp white dress shirt, pinned with a silver cuff link, while the amazingly realistic pale-plastic hand sports a matching wedding ring. A delicate trickle of blood traces a path down the palm. We snap it up, christen him Fred, and head for Cape Town with Mom looking apprehensive.

For a hundred dollars a week, we're living in a paradise on the hills of Constantia, overlooking the city. The whole place is filled with light and soft new carpets to wiggle my bare toes in. This is the first time I've ever lived in a house and I'm fascinated by the endless space. There are so many bedrooms that we have two left over and use the biggest one for our various Lego projects and experiments.

I'm allowed to play in the garden but never to venture into the Bush that surrounds the palatial house. It's rumored that blacks, many forced from their homes, are camping in the area, none too happy with any white South Africans who are resisting the end of apartheid. I wonder if we shouldn't get some T-shirts made with *Professional Sikh Nomads, Just Passing Through* emblazoned across the front to make our position clear.

In any case, we're studying judo twice a week, learning how to repel murderers, thieves, and goddamn bureaucrats. Today, Frank triumphs in his group of fifteen-year-olds, and I get flattened as usual by the same red-headed boy who's been destroying me for weeks. Adhering to the family code of never showing weakness in public, it's only once I'm in the car on the way home, that I finally start to sob. "I don't want to go anymore!"

"That's just avoiding the central issue." Dad steers down the road, flanked by rich red South African earth. The setting sun, so large and shimmering here, lies low on the hills of the vineyards. "Do you want to go through your life running away?" he asks.

I try to stop crying, gulping for air. Isn't running away what we do best? Mom seems about to say something, but he silences her with a look and turns to me. "Sweetheart, did you know that there were three skeletons discovered on a beach, once?" Staring at the back of his head, I try catching up with his brain. "Scientists analyzed the remains and found they died from dehydration. Imagine being right in front of an ocean of water, not being able to drink it, and slowly dying of thirst." I listen, wide-eyed. "Do you know what else they found?"

"No," I sniff.

"Four feet under the sand was a reservoir of fresh water. It was there the whole time, just a meter away. If they had only dug. So don't think there's no solution. This boy is not invincible; he's just some kid. Dig deeper."

I'M ALWAYS AT my most determined, or maniacal, when I have a clear goal from Dad. My training regimen is forthwith increased to include judo sparring with Frank every afternoon. We train in the other spare room, duvets stacked to make a soft landing area. "Get below his center of gravity," Frank instructs, bare-chested and miming the correct technique. "If you displace someone's balance, you can throw anyone." Towering over me in cutoff jeans, he shows me how to grab one of his arms, turn while bending my knees, and then use my lower back to lift, hurling him over my shoulder. We also practice a stranglehold, just in case "things get rough," as Frank hopefully puts it.

A few weeks later, the doorbell rings just as Mom is making our morning glass of carrot, celery, and cucumber extract. Mom looks up from the juicer, while the rest of us freeze. It is our firm family belief that no good can come from unannounced visitors. In a coordinated move Mom, Frank, Chiara, and I leave the kitchen, which is in full view of the ground-floor windows, and relocate to a hidden alcove off the living room.

Dad stealthily approaches the front door. Barefoot and in his flowing black and green kimono, he advances like a blond, bearded samurai. A force to be reckoned with. My palms are clammy as I press in next to Mom. There's a side effect of fear: It clarifies everything. In just an instant I realize how desperately I need my family to be safe. These four people are all I have, all I know. The rest of the world is just a collection of strangers.

Straining my ears, I hear the light padding of Dad's bare feet. I know he's checking through the front windows, before even nearing the door's peephole—it's what we always do before leaving the house. Because when people come to get you, they don't stand all politely on the front porch. They circle to the sides.

There's an ominous silence, followed by a clicking sound as Dad opens the door. I hold my breath as muted unintelligible conversation filters back to us, the reserves in the trenches. *Slam.* Dad storms into the living room, red-cheeked. "At ease, troops. Goddamn Jehovah's Witnesses."

Frank and I tumble outside, our adrenaline still running high, with nowhere to go. Beyond our backyard, the forbidden Bush beckons. We share a silent look and move forward, slipping into the unknown. Sun-baked twigs snap under our sneakers and catch hold of my poofy dress. By the time we emerge into a clearing, my pigtails have come undone and Frank's sweat-soaked T-shirt is off, stuffed into the back pocket of his cargo shorts.

Together, we squint at the horizon. Sometimes I think South Africa must be the most wildly beautiful place there is, with its crimson terrain and trees shaped like enormous bonsai. Their branches so perfect for climbing. In the shade of a baobab, we sink down to rest and breathe in the scent of sun-dried leaves. "I've got to find a swim team here if we're staying any longer." Frank sighs. "I'm going to get out of practice."

"But you're so good at judo, too." Actually, upon reflection, he's good at everything: drawing, math, karate, charming people, making friends, being cool.

"Swimming is what I want to do," he says.

I nod understandingly. "I want to be a flight attendant."

"Oh, yeah." Frank grins. "Your life's dream."

With all the time we spend on airplanes, I consider flight attendants to be masters of the universe. They control the drink cart and have access to unlimited salted peanuts. We lean back against the rough trunk and pick at the dry, sturdy grass, scattering pieces around us. "If we had just stayed in one place for more than a minute I could be further ahead!" Frank glares at his battered shoes and I know he's thinking of the Olympics. Every time a new coach sees his long body cutting through the water, they get an eager glint in their eye and start planning his ascent to the gold. For Dad, this is obvious. We are expected to be the best; it's simply a baseline to build on.

"You should ask Dad if we can stay somewhere with a swim team."

He lets out a short laugh. "I can't. He doesn't listen."

"Sure he does!"

"It's different with you."

I frown. "Why?"

". . . I don't know. Because you're little, I guess." Frank stands abruptly. "Let's go back."

I sense he is keeping something from me, but he moves on and I follow. We climb a narrow pathway, dense, prickly bushes hemming us in on either side. I'm huffing and puffing by the time we near the summit of a hill.

I don't notice the tall plants around us rustling until three black men step out and block our path.

My mind floods with a hundred warnings we've heard, how skin color is enough to spark violence, on either side. How we can't expect to stroll through a war as if it has nothing to do with us. I start to panic as the men look down at us in total silence.

Frank moves in front of me. His bare freckled back obscures some of my view, but I have time to notice the curved knives thrust through the belt loops at the men's hips. The muscles of their bare chests look carved in stone. I can see we're blocked on all sides. Standing as still as possible, I feel a bead of sweat trail slowly down the back of my dress. From what I can make out of Frank's profile, his jaw is set, not showing fear. But he's just a lanky fifteen-year-old and a foot shorter than them.

They glare down at us, frighteningly still. Frank's hand finds mine and I grasp his fingers tightly with my sweaty fist. Ever so slowly, he starts to walk us forward, toward home. We have to turn sideways to wedge past the largest man, and I look up at his face. The anger in his burning gaze is tightly controlled, like something that's been there for a while. He nods almost imperceptibly to his companions, and suddenly, without a word, they move back, vanishing again into the bushes.

"*Run!*" Frank doesn't have to tell me twice. My legs take off on their own accord, speeding down the hill. At the bottom Frank grabs my hand and drags me in his wake, long legs eating up the distance as I half run, half fly behind. We collapse in our backyard, panting, covered in dust, assorted leaves and twigs.

"We outran them!" I gasp in wonder.

"They let us go." Frank stares at me. "Don't forget it."

As MUCH AS Dad claims to want to avoid drama or attention, it's my growing suspicion that he secretly gets bored after two or three weeks of peace. Case in point: Fred's debut.

Dad and us kids are in the driveway, about to leave for the health food store, when he gets a funny look in his eye and disappears back into the house. He emerges grinning to himself, and positions the upper part of the severed arm over the edge of the trunk, before slamming down the lid. The effect is amazingly realistic. It appears we've stashed a body away and forgotten to tuck his arm in. The trickle of fake blood on the pale hand is truly eye-catching.

On the streets, heads swivel as we cruise by, people staring open-mouthed. Dad keeps chuckling to himself. "Look, did you see how that car dropped back. Ha! He's turning off now. The faint of heart."

When we return, Mom is watering our lone flowerpot on the front porch and sees Fred. "You drove them around like this?" She whirls on Dad, looking terrified. "Tensions are so high, it could have been dangerous!"

"Now listen." Dad raises a finger. "You don't think I've taken all that into account? What better way to navigate a conflict zone, than with a dead guy in your trunk?" He gestures at our car. "No one would dare try anything once you've made *that* kind of statement."

Mom opens her mouth, about to say something, then closes it.

My PARENTS ARE having a Serious Talk. I can tell because Dad is leaning forward, really listening rather than what he often does—dismissing Mom out of hand or making a joke. The violence in South Africa is increasing, and even in our isolated area, the anxiety is palpable. Yesterday, Dad bought masking tape. The boxes and suitcases can't be far behind.

Even though it makes me nervous to hear them discuss the urgency of getting us out in time, I love seeing them like this, a team. They face each other on the living room's big white chairs, silhouetted against the floor-to-ceiling windows with a bright view of the garden. My parents look so sophisticated to me: my tough-looking father watching my beautiful mom, her dark hair wound in a simple chignon. In these moments, I am so proud to be their kid. There are the times when I am not, when Dad is shouting and she is silently absorbing it. But now they are united, invincible, and capable of fixing anything.

I sit on the stairs, unobserved, legs crossed like Mom and tilting my chin in what I hope is an imitation of her effortless class. It is my ambition to become an elegant woman one day, the kind with heels that go *click* and long, floaty dresses that whoosh across ballrooms.

"What's wrong with you?" Frank is standing behind me on the stairs.

"Nothing."

"You look like you've thrown your back out."

I drop my pose.

"Anyway, I have a project for us," he says. "C'mon."

In his room he reaches deep into a pile of T-shirts, releasing musty boy-smell, and retrieves a small wooden box, which he lovingly presents to me. I pop the lid and am confronted with an assortment of huge spiders. Leaping back in shock, I drop the box, and the creatures sprawl across the carpet, immobile.

"Realistic, right?" He picks up a hairy black one with tiny red eyes. "Keep watch in the hall while I put one of 'em in Chiara's bed." I'm practiced at standing guard, and without knowing why, I seem to do it well. Both Frank and my father believe it has something to do with intuition. But maybe it began out of necessity; to sense people so acutely, their shifting moods, to feel danger coming.

I lean against the wall outside Frank's room as he moves stealthily down the hall. It's not the first prank of this sort. There were the plastic ants in Australia, and the snake in Kyoto. It's usually in retaliation for some slight in their ongoing war. Often I feel guilty, not so much for my complicity, but because I know Chiara wishes I would be, just once, on her side. When Chiara says *I love you Bhajan*, I believe she is telling the truth. It's when I say it back that I'm unsure.

I would not know how to put it into words, but it's always there, a feeling that Chiara is hiding some part of herself. Or maybe there is just a missing part?

Footsteps climb the stairs, and I whistle low. Frank, his mission accomplished, drags me into his room where we hurriedly sit on the remaining spiders. Mom pokes her head in, announcing that we are going to blow town in forty-eight hours. While nodding innocently, I begin mentally saving the essentials.

Mom is in charge of packing and therefore personally responsible should any important document, teddy bear, or item of clothing go missing. Dad's filing system—a giant pile of tea-stained papers spilling off the coffee table—must be transported intact and never shuffled in any way, lest another kind of hell break loose. Watching Mom work steadily, I frown. Dad is always so strong and daring in his decisions, but it's actually Mom who seems to pull it all together. I hadn't noticed it before. . . . I guess you rarely notice the person doing most of the work, because they're always busy and the other one has more time to talk.

Late into the night, masking tape squeaks across boxes and flights are booked, our routine broken only by a bloodcurdling scream from the direction of Chiara's bedroom. Frank pauses, a box in his arms, and winks at me.

THE TRUNK IS stuffed with luggage when we all roll up outside the judo gym. Our plane is leaving late this evening, and I have just enough time to set things straight. Chiara helps me tie the white belt of my *gi* tight and pats me on the shoulder reassuringly. I walk out onto the mat with the other students as my family watches through the observation window, encouraging me with a variety of hand signals.

My redheaded nemesis is looking particularly tough today, and my hands begin to sweat. By the time it's our turn to spar, I'm panicky, trying to appear nonchalant while remembering the moves I've been taught. When the moment comes, it's not quite as I had practiced in my visualizations with Dad. We are dragging each other around the mat when he grabs my belt, trying to lift me off balance. My *gi* starts to come undone, and squirming wildly, I wrench my arms out of the jacket, charging forward in under-shirted glory, abandoning all technique.

Puffing like steam engines, we wrestle desperately. Just as he lunges at me, I take a big step forward to catch my balance, and he accidentally falls over my extended leg. He hits the mat with a *splat*, whereupon I promptly trip on his foot and land flat on top of him. At the last second, I manage to position my elbow so it digs into his shoulder, hard.

Looking up hopefully, I see the startled face of our sensei, and my whole family grinning behind the glass, pumping their fists, as Dad mouths "fan-tas-tic!"

And that's how we blow town.

5: Vancouver, age 6

Why is it that the more ordinary a situation is, the more it paralyzes me with anxiety? I'm quite sure I could walk into war without hesitation, but socializing with my peers . . . *Oh God, make it stop.*

I watch the girl gymnasts near the uneven bars, applying chalk to their handgrips and clapping once or twice, releasing small puffs of white. They look decidedly cliquey. For now, I'm safe in the observation room among adults. There's a scattering of parents, including Mom, who lifts a pen and signs my registration form. "Okay, let's go!" Paul, the assistant coach, rubs his hands together energetically. I'm about to be flung out among *other children.*

We walk along the edge of the blue floor exercise mat, the fuzzy texture soft beneath my bare feet. "You're pretty quiet, huh?" Paul ventures, looking down at me.

I'm not sure how to answer, so I just smile, my default expression. But I think I know where his misconception is coming from. It's the sugar. Or lack thereof. Like most unhealthy foods, I've never even tasted the stuff, and only get treats in the form of honey or fruit. This perpetual lack of a sugar high may be what gives me a deceptively calm, almost serene, disposition. It also further alienates me from my peers, whom I've noticed spend large portions of their day either bouncing off walls or sulking. Not sure if it's the difference in diet, or the high standards I'm held to, but people regularly mistake me for a mellow, noncompetitive child.

They could not be more wrong.

In my head, I'm just beginning a campaign of world domination. In addition to gymnastics, I've joined Frank's swim team, much to his delight, and now wedge in an extra three workouts a week in the water. I may only be six, but I plan to be the fastest, the cleverest, the best—at everything. I'm just methodical about it.

We near the uneven-bar area and the girls turn to stare at me. Six of them, mostly a few years older than me and muscular. "This is Jen, Ashley, Megan, Ashley L., Shannon, and Ashley C.," Paul says.

"Hi." I smile, lifting one hand in a small wave and gesture of peace.

"Girls!" Paul drops a hand onto my tense shoulder. "This is Ha-babb-gin." He mangles my name. "From all over the place and India!"

The girls exchange smirking sideways looks and I think, *Oh Bhajan, brace yourself.*

FOR MOST OF our forty-five minute drive home, I sob uncontrolla-bly. In the course of the three-hour training session, I've had my hair pulled while being asked why it is so freakishly long, been sprayed with water and sprinkled with chalk while practicing bars, and been told that my name makes me sound like an incurable disease. They let up for a while after the head coach gave them a look, but rallied toward the end to shove me aside and inform me that my Aussie/South African hybrid accent was impossi-ble to understand. When I tried to explain, the ringleader, Shannon, said, "Whatever."

"Whatever what?" I was genuinely puzzled.

"Just whatever!" snapped Ashley L., her fists clenched.

As we drive away, the thought of returning is terrifying.

"Why are they so mean!?" I wail. "Nothing they say makes any sense. Not one of them argues logically!"

"They've been raised differently." Mom says. "That's how kids in school interact with each other. That's why we wanted to teach you at home."

"But why do they hate me so much?" I wipe some chalk off my leg and drag the sleeve of my *Kundalini Yoga* T-shirt under my nose.

"You're not like them. They've lived in the same place, with the same people their whole lives. Then you show up."

"I don't want to be different all the time!" My voice breaks. Mom takes her sympathetic eyes off the highway for a moment as I kick the underside of the dashboard repeatedly for effect.

"You are different, darling, and you always will be. Just remember—you're Harbhajan."

They always tell me this in moments of adversity, and I just don't get it. "That's part of the problem, Mom! Life would be so much easier if I were called Ashley."

For a long while she is silent, turning something over in her mind. "You know, being the same isn't all it's cracked up to be. It can be torture to find your way out of that . . . out of a place where everyone is afraid to be bold." A shadow settles across her face. "I grew up like that."

I am hardly breathing. She so rarely talks about herself that I keep my voice low, trying not to startle her, to keep her going. "When you were a kid in France?"

"Mhmm, and it wasn't until I met your father that I realized how important the way you think is. Having an open mind, believing in truth . . . believing in life." She turns to me with that look of hers, mischievous and almost shy. "I hope one day when you're older, when you're a woman, you'll realize why I'm so happy that you're different. That you are you."

But it just seems so far way. This childhood thing is lasting forever, and I don't know how much longer I can stomach the situation.

As we pull into our darkened driveway and the tall carved gates slide shut behind us, I'm cheered at the sight of our home. A two-story mansion overlooking Greater Vancouver, and surrounded by trees, hidden from the rest of the world, just the way Dad likes it. The big backyard, bursting with flowers, tumbles down a hill to our private swimming pool and a full-size trampoline—my favorite birthday present ever.

Pushing open the heavy door and kicking off my shoes, I trudge into our wood-floored living room. The only objects gracing the area are five plastic outdoor lounge chairs, with flowered weather-proof cushions. It seemed like a good temporary option when we moved in, and now, almost a year later, most of the house is still furnished with lawn paraphernalia. Sometimes, like right now, it irks me. Without the benefit of shelves, our collection of books are stacked against the wall, and papers and documents spill off the beige plastic picnic table in our dining room. Why can't we even try to appear normal? I pitch face down onto the rough fabric of the lounge chair and lie inert.

While we eat dinner, Chiara looking moody, Frank smelling of chlorine, and Mom spending more time serving us than actually eating, I search the darkness outside the window for the confident sweep of light that marks Dad's new Lincoln turning in. Lately, he seems to time his arrival to coincide with the end of family dinner. For a man with no real job, Dad spends a lot of time gone. It began shortly after our arrival in Canada, the absences, the increased strain between my parents. There is a slight tension in the room, an almost imperceptible shifting of molecules when he is home. We all sit a little straighter. Mom's gestures become more self-conscious. For once in my life I think know why: It was the interrogation.

Dad flew into Canada first—the rest of us were still laid over in Vienna on the way from South Africa. When he went through Vancouver airport, Dad set off alerts by refusing to answer a number of questions, and when we followed forty-eight hours later, Mom led us through customs and right into a trap. We were all separated for three hours and questioned. I was isolated in a small chilly room, with two pasty-skinned immigration officers popping in and out and repeatedly asking the same questions. "Where do your parents come from?" the man said sympathetically, blinking his pale watery eyes.

"I don't know."

"Where were your parents born?"

"Please ask my dad."

"We are asking you, honey, and you have to answer us."

Their manner hardened and a horrible dread traveled through me, making my legs go numb. They exchanged a look and then smiled thinly at me. "Here, have a candy." The female officer held out a brightly colored oval, shiny under the interrogation lights.

My fear was immediately replaced by anger. "I'm not allowed to eat sugar," I said, gripping the table edge with one sweaty hand. Shifting away,

I noticed the damp outline my fingers left on the table. *Prints.* I wiped surreptitiously at the impression with the sleeve of the sweater Mom knitted according to my exact specifications. A fuzzy white pullover with a holy cow from India and a lion, my birth-sign, holding hands across my chest.

The man paused his rhythmic tapping of a pen as if registering what I had just done; then he frowned, seeming to dismiss it as impossible. Six-year-olds don't wipe prints. The interrogator leaned back, tapping his pen again and watching me. The contrast of his slight, soft hand with my father's strong, tanned one helped me lift my chin. I looked at the agent directly for once.

"Why did your parents—"

"Ask my dad." I snapped.

When we were finally reunited, Mom was furious that I had been taken away alone, but I think what truly upset her was the fact that Dad gave us no prior warning. I've intuited all this from expert eavesdropping: it's the only way to figure anything out in this family.

Now, as we eat at the table, headlights sweep through the kitchen window, and I breathe out with relief.

"Greetings." Dad places some papers and his tea thermos on the counter and walks through to the living room without pausing. I watch him pass, sensing this new unease. Or, perhaps it's been here for a while, and I was just too young to notice?

AT NIGHT WHEN the house is dark and quiet, I sometimes wander, deeply pleased with the sheer permanence of it. Padding across the cool brick-colored tiles of the kitchen in just my oversized swim team shirt, I hear raised voices from upstairs.

The fluffy white carpet tickles my naked feet as I climb the steps in slow motion and hesitate outside my parents' door. "I think it's tempting fate again, it's dangerous! Why would you do this just when we're finally making a life here?" My mother's voice is confused, but not angry.

"It's only a few interviews on the gold market."

"But we're using a different identity here. Your photo was in the newspaper! What if someone recognizes you?"

"I haven't lived here in years."

"It's still opening us up to being found. You used your real name!"

This catches my attention. I have no idea what my parents' real names or birth dates are. Neither do my siblings. Chiara said she used to know when she was small but can no longer remember. I'm always told it's for my own good, in case I'm ever questioned—and it's true, the airport interrogation was made markedly easier by the fact that I don't know squat.

What family history I do know begins when my parents met, with only vague details on anything before that auspicious day. I know my mom is French and was working in a French bank when she met my dad. I love hearing the story of how she opened the door of the private bank to a new client, asking the requisite "how are you?" and expecting a stock answer. The man on the doorstep spread his arms as wide as his smile and said "fan-tas-tic." They married after a year, and a couple years later Chiara was born, followed quickly by Frank. After a ten-year gap, "to prepare for magnificence," as Dad likes to say, I burst onto the scene. These things I know. The rest is vague, like the fog that settles over Vancouver some mornings. Dense and unmoving. If you wander out into it, it makes you feel lost and disoriented—but also shielded from the world. Insulated on all sides by a cushion of white.

"We've been so careful about the new names, the backstory, everything, and then you give an interview using your real one. He can track that. He could find us—"

"Relax, I've got it handled. It's business."

"We have enough money; it's unnecessary to publicize yourself."

"I'll handle it," he says with finality.

Back in my room, I curl under my comforter and stare out the window, watching the lights sparkle across Lions Gate Bridge. The problem with eavesdropping is that you are left alone with all this information and no one to talk to about it. Closing my eyes, I try to relax. *Dad will take care of it. Doesn't he always?*

But one question won't leave me in peace . . . who is "he"?

"Now listen, don't let these nincompoops bother you." Dad is driving, one hand on the wheel, the other gesturing to emphasize his point, as we speed toward gymnastics practice. "They're just a bunch of undeveloped followers; of course they're going to gang up on you, my little independent thinker."

"But what do I do? They're scary!"

"Smile. Never let them see it getting to you. Deny them the satisfaction of upsetting you."

I gape at him. "But they *are* upsetting me."

"Sure, but they don't need to know that. True strength is in how you handle adversity. So smile and bounce it back on those philistines!"

I gaze doubtfully at my bare knees, wondering exactly what philistines are.

"I'll be there the whole time," he says. "Come get me if you need anything and we'll bash some heads together."

In the locker room, I pull on my favorite blue leotard and take a deep breath. Things will probably get better when I get bigger—it's *got* to get easier. Squaring my shoulders, I walk out onto the gym floor where the other girls are stretching. I start to falter, debating the idea of just heading back to the locker room and waiting out my childhood. But somewhere behind the observation glass, I sense the presence of my father. Lifting my chin, I turn to the girls and *smile*.

Shortly thereafter, I notice myself beginning to go deaf.

It starts slowly. I'm waiting to practice my tumbling lines with the other girls when I realize it's almost impossible to hear them. I ask Ashley L. to repeat herself, but I'm only able to catch every second or third word.

"Do you have a hearing issue or something?" Even Shannon looks slightly concerned.

Two days later, I have my first appointment with an ear specialist. I've hardly ever been to a doctor, never been immunized, and being surrounded by all these clinical-looking metal probes makes my heart thump.

Dad stands at my side. The doctor enters, appearing both chummy and insincere, and starts poking and prodding with steel instruments.

"Well, I don't see anything wrong at the moment," he shrugs, "but we can run more tests. Are you hearing fine now?"

"Now it's fine, but it comes and goes."

"Hmm. I can't see anything wrong. Are you sure you're not imagining it, dear?"

"Quack!" Dad harrumphs as we leave the building. "Typical of the mainstream medical profession."

"I know!" I stomp along indignantly by his side. We rectify the situation by going to our favorite place in the world, to sprinkle cinnamon over hot Starbucks apple cider, and recover from our brush with conformity.

But it keeps happening.

I'm in a handstand, upside down on the balance beam, four feet above the ground, when someone hits the beam sending vibrations down its length. Losing my balance, I fall to the mat and look around in confusion.

"Didn't you hear us!? It's Ashley's turn!" The girls are staring at me, looking concerned. It seems smiling in the face of their bullying is making them more considerate. If I am going deaf, at least I have this small comfort.

Two days later, I'm taken to get my ears cleaned. "Now, this will only hurt a bit," the doctor says, patting my hand as the chair hums into a horizontal position. She is a colossal liar. The fifteen minute cleaning is so painful that it's difficult to stand afterward, my equilibrium thrown off. As I'm led out to be medicated at Starbucks, I vow never to go back to one of these people in white coats again. I much prefer the hippie-skirted, patchouli-scented healers we normally frequent. Smash up some herbs and call it a day.

And then—in the middle of a gymnastics competition—I figure out that I've been had.

My teammates and I are looking slick, suited up in our matching long-sleeved team leotards, red with a silver maple leaf, hair pulled back and secured with a liter of hairspray. We're warming up for the first event when a thunderous whoop sounds from the audience, startling me. Dad's trademark battle cry. Then again, ever since I've had my ears cleaned, everything sounds *so loud*.

Ashley touches my arm and says something. But I can't hear her. I strain forward, a familiar sense of panic setting in. Shannon is next to me, her hands gesturing urgently, but still I can't hear a thing.

A girl from another team notices us. "Why are you guys doing that?" she looks at my teammates questioningly. I realize I can hear the new girl perfectly. "Is it a joke or something, just moving your lips?" she asks Shannon.

I can feel my mouth hanging open, but I'm unable to close it. My teammates are suddenly busying themselves with all manner of activity. Stretching, jogging in place to stay loose, staring intently at the ceiling.

I'm filled with a hot rush of humiliation. They've been conning me this whole time, pretending to speak, emitting no sound, making me feel I'm going crazy. Instinctively, I search the bleachers for help. My family has noticed that something is wrong. Dad gives me his stern look and points to his eyes. In the repertoire of hand signals familiar to anyone who's done competitive sports, it means *focus*.

Shaking the pins out of my legs, I try to erase the hurt from my face. So maybe smiling at my teammates wasn't the wisest approach. But since I've gotten this far into it, it's hard to double back or change course. What else can you do in this kind of situation? Show up looking massively depressed, and hope for mercy?

The judges raise their red flag and it's my turn. I swallow hard, lift my arms to acknowledge each of the arbiters, and smile.

Is that how these things start in life? You're not even sure it works but it seems like a good idea at the time, and then off you go, smiling against all odds.

IT'S A CREDIT to the blind optimism of my mother that she refuses to give up trying to socialize me. Personally I feel I can do without my peers, but Mom is now the founder of a local Vancouver Abacus group, a children's puppet theater, and an art class taught by a giant woman in multicolored muumuus who says I use too much paint. Apparently I also use too much glue, clay, paper, glitter, and reserves of her patience.

The other kids are well behaved, good British Columbians, recruited by Mom at the Wild Oats health food store or our swimming club. They understand the concept of moderation, whereas I only understand yes or no. Either I'm forbidden to have something, like sugar or a negative attitude, or it's full steam ahead. In short, I am every art teacher's nightmare, and every sports coach's dream.

Today I've been instructed to put on my nice pink dress and report for duty downstairs at the ungodly hour of 7:30 a.m. The whole gang assembles to drive me to a new place called Sunday School. I'm confused by this Western ritual and ask a few times why it has to be on this day, when we could all be sleeping in. I mean, couldn't it be moved to a Tuesday?

"Sunday is when Christians go to church." Dad turns down an unfamiliar tree-lined street.

"I'm going to a church?" I sit up straighter. So far I've only been to temples and ashrams. *A church—exotic!* I straighten the hem of my dress as we pull into the parking lot of a large building with a pointed top. A convoy of minivans are already pulling out. Frank smirks at me, Chiara pats my shoulder a little too encouragingly, and I'm delivered to Miss Laura, a very happy-seeming woman who asks me how I'm doing in a startling clear voice, as if I'm slightly brain-dead.

We're late as usual, and a group of twelve kids are sitting in a large circle on the floor, looking neat and polished. They appear friendly, scooching apart to make room for me in the circle. Fabulous!

"Welcome to Sunday School!" Our teacher tucks a piece of her shiny dark bob behind an ear and smiles benevolently at us. "We have a new friend here today, her name is *Buuuh-khan*. Everyone say hello!"

"Hello, *Buuuh-khan!*" The circle says obediently.

"Hi." I lift a hand. A few kids wave back before we realize it looks weird and turn to the teacher for further instruction.

"Today we will be talking about Jesus and what he means to us." Okay fine, so far so good. I wait for her to elaborate. "How does Jesus affect your lives? Are you close to him?"

I'm beginning to feel uneasy. But everyone else seems to be following her.

"We know he watches over us, and sees everything that we do, which is why it's important to be good. But how do you feel about Jesus?"

Oh no, she's going to make us speak now. *Who is this Jesus guy?* And why are we all supposed to know about him? Is it something they covered last week?

"Megan?" The teacher points to the pretty girl beside me, wearing an emerald ribbon at the end of her braid. Why don't we ever have time to accessorize me?

"He watches over me," Megan says with an authority that makes me believe her. "And makes sure people are doing the *right* thing." I'm absorbing this, when I realize I'm sitting next to Megan, and have a 50-50 chance of being called on next.

"Buuuh-khan?"

No!

"Yes!" I say brightly. I can't let my family down, and search my brain for clues. "I think I . . . like him?" Pausing, I watch for reactions, checking if I'm on the right track here. No one seems outraged, so I take a firmer stance. "Yes, I like him. He um, seems nice."

Miss Laura is frowning at me. "But I'm not sure . . ." I conclude lamely, leaving my options open.

"Mmm." She pins me with her eyes, "But what does Jesus mean to you? What does he *represent*?"

Everyone stares at me, and I frantically shuffle through the information I've gleaned. A man. Who watches you. Who makes sure you're behaving . . . "Interpol!" I say triumphantly.

The moment it's out, I know I've gone wrong. I hasten to explain, "Like the cops, you know, watching you."

When it's mercifully over I'm led out to the car by Dad, terrified that

I've blown our cover, and take my place between Frank and Chiara in the backseat.

"How'd it go?" Mom asks me hopefully.

"She got kicked out of Sunday School," Dad replies. He turns the engine on, leans back, and bursts into laughter. Mom's shoulders start to shake uncontrollably and she rests her forehead on the dash, giggling. I'm so relieved that I temporarily forget to be upset at being dropped into a situation without any knowledge to go on.

"Bravo, Bhajan!" Dad turns around to grin at me, proud as can be at my expulsion from the church. "'Interpol'! Well done, that's independent thinking for you."

"You have to brief me next time!" I cross my arms, relief shifting to indignation. "Those people! From the way they talk about Jesus, you'd think he was related to God or something."

6: Vancouver, age 7

THE FIELD IS covered with colorful tents, portable grills flickering to life outside. The aroma of hot dogs and sharp mustard mingle with freshly cut grass. Summer swimming has begun, and the march toward Nationals is on. Continuing my quest to overachieve, I'm still dedicating myself to two sports. Sure, the cartilage in my wrists is painfully worn down from intense gymnastic workouts, and there's a constant ache in my shoulders from swimming; but after almost two years on Frank's team, I'm finally ready to try out for Nationals.

Today are the qualifying races. The only one I have a shot at, fifty-meter freestyle, won't happen for another three hours. So I slip cautiously through the woods, hiding myself behind a giant tree, while the rest of the team—or those of us uncool enough to play hide and seek—search for me. Sunshine filters through the leaves, painting patterns on the forest floor and releasing the warm scent of pine needles and earth. I hear my hunters crunching across the pine carpet. But the trees here are hundreds of years old, with trunks so large an entire swim squad could vanish behind them. British Columbia is ideal for disappearing; maybe that's why we chose it.

Stepping closer to the tree in my bulky red Birkenstocks, I rest my sore hands against the rough bark and breathe in deeply. It's so peaceful here. I know that Mom is, at this very moment, heating water for our organic instant split-pea soup cups. According to Dad, let the competition pollute themselves with donuts and soda; we will meditate, before snacking on almonds and dried seaweed strips.

I'll need any help I can get. Just weeks ago, a consortium of swim-mothers threatened to formally eject me from my age group. They've seen me, stay-ing after every practice with Frank, swimming endless laps. The moms said

I'm trying to become "too fast" and demanded to see my birth certificate, as proof that I'm not a twenty-year-old man.

In truth, I'm not built for this sport. My body is too slim, almost frail-looking next to the muscular build of other competitors. But the other kids aren't as obsessed. They are distracted by the rest of their life, whereas this is my life. By the time we managed to find my latest fake birth certificate, featuring my real birthdate and the false last name we are using here, the moms had kicked me out anyway. At the age of seven, I'll now have to compete against girls who are a year older. This is yet another reason why I wish we would keep the house neater. What's the point of spending thousands of dollars on these pieces of forged paper, if we can hardly ever find them under all the vitamin bottles and books?

Back in the cool shade of our tent, I sit cross-legged on a blanket and blow on the pale green pea soup. "It's so good to see you like this, Bhajan," Mom says softly.

I raise my eyebrows questioningly. Like what? With my mouth full?

"I mean all natural, muddy, with leaves in your hair. It makes me so happy. I really didn't want you raised in those five-star hotels anymore. It's not right."

"Be honest Mom, were you getting tired of my poofy dress?"

"The dress is fine . . ." She winks. "It's more that I want you to know you don't have to be perfect. I like my Bhajan at her most messy." Her face has turned serious and we sit in silence for a moment. Often, when she looks at me like this, I feel protective of her, of the uncomplicated way she sees me. I wish I could express that she's not the one I sense I have to keep impressing. It's not her expression I analyze in the crowd of parents, when I fall short of first place. But instead, I take a big mouthful of soup and we smile at each other, me with a split pea stuck to my front tooth.

At dusk, the swim meet over, Frank, Chiara, and I sit outside, spent and freckled, watching the fireflies dance in the air as the last flames of the grills flicker out. Adults are always saying that kids don't know enough to appreciate their youth. But I disagree. My siblings and I feel the magic of this summer. After moving around constantly, these endless days, the smell of chlorine and sunblock lingering on our skin, are special. For the rest, there will always be next summer, next year. For us, everything we are tasting may be for the last time.

DAD'S INNOVATIVE NEW project is born while chatting with a father named Stephan at swim practice. When he learns that Stephan has patented something called the Spinner they decide to partner up and make a few million. A flat piece of plastic with a smooth curved bottom, the Spinner—only $9.99!—is meant to be placed on a bare floor, allowing the user to stand on it and practice skating spins.

Our child-labor assembly line is set up in the dining room next to the big plastic table, stacked high with Spinner paraphernalia and packing materials. Chiara is in charge of writing addresses on the boxes before passing them to me for filling, and then I hand off to Frank for sealing and taping. After an hour we have a nice rhythm going.

It's very pleasant to sit in our lovely house with the view over the bay, busily at work on an enterprise of this glamour and magnitude. Family unity is intoxicating to me. We may not always eat dinner together, but we fulfill orders like a well-oiled machine. Dad keeps an amused eye on us while sorting mail and reviewing what looks like the new Spinner ad he designed in his usual bold strokes. Taking a break, I check out what he's come up with. The final print is brightly colored and eye-catching, with a large red star in the foreground containing the words: *As seen on TV!*

It has, of course, never been on TV.

"Can you spot the inserts?" he asks, handing me the paper. From our mountain of books, we've recently been studying one on subliminal images in advertising—poring over the photos to uncover, for example, skulls in the ice cubes of whiskey ads. Wherever we travel, and no matter how fast we leave, the books never get left behind. At least one suitcase is filled to bursting with his esoteric volumes on religion, history, world politics, and conspiracies. He always seems to be searching for answers, for the real story. And since we rarely have a TV, us kids follow suit, devouring the unusual by the stack. I need a lot of Dad's help to grasp anything he assigns me to read, but luckily he loves to talk. Still, it came as a shock to me that concealing symbols of death in ads is a highly effective way to sell certain products.

"You put a skull in here?" I squint, searching his Spinner ad.

"Well, I was thinking of adding something like that, but we've got the wrong demographic for death. That's more effective for alcohol and cigarettes."

"Oh," I say.

"In life, you have to know your target market. So instead, I've put the word *fun* in subliminally."

I nod admiringly. A well-thought-out decision, if you ask me.

On my rare days off from training, I love to ride along with Mom and pick up Chiara from herbal college, where she is studying for a degree in natural healing. It's a reputable school, one of the best places to study alternative medicine, but that doesn't stop me from making fun of the students, who never cease to crack me up. My favorite is a girl who thinks she's an angel, wears only white, and will only eat vegan white foods. She's studying nutrition but subsists on a diet of white bread, soy butter sandwiches and steamed cauliflower. I've asked the angel about this contradiction a few times, but she never seems amused.

Chiara, annoyed after one of my cross-examinations of her classmate, sulks in the front seat next to Mom.

"What about bananas?" I venture from the back.

"Bhajan, stop it." Chiara sighs.

"It's a valid question," I protest. "Can the angel eat something that is yellow on the outside but white on the inside?"

"Ugh."

"That's okay," I grin. "I'll ask her myself next week."

"I'm sick of her making fun of them!" Chiara turns fiercely to Mom. "It wasn't even my idea to go there in the first place. I wanted to go to normal college."

"But you like going there now!"

I slide down guiltily in my seat. This is a continuation of a fight they've been having on and off for weeks. Dad is impossible to argue with, so Chiara's been taking out her frustration on Mom, who sympathizes with all our struggles.

"I like it now, but not at the beginning!" Chiara is nearly hysterical; her face flushed, hair all over the place, "Everyone else my age is free to do what they want! I'm always being supervised!"

"Doing whatever you want isn't always a good thing." Mom unlocks the front door to the house and we follow her in. "If you get out of your head and *think* about it a bit—"

"Stop telling me what to do!"

Without warning, Chiara lifts her knee and lands a firm kick on Mom's shin. There is a sharp *smack* as her foot hits Mom's bare skin. I hear myself gasp, and with surprising vehemence, Chiara goes in for another kick.

What happens next seems to occur both very quickly and in slow motion. Dad climbs the steps from the living room to the foyer. In four long, athletic strides, he's in front of Chiara. His hard punch lands on her jaw, making her legs buckle, and she goes down. "Enough!" he snaps at Chiara and then turns, leaving the room. I jump back instinctively as he passes, my body tense.

A strange sense of unreality descends; we're frozen in position, forming a silent triangle. Mom and me on our feet, Chiara crumpled on the floor. Then, avoiding eye contact, Chiara stands, gathers her bag, and climbs the stairs. After some hesitation, Mom goes up as well, turning the opposite direction down the hall.

I look around the empty place, my heartbeat the only sound. Everything looks normal; the house is still, not a mark on the wood floor. I place my shoes neatly side by side near the door. It almost seems as if nothing has happened.

7: British Columbia, age 7

IT'S BARELY DAWN as I climb to the top of a gentle rise overlooking the huge Olympic-size swim complex where Nationals are being held. The massive structure looming out of the fog would be intimidating enough, but the sprawling field outside is packed with tents. It resembles an army encampment, one dominated by kids in tracksuits who have beaten a whole bunch of other kids to qualify. I stand on the grass, dew shining like tiny droplets of light, and breathe in the slightly chill air. All those hours of training distilled into one summer day outside Vancouver.

"A dollar for your thoughts." Dad has stayed beside me on the hill, while the others look for a spot below.

"Isn't it a penny?"

"Inflation, Bhajan." He tilts his panama hat back and we contemplate the vista.

"It's just . . ." I shuffle my damp sneakers. "The faster I get . . . the less people seem to like me." I'm thinking in particular of Sara, my closest friend on the team, and always faster. But lately only by a bit. There is a difference in the way she looks at me, now that only a second separates us.

"Well, there it is." Dad heaves the folded tent to his other shoulder. "Sometimes you have to choose between being accepted or being the best."

THE ROARING FROM thousands of spectators echoes around the pool as we file in to compete. Hardly anyone thought I would qualify for the final in this age group and my legs feel strangely weak. When we slow for a moment, I close my eyes and visualize the race the way Dad has taught me. Trying to conjure every detail, every sensation.

The cheering quiets as we strip off our tracksuit jackets and line up behind the starting blocks. This is it. Sara and I, next to each other in the center lanes of the pool. We avoid eye contact.

"Swimmers, take your places." We climb onto the blocks; the water shining like cold glass below.

"On your marks." I give my special black swim cap one last tug. Unable to resist, Dad took the words of the consortium of mothers to heart, and had *Too Fast* printed next to the Speedo logo above my left ear.

"Get set . . ." The gun sounds, and we're flying through the air. As soon as the water closes in around me, I know it's a good dive. But pushing off for the final lap I see the last thing I want to. Feet. In front of me.

Sara has passed me—as usual. I'm gritting my teeth trying to at least get closer, when she does something truly surprising. She looks back. Under the water, I see her angle her head awkwardly to check where I am. We're taught never to do this because it slows you down, and that's what gives me hope. She's worried. About me.

I stop breathing to save time. The water turns white from my windmilling arms and I see nothing. Just swim, head forward, heart pounding, as fast as I can. My lungs are burning as my hands hit the sensor board and I surface, gasping desperately for oxygen. On my left, Sara is holding on to the side of the pool, breathing heavily and looking up at the large electronic scoreboard. A few seconds pause, and our names appear. Scanning quickly I see mine sixth down on the board, with Sarah one place ahead, a number 5 next to her name. Here, at Nationals, we aren't even near the top.

Ah, well. I pull my cap and goggles off and sink down briefly under the water to cool off. Resurfacing with my head tilted back, the first thing I see is my starting block, with its white background and black number: 6. Only now, do I realize what everyone else has already figured out. We're listed in order of lane number. And there it is, to the right of my name: 1st Place.

Without thinking, I reach out to touch Sara's shoulder. But she tosses her cap and goggles onto the ledge of the pool and starts to get out, face hard.

Ten minutes later, I stand barefoot on the grass outside the stadium door waiting for the gang to come down from the bleachers and find me.

Sara is a few meters away, looking in the other direction, still ignoring me. The arena door opens and her mom comes out, moving briskly, shaking her head. She hands a towel to Sara, who tries to say something, almost pleading. Her mother dismisses her with a disgusted wave and walks toward the tents.

Sara is left alone, hugging the towel around herself and chewing a corner. I fear exactly what she must feel, to have fallen short of all that was expected of her. To have wavered and looked back at me, the girl who isn't as fast, but wanted it more. Watching Sara move away, a sensation of loneliness mingles with my glow and I stare at the ground. Have I sacrificed a friendship just because I wanted to win, to be the best in his eyes? Her figure has become small, just an outline on the field of green, by the time I sense this was never really about us.

This day, this race, will stay with me like no other. But not because I've won. Because, standing barefoot on the grass, I'm finally beginning to grasp why my father sets expectations so punishingly high, and then doesn't care about medals or other people's praise. It was never about coming in first, because I already had. Many, many, times. He's been showing me for months how to visualize the impossible so clearly that I could feel the water, the rush of my blood. Physically, I was not strong enough to make it. But he made me envision it. I believed, and it happened. It's as if magic is right here, a thing you can bring to life.

The metal door to the stands crashes open and my family rushes out onto the grass. Dangling upside down off Dad's shoulder, with Frank tickling my tummy, the world begins to realign itself. I guess this race has proven Dad's life philosophy was right all along. No matter how scared you are, or how many people are chasing you . . . never, never, look back.

8: Vancouver, age 8

THE RINGING OF our front doorbell signals the beginning of the end.

I've never actually heard the chimes before, and look around in confusion for the source. It's 9 p.m.; no one knows where we live. It only takes an instant for us to panic. Mom peeks out the side window. "It's Stephan. He looks angry."

Stephan, Dad's partner in the Spinner business, has been asking too many questions lately, especially about why my father doesn't want his name on any of the formal documents.

"Dammit, how did he find us?" Dad hisses.

"He must have followed one of our cars home." Mom edges away from the window.

"Didn't you check for a tail?"

"I always do. You know that," she says defensively. It's actually Dad who sometimes doesn't check. We are frequently distracted when he lets me steer during the last leg of a car ride, or when I get out and cling to the hood while he swerves around gently, pretending to try to dislodge me.

The bell sounds again. "I know you're inside!" Stephan's voice carries through the door. "If you don't open up I'm going to call the police!"

Mom's face loses all color. It doesn't matter if Stephan has anything on us or not: We must avoid contact with the cops at all costs. "You go talk to him, calm him down," Dad directs Mom. He turns his back and moves swiftly out the back door into the dark garden. A moment later, I make out Dad's silhouette running down the hill leading to our pool and then vanishing into the forest.

Mom breathes deeply, steeling herself to open the door. I'm hidden behind Chiara's arm when we hear their raised voices. "He can't agree to start a business and then say he doesn't want his name on anything. I've invested a lot, and suddenly he wants out?!"

"He's letting you keep all the money, so I would think that's quite a good deal."

It's typical of Dad to start something, turn it into a success, and then abruptly lose interest.

"Why are you people so secretive? I think you're hiding something." Stephan is yelling now. Chiara and I exchange worried looks while Frank walks over to stand beside Mom. Fully grown at eighteen, Frank's muscular six-two frame seems to check Stephan, who lowers his voice. "Something's off here. And I intend to find out what it is."

I glimpse him raising his chin before Mom closes the door.

An hour later, Dad slips in from the night, and that's when everything falls apart.

Frank, Chiara, and I wait tensely in the backyard while our parents talk inside, their figures illuminated by the kitchen light. After a time, Mom steps out, looking exhausted. "We're going to have to leave."

"What? Nooo!" Chiara starts to sob. "But I'm finally doing well in college—"

"Look, I'm sorry. But your father says it's too dangerous to stay."

I can see Mom's been crying, and my heart tightens. "It'll be fine, Mom," I say automatically, climbing the steps and putting on a smile.

"Nooo it won't," Chiara wails behind us.

"Shut up!" Frank yells.

Mom puts a hand to her forehead. "He wants to leave tomorrow morning at the latest, so we have to pack tonight."

The breath has been knocked out of me. I'm used to blowing town with no warning, but those were places we were just passing through. I've actually made friends during our time here. There's a birthday party at the roller rink in a few days, gymnastics competitions coming up, summer swimming next year . . .

By 4 a.m., it looks like a tornado has torn through our house. Clothes, books, and toys are scattered on the floor, interspersed with rapidly filling suitcases. "I just don't see why this is necessary! We haven't done anything wrong." Mom's voice carries into the big kitchen from the living room, where Dad is burning business documents in the stone fireplace. We stop packing and start eavesdropping.

"So, you want to put everyone at risk just to stick around." Dad's voice has a menacing edge to it.

"But we *aren't* at risk! And the kids are finally settled here. We've built a life! It's taken two years. They have friends and they're doing so well—"

"This is how people get caught. They get soft and sentimental. So if you want to sabotage the whole operation and put everyone in danger, then by all means, let's stay."

There is silence, and when she speaks again I can tell she's fighting tears. "All right, all right. I just worry about them having to start over so many times."

"It'll do them good. They need to get toughened. Let's finish packing."

Three hours later we are at the airport, bleary-eyed, with four-teen suitcases and assorted bags. Most of our possessions have been left behind, anything with names burned or thrown away in random gar-bage bins on the way to the airport. Chiara, Frank, and I move our lug-gage while Mom and Dad peel off toward the ticket counters, trying to find a charter flight we can get on without appearing in the passenger log.

I shiver in the brisk, early-fall wind as airplanes roar overhead, drown-ing out my thoughts. I've had no sleep, no time to stop and think, and I'm not sure I want to. Loading our bags onto trolleys, Frank looks over at Chiara and sighs. She is dressed, as usual, in baggy layers of worn clothes, all varying shades of brown or gray. We suspect she does it just to annoy us, and it works. "Why do you insist on trying to look homeless?" Frank leans on one of the trolleys, frowning.

"Do you really think this is what we should be worrying about now, Frank?" She purses her lips, raising a bushy eyebrow.

"Yes, I do." He nods. "I really do."

I'M ALREADY BUCKLED into the window seat of a plane when I find out we're on the way to Toronto. Or, at least, we're going there for now. Direct flights are for amateurs; a layover is essential for breaking the trail while getting out of the country. In Toronto International Airport, Dad decides our future country of residence by scanning the departure board to see which flights are leaving soonest. The numbers and destinations change with brisk clicks as well-organized strangers glide by, each towing a single neat black roller suitcase. This concept of "traveling light" fascinates me. It took me until the age of five to figure out that other people didn't take all their worldly possessions with them to airports. I just assumed they only owned a small carry-on bag's worth of things.

Dad picks a flight but I'm still in the dark. While I'm watching, Mom puts a hand on his arm and discusses something quietly, almost as if asking a question. Then she walks away, an international phone card in hand. It must be sensitive. An untraceable call from the airport of a city you are about to abandon is as careful as you can be. At a phone booth across the shiny white terminal, Mom's body undergoes a strange transformation. She seems to become smaller, folding in on herself.

I slip away from the others and walk toward her. She is speaking a language that I've never heard before, all harsh consonants, and her face is streaked with tears. I am reaching out instinctively to touch her when someone grabs my shoulder: Dad. Angrily, he marches me back to my siblings, fingers digging into my arm, before releasing me to go keep an eye out for our gate number. Desperate to know what's wrong, I pester Frank and Chiara for information until she stalks off; but he begins to waver.

"Please," I whisper. "No one ever tells me anything. I can keep my mouth shut, you know that!"

"You want to know?" Frank looks straight at me with his dark eyes. "Fine. That's her father she's calling."

I need a moment to absorb this; I always assumed her parents were dead.

"Then why is she sad?"

When he answers, it's in a strange voice that makes me step back: "Because he's the one chasing us."

9: Germany, age 8

FLUORESCENT AIRPORT LIGHTS, a baggage carousel like a winding silver snake, more people with neat black roller bags. Outside, the cold air slices through my light jacket as we pile into two taxis, luggage overflowing. I try to flex my stiff wrists, but pain shoots up my arms. It's been getting steadily worse in the last months and there seems no way to reverse the damage.

"Okay! Here's the plan," Dad announces when we are standing, thirty minutes later, in Frankfurt's main train station. "We take the first train to Hanover, and we'll switch to another there." Apparently while I was in the bathroom they decided we are going to Hamburg, mostly because of the city's world-renowned Olympic-swim-training facility.

"Don't you think we should get a hotel and rest first?" Mom suggests carefully.

"No. Let's keep going."

When the train roars into the station, its doors open with a pneumatic *whoosh*. "Look at that." Dad glances at his watch. "Right on the dot. German efficiency, Bhajan. That's how they almost won the war."

It seems like we've barely transferred our mountain of bags into a compartment, the landscape flying by outside, when Dad's ears perk up at the next-station announcement. "Is this it? All these places sound the same, BadenWadenBurgerDorf."

Mom scans the tickets. "This is it, our stop's coming up."

"Bags to the exit!" Dad orders, and I shove my feet back into my unlaced sneakers. We're a quarter-way done, when we realize how greatly we've misjudged the timing. The train is already slowing down and pulling into the station and most of our bags are still in our compartment. Frank, Chiara and I lurch toward the corridor in the same instant, getting wedged together in the doorway before elbowing each other out of the way.

Dad has two bags strapped to his shoulders and one hanging around his neck when the doors open. Clumping down the steps, he drops everything outside. Frank starts to follow. "No, no," Dad yells, "Just throw it!" Frank begins hurling our bags out the door. They fly in soaring arcs before landing with a thump on the platform in front of shocked fellow travelers.

Ignoring the pain in my wrists, I grab the last bag and am staggering toward the doors when I hear an ominous click, as they prepare to slam shut. My family stares up at me from the platform. In a cluster, they start running toward me, arms outstretched.

"Jump, Bhajan!"

"Bhajan, get out!"

I leap off the second step, the train doors snapping shut behind my ankles, and land twisted to one side. Automatically, I bend my knees, going into a shoulder roll and come to an awkward stop on my back.

And that is why all kids should be put into judo class. You just never know when you're going to need to drop and roll.

WHEN WE ARRIVE in Hamburg, everything is gray: the sky, the buildings, even the busy street. I haven't really slept in more than forty-eight hours and have no idea what day or time it is. All I'm sure of is that I'm standing outside the Hauptbahnhof, local code for train station, shivering and ravenous, while Mom is in a phone booth trying to find us a place to live.

"Accechtung!" a deep voice yells and a man on a bicycle swerves past me. I rub my eyes, watching him pedal away at warp speed.

"Fahrradweg!" A lanky woman bellows, barely missing my foot. Come to think of it, I've never seen so many bikes; thousands are locked to metal railings outside the station and more keep whizzing by, ringing warning bells, carrying angry people who scream at me.

As my eyes fill with tears, a hand grabs mine and yanks me backward. Mom has left the phone hanging by its cord and is standing in front of me, her edges blurred. "That's a bike lane! You were standing right in the middle of it."

"How was I supposed to know that!" I hear a faint note of hysteria creep into my voice.

"Just sit with the bags, I need to get back to the phone. Your dad wants a place with a kitchen."

I doubt this is the time to be so particular, but I keep my mouth shut and go sit outside the station on our pile of possessions.

After what seems like hours, I'm sleepwalked into a taxi, and then unloaded on a different, quieter sidewalk in front of a four-story apartment building. A wizened elderly woman emerges on the front stoop and looks us over with a disapproving gaze. "You are ze American family Roberts?" We smile at her. Greetings! Her white eyebrows draw together with terrifying slowness. "You are *late*."

"Welcome to Germany," Frank sighs, heading up the path.

8 A.M.: Wake up. Go promptly back to sleep.

8:10 a.m.: Wake up again. Chiara is already up and about, her face blank. I wish I could read her, could either actively like or dislike her, but the main sensation she stirs is one of unease. Of not being able to fasten onto who she really is. Sometimes she catches me staring, and when I rise from bed, she meets my eyes sharply. One thing's for sure, nothing gets past her. My sister and I are sharing the main room of the two-room furnished apartment, with Frank in the bedroom. Mom and Dad are in an interconnecting studio. If you can't find a three-bedroom on short notice, *make it work*. I've made a purchase that gives me hope our new life will have some permanence, and I squint at my three goldfish through sleep-heavy eyes. My favorite, Lionheart, swims up to me and hovers in place, easily distinguishable with his extravagant orange fins.

8:30 a.m.: Frank plops down beside me at the breakfast table and starts shoveling muesli into his mouth. Or should I say Roy? As soon as we woke up the day after arriving in Germany, we were told to choose new names. This time we're making a complete change, not just our family name. Thus, Chiara is Sara, Frank is Roy, and I have become Crystal. So far I've tripped up a few times, calling Frank or Chiara by their former names in public, but we usually get it right. Carefully I pick all the raisins out of my muesli and hand the offending fruits to Frank, who actually likes extra shriveled grapes in his cereal.

9:00 a.m.: At my desk, I plow through a page of math problems that Mom has given me. Really, the only good thing about having to run away from a place is that my schooling is always suspended during the escape.

11 a.m.: I've never felt a winter like this. An icy Siberian wind gusts through Hamburg, gluing my watery eyelashes together. I try to vanish further into my jacket as we trudge through the snow to the U-Bahn. Chiara and Frank are off to German class before Frank's swim training—where he's already at Olympic level—while I'm heading to gymnastics with Mom. Six days a week, we take the subway out to a gray concrete factorylike building, where I train for three and a half hours. I'm beginning to realize I made a pretty big mistake.

After our arrival in Deutschland, in addition to a new name, I was told to choose between gymnastics and swimming. In order to impress my parents, I opted for gymnastics, which is harder, more dangerous, and which I'm worse at. Now I'm stuck. Because they went ahead and hired me a private coach.

"Hey, wie gehts?" I walk into the still and silent gym, wearing my leotard, hair tied into a tight bun with ten elastics.

"Nicht schlecht," *Not bad*, Anatoli says with a typically Russian one-shoulder shrug. I'm just beginning to learn German, and since he speaks only German and Russian, our early training sessions resemble two cavemen trying to coordinate a bison hunt. A lot of exaggerated arm movements followed by agreeable grunts. Patiently, he shows me why my wrists hurt so much. In each impact-filled tumbling-line, I've been pointing my hands outwards, eroding the cartilage. I was skeptical, since no other coach even noticed before. But after five months of drudgery—re-learning the simplest of skills in the echoing empty gym, I realize this calm man, short and muscled, with wiry white hair and very sad blue eyes, is always right. He is just so quiet that it takes a while to notice.

3:00 p.m.: We go home to drop off some groceries and refuel with whole-grain pasta. I peek in on Dad, who is on the couch in his favorite black bathrobe, downing Earl Grey with a dash of milk and watching the German news. It can only be for the stock prices, since he refuses to learn any German except *Guten Tag* and *Fantastisch!*

"Got some goodies at the store, pal?" He smiles, offering me a sip of his tea.

Sitting beside him, I counter with a handful of macadamia nuts. "I stole these."

"Hmm. Where from?" He raises one wild blond eyebrow.

"The supermarket, of course!" I huff indignantly.

"That's my girl."

He started giving me tips on shoplifting when I was about six. We're not stealing to save money, but to make a point. As with everything in our family, there are our own internal rules. We're Sikhs, but street-smart Sikhs. Dad only sanctions ripping off large chain stores, never family-owned operations. Mom once questioned whether this was a good idea, especially since we're living under assumed identities. But Dad says that knowing how to steal is good practice, especially in a global society facing near-certain economic collapse, or an even-likelier military takeover. "You don't want them to be helpless, do you?" Like most of his arguments, this one is pretty hard to argue with.

4:30 p.m.: "Halt!" I grit my teeth, holding my leg up, the shin a few inches from my nose, without help from my hands. "Plié." Hawklike, Olga watches me as my legs burn and beg for mercy. She has been hired, at Anatoli's suggestion, to make sure I move with elegance. I have mixed feelings about Olga. In one way, of course, I hate her guts. No one person has ever caused me so much pain, and been so impossible to please. But I also refuse to stop the daily ballet sessions. She's good. I know it, and I want to learn to be the best gymnast I can. Even if she has to bleed it out of me.

6:00 p.m.: We roll up to the sprawling sports medicine complex near the university, which, according to my parents' extensive research, has the best doctors for athletes. I have never heard of any other parents putting this much effort into finding the best experts to care for their kids.

Everything they do is tailored to me. It often makes me feel obligated to do something just as extraordinary in return.

I sit in the waiting room surrounded by posters of muscle anatomy while Mom fills out forms. Across from me are three tall, muscled guys who look about sixteen, with various braces on their legs. Dark smudges under their eyes prove they train just as much as me, if not more. One even has a futuristic-looking metal brace clamped on his knee over the tracksuit pants. "Hallo, was für Sport machst du?" he asks, leaning forward.

"Kunstturnen," I answer, flattered that such gorgeous boys want to know what sport I'm in. "And you?"

"Fussball," they say in unison.

We sit back and smile at each other, united by the fact that we spend almost as much time working out as other kids spend in school. "How old are you?" asks one of my future husbands. I tell them I'm eight, and their eyebrows rise. Smugly, I smile to myself. It has taken their sport an extra eight years to land them in intensive physical therapy. Mine has nearly destroyed the cartilage in my wrists in half the time. I can tell they are impressed.

8:00 p.m.: Frank comes out of the kitchen holding two giant chunks of dark bread sandwiching some cheese. "Hey Bhajan. Wanna prank someone?" My siblings are forbidden to date, and outside friends need to be approved by Dad, so we need to be inventive when it comes to entertainment. We open the phone book and skim down until we find a name that annoys us. Anything too uptight or snooty-sounding will do. I dial the number of a Herr Manfred Von Brockenburg.

"Hallo?"

"Hallo," I say in German, pinching my nose. "May I speak to Christian?"

"There is no Christian here, you have the wrong number."

"Oh, okay, sorry." I hang up.

Frank waits five minutes before calling and also asking to speak with Christian. By the fourth call, ol' Manfred is getting very heated about the fact that no one by the name of Christian lives there.

We make ourselves some tea, clink cups, and go in for the kill.

Ring, ring.

"Hallo?"

"Hallo," Frank says in German, "This is Christian. Are there any messages for me?"

10 p.m.: I crawl into bed, every muscle exhausted, and turn out the light. It's Wednesday night. Only three more days until my day off.

I KICK AT dirty snow while Mom wedges the receiver between shoulder and ear, scratching the international phone card with a coin until the security code comes into view. Once again I wait while she makes an untraceable call. It's so cold that I'm jogging in place in my Moon Boots by the time she comes out of the booth, looking equally frozen. "Okay, chérie, let's go get a tea."

I fall into step beside her. "Did you get Our Friend?"

She nods, pulling her pretty green cloche hat farther down over her ears. "She finally picked up. Sometimes I have the feeling she avoids answering because she hasn't done any of the research she promised. But of course, she operates in her own time zone." Mom smiles, pushing open the door to a corner bakery. We hurry in, escaping the freezing wind and enveloped by the warm scent of freshly baked bread.

This is pretty much all I know about Our Friend: She is a woman; she lives somewhere in Brazil; and she's the person who gets us our forged passports. I don't even know her name. Neither do my siblings. But then, we don't even know our own real last name.

Our parents have decided it's time for completely new documents, in case Mom's father has found out our identities from while we were in Vancouver. "Why does your father keep chasing us?" I lift my peppermint tea, slowly-thawing fingers wrapped around the glass cup.

Mom looks down at the table. "He's a person used to always having things his way. That's the problem with having power in a small town."

"So he was important where you lived in France?"

"Mmm." She takes a sip. "He never wanted me to go away with your father, and he's still very angry . . . maybe more so now, because even with all his resources he can't find us."

"He didn't like Dad?" This seems impossible to me. My father is so much fun. Well, as long as he's in a good mood and not hurling a punch at my sister.

"No." She smiles wryly. "He didn't. He is the main reason Interpol is after us. My father insisted they put alerts out."

"How could he manage that?"

There is a long pause. "Because in that country, he's a high-level operative in the secret police."

My God. I sit back, feeling disoriented. The thought of my mom's father—my grandfather—hunting us all these years! My mother tells me that he is trying to put my dad in jail, trying to take us kids away.

"Why?" I ask.

She hesitates again and then lets her shoulders drop. "Bhajan, everything we did, we only did because we wanted to keep you safe. I want you to know that." Her words come in a rush. "Sometimes when someone starts treating you like a criminal, you have to become one to escape. Your father had to have money to get us away, we had to—" She cuts herself off. Just as quickly as she opened up, I see her face change, and draw away, remembering not to risk sharing information.

For once, I'm not sure I want to know more. There's something dark running through this story, and I just want things to be nice and stable. "But you have three kids together now," I venture hopefully. "Don't you think he'll stop chasing us soon?"

"No." She looks straight at me. "No, I don't think he will ever stop."

10: Heidelberg, age 9

THE GRASS IS soft and a fresh spring green, dotted with flowers beside the river, perfect for passing out after rollerblading along the Neckar, with a bread roll in one hand and a banana in the other. Classical music chimes from a little cart selling fresh milk, while locals in various states of undress sun themselves nearby, faces tilted up to the warmth.

I rest my head on Frank's outstretched arm, the breeze tangling our long hair, and breathe in the scent of lilacs and freshly cut grass. Though sleepy eyes, I watch a rotund bumblebee. He hovers heavily, with no direction, as drunk on the sweetness of summer as me. But as usual, whenever I start to fully relax, the anxiety slips back in.

The southern city of Heidelberg is so very different from Hamburg in the freezing winter, and yet, the beauty of our surroundings no longer masks the terrifying reality that our family is fraying. We just never seem to be able to rest, to catch our breath, before we have to run again. The threat from Stephan and his Spinner-scheme in Vancouver came from the outside; we could deal with that. But now the strain is from a far scarier place—inside our gang.

I turn on my side, touching Frank's chest. "Do you think he'll start speaking to you again soon?" Right before we moved to Heidelberg, Frank argued with Dad over something so small I think we've all forgotten what it was. But Dad simply stopped speaking to him. At first I thought it would pass; it seems ridiculous to live with someone every day and yet never make eye contact or exchange a word. Nothing like this has ever happened before. But months later, the standoff has taken on a terrifying semblance of permanence. There's a coldness in the apartment that never existed before.

"Not unless I start groveling . . . and even then maybe not." He picks at the grass.

"Maybe if I talk to him—"

"Stay out of it Bhajan. I'm serious." He sits up abruptly, refastening his rollerblades.

We stop at an outdoor market, buying enough peaches to give a comforting weight to our backpacks, and skate off together, jumping high off the curb. As night falls all around, we sail through the quiet lanes of the park, the wheels of our inline skates humming rhythmically in the silence. I close my eyes for an instant, arms outstretched, waist-length hair flying loose. The air is like silk against my skin.

Some feelings stay with you, even as they are happening. Me and him, gliding home together in a darkness so absolute it seems like it will last forever.

But then, two days later, Frank comes home late from swimming practice and my mouth drops open. In a radical move, he has gotten his traditional Sikh ponytail cut off. My brother saunters in sporting a normal-guy haircut, a couple inches long, with some dark curls falling on his forehead. I guess he decided that since Dad is pretending he doesn't exist, there's really nothing to lose. I'm deeply impressed. The lack of hair sets off the beauty of his face, the straight nose, slanting cheekbones, and strong chin. But his eyes will always remain his best feature, dark and warm, and they are what give him away. I realize that Frank and I are hoping, hoping for the same thing: Surely going against the laws we were raised with will make Dad say *something* to him.

Dad registers it with a cool look, pauses, and then walks through to the kitchen without saying a word. Frank picks up his swim bag, eyes downcast, and quietly goes to his room.

TWO BARELY HEALED blisters on my palms have torn off, leaving streaks of blood on the high bar. Far below, Anatoli stands in his polyester tracksuit with the green stripe on the side, spotting me in case anything goes wrong. Dad started paying him a full-time salary so that he and his family could relocate to Heidelberg. There is no way for me to ever quit gymnastics now. The sport I used to love has morphed into a daily four-and-a-half-hour endurance test I can't escape.

I focus on straightening my body into a handstand, preparing for a full rotation around the bar. When the pain hits, it is so blinding and sudden that my scream echoes off the concrete walls of the empty gym. I lose my grip on the high bar and the ground rushes up. If I land on my neck from this height, it's going to be ugly.

From below, I feel hands on my shoulders as Anatoli dives under me. I crash on top of him, elbowing his stomach and hitting the mat with a resounding *smack*. He has probably just saved me from destroying my spinal column. In thanks I let out another scream, directly into his eardrum. Moving me gently off his body, he runs toward the freezer at the far end of the gym where the ice packs are kept. Through the glass of the observation area, I see Mom's face as I curl into a ball.

"It's broken," Anatoli says, carefully covering my rapidly swelling toe with a gel pack. I'm sobbing, something I never allow myself to do in public. Mom stands above me now, her body tense. "She has to go straight to a doctor," Anatoli says, cradling my shoulder. A doctor sounds like a wonderful idea right now, and maybe some morphine, too.

"Why weren't you paying attention?" Mom snaps at me in English, her voice uncharacteristically hard. I'm so stunned that I immediately stop crying. "Do you know how much trouble you're causing?" Her voice is a whip. I forget all about my injury. This is far worse. Could this be my mother, who always comforts me and stays up all night when I'm sick?

Anatoli lifts his hands. "Bitte, bitte." He seems as surprised as I am by the transformation in my normally sweet mother. "This is one of the most dangerous sports in the world. She didn't do anything wrong."

Mom shakes her head as if she can't bear to look at me, then walks away. I've had guns pointed at my head, but this is the most scared I have ever felt.

"It's all right," Anatoli says, kneeling beside me.

I lie back and stare at the chalk-covered metal foundations of the bars.

"Put these on." Mom is back. She drops my sneakers next to me on the mat.

"Why are you angry?" I ask, my voice unsteady.

"Put them on and let's go. If you need a doctor you can walk there."

We make it to the clinic an excruciating fifteen minutes later. The stocky woman behind the desk eyes me with suspicion.

I look at Mom. "Are you going to talk to her?"

She shakes her head. "You're the one who decided to injure yourself."

Anatoli was right. It's broken. Braced and bandaged, I'm home on my bed a few hours later attempting to process the situation. I hear the slam of the front door as Dad comes home. There's the sound of their voices, then my door bursts open. "Bhajan, pal! Are you all right?" He sits on the side of my bed and I press my face into his warm neck, hiding behind his bristling beard. "Princess, don't worry." He wraps his arms around me, and it's like coming in from the cold.

"Why is Mom mad at me?"

"She's mad?" He leans back so he can look at my face.

"She made me walk to the doctor."

"What? I'll have a talk with her, you poor thing. Don't worry about it anymore."

When I wake in the middle of the night, my toe is on fire and I limp to the kitchen, feeling my way along the wall in the dark. I'm rooting around in the freezer for one of the many ice packs we keep on hand, when a soft thump sounds from the adjoining apartment. The studio where my parents sleep. As carefully as possible, I walk on my heel to the interconnecting door and press my ear to the cool white wood. I can hear Dad's raised voice, deep and angry, but only a few words filter through.

"What's . . . point . . ." There's another thud, and I'm certain he's throwing a book or other hard object against the wall.

"You're there to prevent . . . broken!"

So this is about me . . . about me hurting myself, and her somehow not preventing it. He pays Anatoli so I won't get injured, believing that with enough vigilance, safety can be bought, can be planned. To my father, an accident is a mistake, and someone must be blamed. Just never him.

Something else is thrown against the wall, and I flinch guiltily. I think I understand why Mom got so upset today. She knew this was coming, the punishment. Not only does my mother feel my pain, but she must take responsibility for it, too. The same way I sense her sadness now, deep in my bones.

11: Frankfurt Airport, age 9

OUR FRIEND IS surprisingly small. I suppose I've built her up in my mind to be a large and dangerously glamorous person. But a petite woman, dressed all in black and walking with the aid of an ornately carved wood cane, separates herself from the rest of the travelers and limps toward us in Frankfurt airport. I stare with open curiosity. Our Friend is a fellow outlaw, but that doesn't mean we trust her completely; we'd never think of meeting her at the airport of the city we are actually living in.

My family raises their eyebrows at me significantly as Our Friend nears us at the information desk. Okay, I won't ask her what happened to her leg. Jeez!

The worry on my mother's face is fading ever so slightly, and I realize she's been afraid Our Friend wouldn't show. We've all been on edge since she was unable to explain over the phone from Brazil what happened to the first ten thousand dollars we sent. Something had gone wrong. But while Our Friend may be a criminal, Mom doesn't think she's a thief, so my parents agreed to send another five grand. That was three months and many strained conversations in Portuguese ago. Now, I take a deep breath and prepare to meet my new identity.

"Querida, you are Harbhajan?" Our Friend stares at me.

Well, with her help, probably not for much longer. But I nod.

"Que menina alta!" *What a tall girl!* It's true; I'm almost Our Friend's size, with most of the height taken up by my skinny, knobby-kneed legs. It's a mystery how I can work out four hours a day, six days a week, and somehow manage not to gain any visible muscle mass. I resemble a very-well-toned pencil.

"Before," she smiles at me, "you were so little." Her eyes mist over. The next thing I know, my face is squished against one of her large breasts as she embraces me. She smells good, some kind of warm, musky perfume that I decide marks her as a woman of the world.

We head to one of the airport restaurants and take two tables as businesspeople hustle by. Mom hammers out the details in Portuguese, Dad right next to her. I'm not supposed to be listening, at a separate table with Frank and Chiara, but it's all we're doing as we pretend to read our books. Something seems off. I can't explain what exactly, but Our Friend's smile is too forced, and my mother looks like she's on the verge of extreme frustration.

Mom seems to be asking the same question over and over, her voice soft yet insistent until Our Friend's shoulders slump, and the color drains from Mom's face.

"What did she say?" Dad snaps.

Mom's voice is barely audible. " . . . The embassy contact . . . they took him out."

I turn to Frank, sotto voce, "What does that mea—"

"Shut up." He pushes my book at me in a way that defies argument. "Read. It's nothing."

To my delight, our parents come over to our table and buy us a rare treat of French fries before going off with Our Friend. When they reappear half an hour later, they stand close and hug. An air of sadness lingers as Dad motions for us to come say goodbye—reaching into his shoulder bag to give her a small stack of German fashion magazines. Impossibly beautiful girls shining on the covers.

Our Friend embraces each of my siblings, then smiles at me. "Para tu, querida, para a su vida. For your life." She presents me with a box of brand-new Legos, a bow tied around it, and I thank her awkwardly.

She crushes me to her breast in a comforting good-bye hug and strokes my hair. Then off she limps, vanishing back into the mass of people rushing for their flights.

Standing in a group, we watch her go. "So what did happen to her leg?" I ask.

"Bhajan!!"

We take a cab to the Hauptbahnhof and begin the return trek to Heidelberg. I buy some pistachios and a normal magazine for the trip. The kind where we haven't glued the pages together at regular intervals to conceal fifteen thousand dollars in cash.

Back home, we climb the long flights of stairs to our apartment and I sprawl out on the living room carpet with my gift. Outside in the small courtyard, the neighborhood kids kick a football rhythmically back and forth as dusk settles over the colorful buildings.

I'm happy to discover there are actual Legos inside the box she gave me. Along with five brand-new forged Brazilian passports.

12: Heidelberg, age 9

THE PHOTO SHOOT is taking place by the river, with Frank standing on a rough boulder, looking soulfully into the distance. He's been scouted by a local modeling agency that wants to send his pictures to Paris. Frank's nineteen now, a man, and with his solemn face he could easily pass for twenty-five. The shoot is adhering loosely to reality: He's in his competition Speedo swimsuit, attracting gaggles of girls who find excuses to walk by repeatedly.

The photographer, Alixx—sure as hell not his real name—has a funny way of standing completely still, as if meditating, before being hit with an idea and moving suddenly and drastically in a tangle of arms, legs, and camera equipment.

Although Dad and Frank have not spoken for a year now, Dad surprised us all by being in favor of the shoot. I thought it might be condemned as a venture of massive potential corruption. But, side by side, Dad and I observe the activity around Frank, who is balanced on the rocks, his body outlined against a moody gray sky. For just an instant, when Frank laughs easily at something the lighting guy says, a look of love and pride transforms our father's expression. His son: this vision of perfection.

"It's cool, huh?" I ask in what I hope is an encouraging yet not overly eager voice.

"Yes." Dad stokes his beard. "And good for his career."

Tracing his profile, it occurs to me how often he hides his feelings behind talk of Frank's career, of advancing him into the right position. It's as if my father's emotions speak a different language from mine, thought-out and calculated, rather than instinctive and unstoppable. But I suppose that's fine, as long as the truth is in him somewhere.

After the outdoor portion of the shoot, we accompany Frank to the photographer's studio for part two. The place is all white walls, white back-drops, and masses of black cables snaking across the concrete floor. Not since Chiara's time at herbal college in Vancouver have I encountered such an interesting bunch of characters. The stylist and assistants are pierced all over the place and seem to exist in some ephemeral plane between reality and the complete detachment therefrom.

Frank, now wearing only jeans, stands in the center of a long sheet of white paper that is suspended from the ceiling and runs down along the floor. The camera flashes in staccato bursts. "You should take photos of her," Frank says in German.

The photographer looks confused. "Wer?" *Who?*

"My little sister." He nods toward me. "If you like photographing ath-letes, she's a gymnast and dancer."

Alixx turns and scans me with an expression of deep doubt. I shift uncomfortably in my worn sneakers. I know he sees a girl with overly long legs, disproportionately large feet, and a complete lack of any hairstyle.

"No really." Frank insists, "Come here, Bh—Crystal. Show him one of your jumps."

I start to pull off my sneakers before they change their minds and catch a glimpse of Chiara, hair pulled into her hallmark ruthless bun, stocky fig-ure hidden by an oversized sweatshirt; she glares first at Frank, then at me, and back again. It is the first time I have seen her include me in a look of hatred, and it makes me step away, closer to Frank in the center of the backdrop.

When we get back home, Frank's and my egos significantly inflated, I make myself a sandwich while my siblings bicker in another room. Without warning, a howl of pain issues from the living room, and I nearly choke. Frank hops down the hall toward me, clutching one knee, eyes bugging out. "She stabbed me!"

That's the thing with Chiara: You just never know. In the course of an argument over whether or not having your photo taken is stupid, it's totally plausible for her to pick up a recently sharpened pencil from the coffee table and ram it into your knee. She has mostly been gentle and caring with me. But it seems the older and more formed I become, the more she withdraws and watches. Or maybe it's me, watching her.

"You're not getting away with this!" Frank screams down the hall. But it's an empty threat: he is not prone to informing. The only reason Mom finds out is because she comes in to dispense spirulina and finds me trying to squeeze the lead out of his knee while he finishes my sandwich.

I'M IN THE little neighborhood park with Mom, talking to a girl from a nearby street who is buying a Cornetto ice-cream cone from a tinkling truck; I watch as she peels it luxuriantly to reveal smooth white ice cream. She knows I'm not allowed to eat sugar, but we figure I may be able to get away with trying a little bit while our mothers are distracting each other. Just a bite. Stealthily, we move toward a bush and out of sight.

I don't even register if I like the taste because Mom—who has incredible intuition for unhealthy edibles—walks around the shrub and sees me taking the first lick. I am marched home in ominous silence, hanging my head in shame.

"That was a really bad idea," Chiara offers from our desk where she is reading, while I lie on my bed, face turned to the wall. Once you start with refined sweeteners it's hard to go back; I wonder if I'm already addicted.

"Thank you so much for the clarification," I mutter, and then turn my head sharply at the sound of a heavy step in the hall.

The door opens and I see an electrical cord. Dad is twirling one end, the rest wrapped around his knuckles. He has actually yanked the cord out of something, because one end has the plug, and the part he twirls is a sharp fray of copper-colored wires. Chiara stops reading and doesn't move. He comes forward slowly until he is standing beside my bed, huge from my perspective. The cord dangles like a threat in the air. Dad spins just the end again and the faint whoosh is perfectly audible in the total silence. A feeling of indignation starts slowly in my chest. I want to sit up, but the cord is right there and he knows it, so I'm forced to stay flat on my back.

He says something about my disrespect for all the work they do, giving me all the tools I will need to succeed, but I just see the cord. The frayed end lashes once, hard, against my bare leg, where my cutoff shorts end.

Snap.

The pain is not the worst part, it's the blow to our trust. I am good almost all the time! It was one mistake! I take my eyes off the wire and focus directly on his. He's saying something but I keep watching him, my jaw set. If he's going to do that again I want him to have to look at me first.

He coils the cord around his hand, and tilts his head to one side. "I don't enjoy this," he says in a different tone, "but you must have will power if you're going to survive in life. You can't cave in just because everyone else is doing something. Understand?"

I nod.

He goes, closing the door behind him. Chiara remains at our desk; her back is turned to me and she still holds the book, but her hands are shaking. After a while, I get up and feed the goldfish.

KLAUS, OUR LANDLORD, is getting increasingly suspicious of us. When we moved in, he asked for ID and since the new documents from Our Friend hadn't come through yet, we gave him an entirely different last name. Now he won't stop hassling us to hand over our passports so he can photocopy them for his records. Like most bureaucratic measures, we didn't take it seriously at the time, and now, as our landlord says, "Ve have problem." We've been attempting to distract him with excuses and wit. But, as a people, the Deutsch are not gullible enough to be susceptible to charm, and not dishonest enough to pretend they like you. That doesn't leave us much to work with.

I know by now that we will solve this the way we do, by running—but who will take my goldfish? We transported them here by train in a plastic bag full of water, and that'll never work on a plane. In bed a few nights later, I make a mental list of my important possessions, sorting them into suitcases to come along and boxes to leave behind.

The door to the dark hallway opens silently. Chiara is not in bed so I figure she is just now coming home. But it's Frank, in his sleep-uniform of boxers and rumpled hair.

The mattress dips to one side as he sits down and lies back.

"Hey," I murmur, rubbing an eye. He pulls some of the sheet over for himself.

"Nightmare?" Usually I'm the one rushing to his room, clutching at his shoulder and asking what such a terrible dream could mean for my future.

"Nah, came to say hi." He puts his arm out so I can use it as an extra pillow. He smells comfortingly of chlorine and the blue, mountain-breeze soap he likes. Closing my eyes, I let the lists fade away.

Sometimes you have no idea what is going on, and at the same time, by some instinct, you know exactly what's happening. When I feel his hand moving up my bare leg, beneath the oversize T-shirt I wear to bed and pulling down my underwear, I am completely confused, and simultaneously open my eyes in recognition. For one moment our eyes meet. He looks different, with a kind of unfocused intensity. I feel him move and he is on top of me, skin warm against mine where he has pulled my shirt up. The sheer strength and size of him makes such an impression on me that it blots out everything else.

My world tilts and narrows. All that's left are the muscles of his back in the moonlight, the feel of his stubble against my cheek, his face buried in my loose hair. Even my confusion seems to go numb. I never realized how tall and strong he is until this moment. It's strange how you can live your whole life with someone and never notice certain things about them. The span and firmness of his hands. The same hands that held mine, encouraging me to walk, crossing thousands of streets all over the planet, guiding me forward. His same long, square-tipped fingers that traced the lines of Dr. Seuss, teaching me to read. The arm that reached through the waves to drag me out of a riptide off Bondi Beach as I swirled underwater. And now . . . this familiar stranger.

When he tangles his fingers in my hair and whispers, "Bhajan," his voice is gravelly, tortured almost. I try to turn my face toward his, to see him, my hands braced on his freckled shoulders. But he looks away, and when I feel something hard against my leg, once again I cannot understand, and yet comprehend everything.

I lose my sense of time, but when he stops, I have the feeling he was holding back from doing something. He stares at the ceiling for a while, at the fluorescent planets I've stuck there; I can tell from his profile that he's frowning. Briefly he squeezes my hand, saying words I don't quite catch. The door closes with a soft click as he leaves.

I am nine, he is nineteen, and I know things will never be the same.

Much later Chiara comes back, moving quietly so as not to wake me. I have pulled my underwear and shirt back on and am lying on my side, faking sleep. My thoughts ricochet in all directions, disorganized and random.

When I open my eyes again it is morning and I have a sensation of swimming up from the deep. Mom, Chiara, and Frank are in the kitchen, adding muesli to their bowls. Frank appears normal. So I guess I must as well.

For a moment our eyes touch, and there is agreement there. This family functions on the edge of a precipice; if tasting ice cream is a big deal, I don't want to think what may happen if something really pushes us off track. Nothing has happened, I must believe that. Must repeat it, until it becomes true.

13: Romania and Cairo, age 10

WE SKIP TOWN at 2 a.m., slipping past Klaus's door.

It's tricky to carry twenty bags down the narrow staircase silently. Steps three and twelve creak, so they have to be avoided while making sure not to hit the wall with a suitcase. My goldfish are gone; I put them in a plastic bag of water earlier today and cycled them to a pet store, much like the one where our relationship began. The three of them were poured back into a large tank, vanishing among the other fish. I allowed myself just one backward glance at my pal Lionheart. He was following me along the tank, just as he did at home.

Mom is on the phone talking quietly to a taxi company in German, directing them to an address on the next block. "Are they coming now?" Dad asks, red-faced from exertion.

"They . . . yes, um . . . they need a, a pair of minutes, and they'll meet us um die Ecke." She translates while hurriedly checking a drawer to make sure it's empty. "Did I take the . . . oh yes, it was there, now the—"

"Stop stuttering and tell me exactly when they will be here," he snaps.

My stomach tightens. Dad's communication style is getting straight to the point, and Mom's brain always likes to take the scenic route. When he gets angry, she becomes increasingly nervous, and then the whole thing spirals toward disaster.

Her hands pull at each other. She can't get the words out. "Well . . . He, um."

"Ein paar Minuten?" I ask, she nods.

"Two minutes Dad, around the corner."

"What would we do without you to translate English to English for your crazy mother?" he turns away, lifting another bag and opening the door quietly. She sends me a relieved look, but I feel a flash of anger, watching his back.

Mom never used to stutter, and even now, it's only with him. I sometimes find it difficult to switch rapidly from one language to another, and she speaks six. This is a new habit of my father's, calling her crazy, and I worry where he's going with it.

But we all have a good chuckle in the cab at the idea of Klaus going upstairs, knocking on the door, and finding out that he no longer has a problem to entertain himself with.

And for us? Next stop, Romania.

The thing I've noticed about impoverished countries is that they usually have something to compensate for the earth-shattering poverty. *Warm weather, beautiful landscapes, friendly people, ancient monuments . . .* But as far as I can tell, the part of Romania where we end up two days later is one long stretch of sadness, with the exhaustion of deprivation etched into the faces of old and young. There seems to be a queue for everything because there is a shortage of everything. Fruits, vegetables, meat, hope.

Dad, ever on the lookout for ways to help me become the best of the best, arranged our trip after tracking down the head coach of the Romanian Olympic gymnastics team and sending him a video of me competing. When we received an invitation to have a tryout and tour the training compound, it coincided perfectly with our escape from Heidelberg. I would never have thought such a thing was possible. The Olympic team! But growing up with my father shows me, time and again, that often the only reason something seems unattainable is because we believe it is.

"Waste a dime," he tells me with his sunburst smile. "The most they can ever do is hang up."

As per usual, the whole family comes along to watch me try out. These things have a way of gathering speed and size, like a snowball careening down a mountain, until the size and pressure of the project threaten to flatten me into a two-dimensional version of myself.

I'm ten years old. What if I freeze, or make a mistake?

To my eyes, the Olympic training compound in Deva, with its guards and security checks, is like an army barrack. The girls who train here live on-site in dorms with the other athletes, away from their families.

In the observation area of the sprawling gym, we are met by the head coach. I've seen him and the whole team on TV. But in person, he is taller, more imposing. Stripped to my leotard, I follow him onto the floor, my hands sweating. The team is warming up and it's easy to recognize the faces of the girls who really are the best in the world. They come forward to greet me, smiling shyly and kissing me on both cheeks. I'm almost the same height, even though they are over sixteen. Stunted growth and delayed development are side effects of training for the gold.

If the head coach is going to take me seriously, I'll have to prove I can be an acrobat despite my height. He instructs me to perform a full floor routine and slips my cassette into the stereo. After the warning beep, Tchaikovsky starts to play. I feel immediately different, almost free. The pressure, the expectations, the countdown to the Olympics—they all recede. Some say a gymnastics floor routine is one of the most concentrated challenges in sport, and it feels true. Because for one minute and twenty-nine seconds, I can lose myself. I hurl my body into a double back-flip, spinning upside down, high above the ground, weightless. When it all began, I danced and tumbled out of joy, but lately, I'm chasing something else. And I've noticed people observe me intently now. Maybe watching someone strive for oblivion is more interesting.

When my music crashes to an end, I hold the final pose, and the coach ejects the cassette, turning it over in his hand.

"I can see you do a lot of dance training." His expression is unreadable.

That evening, my family assembles in our otherwise deserted hotel restaurant in Deva. A tall, morose young man, his thin body listing slightly to one side as if resisting a strong wind, appears. "Good evening."

"Fantastic!" Dad looks up brightly from the table, "What do you have that's hot and vegetarian?"

The waiter looks completely perplexed but soldiers on. "We are having blue cheese, bread, white cheese, orange color cheese—"

Dad holds up a hand, "What d'you have that's not cheese?"

"We are having blue cheese—"

"Holy cow. Okay, tell you what. Take some bread, put the cheese on it and make it really hot."

"Blue cheese, yellow cheese . . .?"

"Just bring it all. But hot! Okay?"

Honestly, at this point I just want to vanish from embarrassment. But it is a characteristic of my father to take last-minute trips to the ends of the earth and expect, nay, demand, a hot meal upon arrival. Regardless of the economic situation, political unrest, or variety of available products. The rest of us wait nervously, knowing he will scream if they don't get it right. Finally the cheese arrives, melted and steaming over toast. It scalds my tongue.

At the end of the week, Dad lays it out. "The head coach says he'd like you to come train here permanently." I must look horrified because he hastens to add, "We'd all come, of course. You wouldn't live in the compound." I am flattered that the team offered. But the intensity of the concrete training center makes me anxious, and each time we walk through the city, the daily hardship people live with is impossible not to internalize.

"What do you think?" he asks

"Noooo." I shake my head vigorously.

"Excellent." He rubs his hands together, "Let's get the hell out of here!"

WELL, THERE THEY are. The pyramids rise up majestically into a sky so full of light that it makes my eyes burn. Dad stands beside me, beaming at the view. We are wearing our matching khaki vests, and looking rather superb in our opinion. After the darkness of Romania, he voted we take an Egyptian detour before heading back to Europe.

I smile up at my father, the Sphinx silhouetted behind his right shoulder. No matter what, I'm such a fan of the way he thinks. Zero barriers, no worries, just a thirst for life and adventure. When I look at him like this, I can forget about the unpredictable moods, the occasional lash of cruelty, because there is simply no one else like him. No one quite so free.

We have spent two weeks frolicking in the Red Sea off Sharm El Sheikh, the longest time I have taken off from gymnastics since starting five years ago, and I feel as if the salt water and sand have scrubbed me clean. A camel ambles past us, long honey-colored neck moving in time with its steps. In silence, we walk to the base of a pyramid so we can touch the rough ancient stones, and I feel them scratch against my fingertips. Looking up at the incredible height and beauty of something that has endured for thousands of years, I am somewhat comforted. This place has seen everything and survived. Humans should be able to do the same.

That night, so late that it's actually morning, I lie outside by the hotel pool in Cairo. It's 2 a.m., and the soft, warm air cocoons me. Music plays from the bar, where bottles sparkle like jewels, while the majority of the gang sprawl on lounge chairs across the pool. All around, trimmed jasmine bushes give off a delicious perfume, their petals gleaming ivory in the light from the half moon. Since our plane to Austria is at 5 a.m., Dad decided there is no reason to pay for another night at the hotel. For a normally extravagant person, he has these occasional, very short-lived bouts of frugality. Like small, nonfatal seizures.

The same three American songs play on repeat, while waiters lean on the bar, skin dark against their white jackets, hair slicked neatly back, bobbing their heads. Frank is just a lounge chair away, sleeping with one arm thrown above his head. We've gotten tan in the last few weeks, and it has multiplied his freckle quotient significantly. I watch his face, the features so familiar, a part of my whole existence. I know his every expression and what each one means, but now he is a mystery to me.

The first time was not the last. Occasionally, when we are sure to be alone, he comes into my room and slips in beside me, hands almost feverish on my skin. All of a sudden, he is no longer my brother and lifelong companion. I can't recognize him. It's as if a film descends over his eyes and some stronger force takes him over and away. Sometimes when he is right against me, I have the sensation of being more alone than ever before.

I never feel scared, but I know we are doing something wrong. Even if I didn't see how guilty he looks before he leaves, I would know. But what worries me more is that I am not really against what is happening.

Sometimes I look forward to it. With the coldness that has settled over my family, the actual human contact is a relief. I feel a bit more loved . . . yet I am ashamed. And through it all runs a deep fear, that maybe, somewhere along the way, I have lost my best friend.

"What Is Love" comes on again and I roll my eyes toward the stars, clear as diamonds in the desert sky. I don't get these love songs at all. What a lot of blather about things that seem simple to solve. If this guy's hurting, he should just blow town like any sensible person. Change his name if necessary, and stop feeling all these emotions. Done.

Then I happen to look across the silver ripples of water at my mom, tired yet alert in the moonlight, her long white cotton dress spilling off the lounger and swaying in the wind. Dad is sitting up now, facing her and moving his hands as he talks. I think of the midnight rushes to airports, a pile of bags holding our whole lives, new continents, new names, Interpol, building everything up only to run again.

Maybe it's not so easy to get away when you're already on the run.

Frank turns onto his side, face relaxed in sleep, lashes resting gently on his cheek. Maybe it's impossible when your heart is involved.

14: Vienna, age 10

"WHAT'S YOUR NAME?" Dad fixes his intense eyes on me, as we sit across from each other at the coffee table.

"Crystal."

"Why did you move here?" He stares at me, unwavering.

I start to fidget. He notices it instantly and I give a casual shrug instead. "For my dad's work. He's an investor." New city, new backstory.

"What kind of investor?"

"In the stock market."

"Where are you from?"

"Florida, Key West."

"Oh, it must be beautiful there."

"The beaches are nice and it's a quiet area, too." If necessary, I have the agreed upon neighborhood and street name ready.

"Bhajan?" he says.

I frown. "Huh?"

"Bhajan?"

"What's a Bhajan?" I tilt my head to one side.

"Wow." He pours me some tea and leans back. "I threw that one in just for fun."

Fresh white snow drifts blanket the cobblestoned streets of Vienna, reflecting golden street lights. The crisp air is filled with the smell of roasting chestnuts and hot Glühwein, sold from pretty wooden stands and responsible for a lot of the rosy cheeks and jolly smiles. Strings of Christmas lights still sparkle across the city, though we are creeping up on the New Year, and each winding street reveals a hidden café, a carved stone church, a colorful courtyard. Everything appears festive.

But no matter how hard I try to be cheerful, I've started to dread waking up each day. At competitions, I place a smile on my face, the same way I point my toes perfectly during every leap, because it's part of the performance. Often I fantasize about having a life like other kids, where they aren't obligated to do a sport they fear, at a level where injury is just a matter of time. Where they aren't—

I'm trudging along behind Chiara to the U-Bahn station, from my daily training, when the hopelessness becomes too much. Breaking off, I step out into the deep snow of the empty field beside the footpath, and wander farther from the noise of the road. The snow around me is untouched, a smooth silver sheet under the low moon. I flop backward and lie down, arms flung out like a starfish. It feels almost good. The silence, the cool snow on my cheek. I close my eyes.

"What the hell are you doing?" Chiara jogs across the virgin snow and angrily hauls me up by the arm. I am curiously limp and detached from the screaming apparition in front of me.

"What's wrong with you? You're soaked! This is your new jacket!" She shakes me by my shoulders with a surprising amount of rage. I stare at her blankly. "Why would you mess up your coat like that?" Her voice is high, forming puffs of steam in the air. "Mom's going to be angry!"

"Oh, go away." I turn my back and head for the U-Bahn.

Late that night in our apartment, Mom sits hesitantly on the side of my bed, where I'm reading the unabridged *Tarzan*. "Bhajan, is something wrong?"

Where to begin?

"Is it gymnastics? You know you can stop if you want to."

Closing the book, I watch her. She looks so burnt out. It would be difficult for me to answer her question, even if I had any intention of being honest. It's only now that she has noticed something is amiss with me, the smiley-est of her children, when everything has progressed too far for me to talk about it. Even with the daily pressure gymnastics puts on me, it's just a peripheral worry. It's something I focus on to blot out the others; my secret world with Frank, the responsibility I feel to keep my family at peace.

"Bhajan, I know all this moving, all the change, isn't easy on you or your brother and sister . . . that sometimes it makes you all want to act out—"

"Maybe you should stop confusing me with Chiara and Frank." My voice is strangely hard, surprising even me.

A look of genuine confusion passes across her face. I know this can't make any sense to her, but I hear myself lurching forward, going in for the kidney punch. "You don't even see, you don't see me because I'm the one who never argues. So stop lumping me in with Frank and Chiara. I'm sick of it! I'm nothing like them, and they are *nothing* like me!"

"Bhajan, wha—"

"I'm done. Done trying to hold it all together—you're on your own." Even as I scream the words I know it's the biggest lie of all. I would go to war for the woman sitting on the edge of my bed. She stares at me as if I have shifted form into something she can no longer reach. But it has the effect I was hoping for. She leaves, and with her go the questions. Because the truth is, no one really wants the truth.

I DON'T KNOW when exactly Dad decides to become Jewish.

He's always researching, mostly on three topics: mind control and its use by media and government, money and who controls it, and spirituality and religion. The last one is how we ended up as Sikhs. For Dad, religion is about philosophy, not small preconditions like birthplace, race, or family history.

In fact, I don't think anything has ever been viewed as barrier by him. More like an amusing speed bump on the road to certain success. But now, when he stumbles across the idea that Jewish people dominate the world financial markets, the subjects of religion, money, and control seem to converge and crystallize. That's how the plan to move to Israel starts.

I don't have much of a concept of the Middle East, except that it is always in crisis. The minute someone says Israel or Palestine I think of a CNN graphic pulsating on the TV screen, a man holding an Uzi, tanks rolling over the desert, and a forlorn child in a torn, dust-stained T-shirt.

Are we really going to leave our favorite bakery in Vienna for that? We've only been here eight months.

Our conversion to Judaism, he explains, will be accomplished not through years of study or lengthy reading of the Torah, but simply by saying we are.

"Can you do that?" I ask Dad as he cracks a pistachio.

"Why not?"

"Well, I mean, can you just decide like that?"

"Sure. We're researching and crafting an ancestral back story. The new name we got the passports under could be Jewish. No one will know the difference."

Watching his casual shrug makes me uneasy. Being Sikhs never had anything to do with money, connections, or power. It was a moral code. I think it still is. But the longer we are away from India, the more a quest for power seems to draw him forward, even though the money, the magic bank accounts never run out. I don't understand why we need to complicate our lives. Is it just to feel important or invincible? Just to mold people how we want? I would much rather be safe.

The rest of the family is unsure about whether I appear Jewish enough to be believable. If anyone looks like they should have GOY stamped on their forehead, above the blue eyes and below the mop of blonde hair, it would be me. In fact, I've always looked very similar to Dad, but quite different from my siblings, with their dark hair and olive complexions.

"There are a lot of blonde Ashkenazi Jews," Mom tells Frank.

They eye me doubtfully.

Israeli border security is legendary; it will be the most intense check we've ever faced. We'll be attempting to fool the most advanced border-control system in the world with five fake passports, a fake cultural heritage, an invented backstory, and a good deal of charm. But if you're gonna go—go big.

15: Cyprus, age 10

Before leaving for the airport, Dad does a final sweep of the living room, making sure any trace of us is gone, then turns to me. "We're going to make a quick stop before Israel."

"Okay. Where?"

"Cyprus. I've made some money," he continues, "and we've got to get it cleaned."

"Laundered?" I perch on the sofa arm.

"Not just laundered, pal! We're going to get it steamed, pressed, ironed, and perhaps even anointed with a little perfume."

Hours later we march into our Cyprus hotel, right on the beach, with a luxurious marble lobby and deliciously soft sofas. Mixed in with the obvious tourists, whose white socks are pulled inexplicably halfway up their calves, are a few sharp-eyed characters, and I sense them trying to categorize us. One look at my father, at the steely way he surveys a room, noting everything, suggests we are up to no good. But the fact that he is surrounded by an apparently nice family calls everything into question. Confusion is one of our best disguises.

Frank and I walk along the beach, swimsuits under our clothes. It's not vacation season. Dark clouds shade the rough sand and a strong wind sends cold waves crashing against our feet. Frank picks up a long slimy, string of seaweed and drapes it over my head, smiling. A trickle of salt water winds its way down my spine, making me curl my toes into the cool, grainy sand. I hurl the seaweed back at him and run along the packed sand at the shoreline, his deep laugh chasing me. We seem to manage this kind of ease only briefly, often when we are on a trip somewhere new. But then, it's back: an invisible distance filled with all the things we don't say to each other.

Soon enough the weather drives me back inside, shivering, to the hotel's indoor pool. I am swimming deep underwater, relishing the peace, the feeling of being weightless, when something shatters the surface. Kicking upward I take a deep breath, and face the boy who just cannonballed my quiet afternoon. He swims up to me and slings an elbow over the edge.

"Hi!"

I have the urge to look behind me and check if he's addressing someone else—someone he already knows.

"What color is your hair when it's dry?"

I'm completely disoriented. "What?"

"I'm curious, so I thought I would ask."

"Well, it's blonde."

"Capital. Mine, too! I just turned twelve, how old are you?"

"Almost eleven."

He has very direct green eyes that perfectly match his communication style.

"That's a great age. I remember it well." He grins. "I'm Tim. What's your name?"

"Bhajan." The moment it leaves my lips, I panic. Bhajan is not the name I'm supposed to be using on this trip. This guy doesn't progress in a normal conversational manner, and it has thrown me off.

"Bhajan?"

"No," I say.

"No what?"

I realize it's too late to claim I made something like Bhajan up. You would have to have a very rich imagination indeed. "Never mind." I frown, irritated.

Thoroughly undaunted by my expression, he looks pensive. "Well Bhajan, I've always liked unusual names. Gives you something to live up to. What does it mean?"

"It's Sanskrit for Song of God."

"That suits you." He rubs some water from his eye with a tanned fist. "So, are you here on vacation, or to launder money?"

For once, I'm speechless.

"That's okay." He nods confidentially. "I can tell from your reaction."

I've got to get the hell away from here. Hoisting myself out of the pool, I look down at him. "We're not here to launder money. We're on vacation."

The corner of his mouth turns up. "All right."

"What do you mean, *all right*?"

"If you weren't here to do that, you wouldn't even know what it is. You're ten."

I glare at him. "I'm on vacation."

"It's okay!" He smiles, throwing an arm out in a gesture of worldly acceptance. "We're here to launder money, too!"

I can't explain to myself exactly why I stay. Perhaps it's because I've never met someone my age whom I don't have to censor myself around. Someone who doesn't fit in with the rest of the world either. With the chlorine dried off, we walk along the stormy beach in our shorts and loose shirts, as he discusses the situation in England. "Of course Blair is going to win, but I mean, is anything really going to change?"

From Tim's previous hints I gather that Tony Blair is a politician in London, where Tim is from, but that's all I know.

I shrug my shoulders cheerfully. "Politicians are usually a bunch of crooks. But it's legal because they make the laws."

"Exactly! I like the way your brain works, Bhajan." He nods, "My dad always says politicians are like gym socks—they should be changed often and for the same reason."

My shirt is still damp from the ocean wind an hour later, as I stand nervously outside my parents' hotel room. Slowly, I unlock the door, contemplating how I'm going to break it to Dad that I blew our cover—and that the person who got it out of me is twelve years old. I phrase my confession in a way that sounds like I may or may not have dropped my real name. Dad sees straight through it. "Relay the conversation to me," he says, sitting in the armchair by the window. Lately he has been training us to remember large portions of dialogue verbatim, so I'm stuck. He listens for a while and then starts laughing. My shoulders sag with relief. "Where is this kid?" he asks.

"On the beach, waiting. We were going to race out to the rocks and back."

"Well, invite him to dinner with us. This I've got to see."

I raise my eyebrows. My father doesn't usually like to associate with other kids, finding them to be gratingly unadultlike. It's a mystery to him why some parents allow them to . . . act like children.

Dinner is an altogether startling affair, with Tim holding his own the whole way through, discussing politics, literature, and the merits of the English school system with my father. Whatever they are doing at his private school, it's working. The conversation veers so far out of my sphere of knowledge that it brings on a feeling of panic. I often wonder if other kids are secretly far ahead of me. They spend so much *time* in school. While my educational schedule just consists of a few hours a day and a lot of hands-on life experience.

After dinner we play poker, sitting on the plush couches in the lobby. I'm cutting the deck when Tim leans closer and asks me why I bite my nails so short. Hiding my fingertips in a loose fist, I tell him I've got a lot on my mind.

Chiara snorts and rolls her eyes. "Please."

Tim fixes her with an even look. "How would you know, though? You two don't seem close."

Chiara stares, blindsided by his bluntness, and I glance away as he deals.

In two hours, Tim and his parents are leaving for the airport. I have the odd, distinctly uncomfortable impression that I am going to miss this person who I only just met. I try ignoring the rogue emotion and proceed with great cheer; he follows my lead admirably until his parents show up with suitcases. "So, you're going back to Frankfurt after this?" Tim pockets the deck of cards.

Frankfurt is the story I've been given, and I'm sticking to it. "Yeah, I think so."

"You think so?"

"Well, we move all the time, so it's hard to say where I'll be."

"Maybe you'll come to London!" He looks so hopeful in this moment that I hate to crush it.

"Probably not."

Standing up, he walks to the reception desk and returns with pen and paper.

"Here's what we'll do." Tim begins to write. "I don't move. We've been at this house for a long time." He hands me his address and pushes a second piece of paper toward me.

"Give me your address in Frankfurt and I'll write to you."

"Oh," I say, "We're moving apartments, I don't have one yet."

"Do you know where you are moving to?" He's watching me with his steady gaze, especially unnerving in someone so young. Now I know why adults sometimes ask me how I got my eyes, at my age.

"No, we don't know yet."

"Do you know which hotel you'll be staying at?"

I shake my head and I can tell he feels the situation getting away from him.

For once, he just looks his age, instead of like a twelve-year-old waiting to turn thirty. I feel a little flip in my stomach—*he likes me*! Someone so clever and handsome actually likes *me*. A bubbly sort of happiness travels up my spine. The sensation only lasts a few seconds, though, because I can tell he wants to say or do something, to keep trying, but he has reached the end of his experience.

Tim is the most mature, smart, and streetwise person my age I have ever met, and yet there is still so much separating us. So much to hide. Suddenly I have a terrible suspicion that no matter where I go, I will always be apart.

We are standing near the sliding doors when his family's cab pulls up. Tim hands me the folded paper with his address. "You'll write me as soon as you know where you're living right?"

I avoid his gaze. How could he understand, there's no way I would be allowed to stay in touch with someone. Every postmark leaves a trail.

He touches my hand to get my attention. "Do you promise?"

I look up at him steadily. "Yes," I lie.

During the night I cry silently, my face pressed into the pillow of the rollaway bed that has been fitted into the room with Frank and Chiara. This goodbye has hardened me in ways that all the others haven't. It will be easier from now on. The lies, the leaving. But what if that's not who I want to be?

16: Tel Aviv, Israel, age 11

IN THE CYPRUS airport, as we wait to board, I look up and see three young men in plainclothes; fit, sharp-eyed, and scanning passengers. I've been briefed that the Israeli security-check system often begins before you even get on the plane. The operatives are obvious to us, because they're ignoring unnecessary noise and movement, and focusing only on what matters to them. In a sense, it's like wearing blinders. They're watching for a tell, for someone who is nervous and trying to hide it. I focus on relaxing my shoulders, on looking like a sleepy kid waiting in line. Their eyes keep moving past, and I feel a sort of affinity. Just like them, I'd never notice something beautiful or routine at an airport, because all I see—all I watch for—are them.

As we board, I try to ignore an unfamiliar ache in my chest. It's impossible that I would be missing Tim. All my training, all their work, has been to make me immune to any such thing. I look at my family and, as with the border guards, I keep my face blank.

An hour later, when we land, we pass through security smoothly. Near the taxi stand, Dad tucks all our passports into one of his typically overstuffed pockets with satisfaction. "If they stand up to that kind of scrutiny, it's a great product." Mom gives him a look filled with exhaustion. I can imagine what she's thinking, because I'm feeling it, too: *Did we really have to risk everything, just to see if we could get away with it?*

Our taxi careens onto a Tel Aviv highway, windows down, unfamiliar music flowing out on the dry desert wind. Billboards and signs are covered with Hebrew letters, marching confidently the wrong way. The landscape is parched and barren. As we merge onto smaller streets cramped with honking cars, shouting drivers and dust, a shrill, ear-splitting wail pierces my thoughts. All the cars lurch to a stop. "Bomb alert," the cab driver says casually over his shoulder. "Oh, look, there it is."

Men in dark police uniforms converge on the sidewalk, where an abandoned backpack leans against the wall of a building, disturbingly close to the front of our taxi. I lean back, pressing my shoulders into the cracked leather seat, trying to put an extra few inches between myself and possible death. Soon, they seem to defuse it or at least pronounce it harmless, and traffic yells back to life.

My heart is still beating out of rhythm when we pull up to our hotel. I don't mind life-threatening situations, but I like having some sort of control over them, or a chance of escape. In this scenario you're just walking along, la-di-da, and the next thing you know your torso is three blocks away from your head.

Of course, we've come here with a plan: The Maccabiah Games are Israel's Olympics, with the best Jewish athletes from all over the world gathering in Tel Aviv. Frank is certainly an Olympic-level swimmer, and what better way to integrate into a new community than to be a sports hero? His skills smoothed our way into getting a visa for the entire family. I'm too young to participate in the Maccabiah Games now, but that doesn't mean my schedule will be any less intense.

GYMNASTIC TRAINING SESSIONS in the land of milk and honey begin with an endurance test that head coach Zahava likes to call a "light warm-up." Zahava is my new project, since she never smiles, and quite possibly never has. She seems both confused and slightly intrigued by the fact that I do it so often, and I'm trying to wear her down with constant good cheer. It's the same stance I take with myself; refusing to acknowledge the darkness, this shadow beneath my skin.

With the games approaching, the Israeli Olympic gymnastics team is in lockdown mode, training extra hours with hardcore endurance conditioning, and I am along for the ride. We sprint at full speed around the huge gym, me bringing up the rear, clambering over every obstacle on the way. The girls shoot concerned looks over their shoulders at the sight of my red, manically determined face bobbing along behind. I push myself further, enjoying the pain, the feeling of my muscles tearing. It has begun here, the pleasure I take in punishing myself.

In this moment I don't ask why, I don't even question it. And the paradox of sport is that I'm admired for it. When I get nosebleeds from exhaustion and train on, the flow staunched with Kleenex, they say I have exactly the kind of dedication it takes—to go all the way to the Olympics.

Most days, just before dusk, I like to climb out the third-floor window onto the modern, scaffoldinglike design that adorns the outside of our hotel. If you balance carefully, it makes the perfect perch for looking toward the beach, over the honking cars, and watching the sky turn from orange to a deep, rich red. With one leg swaying in space, the other extended on a round metal pipe, I ice my knee, while Frank applies hot-packs to his shoulders. We sit in silence, listening to the sound of the radio from the beach bar. A summer hit plays on repeat, "Ani ohevet et Beni yeled ra." We know just enough Hebrew now to understand, *I'm in love with the bad boy*.

"Why would someone love someone bad?" I shake my head, full of practicality.

"Because it's interesting." There is a smile in his voice.

"Really?"

"Sure, predictable people are rarely fascinating. You have to have some fire."

I look back at the sunset, now fading to purple.

"You've got something of it, for sure." His soft words dangle in the dry evening air between us. At times like this, I sense the power I have over him, and it makes me feel like I am slipping into a freefall.

I'm learning that I have an effect on him—on men—without really meaning to, and I'm not sure how to deal with it. Men seem large and unmovable, but I am realizing they are actually quite malleable. It's just that once they start to move, it can ricochet out of your control very quickly. I've decided to shut that side of myself down but also keep my eye on it. Like a bomb, it's better left untouched.

I watch Frank's profile, painted by the sky, and think how much I love him still and wish we could be friends again, the way we were. We never hug anymore. He never puts me in a headlock and plants a kiss on my forehead like when I was little. To me, the onset of attraction is directly related to the vanishing of affection and intimacy. And lately, once in a while, it makes me angry rather than sad. I blame myself, of course. My anger never seems to rest on anyone else for long, it circles back to the girl in the mirror.

Couples walk by on the street below, holding hands on their way to the beach boardwalk, sometimes stopping to kiss. That's when it occurs to me that Frank never kisses me. Maybe you have to look someone in the eye to do that. With everything else that happens, shouldn't . . . ?

There must be something wrong with me.

I lean closer to the edge, a calloused hand resting on the frayed edge of my cutoff shorts for balance. Honestly, it's probably a good thing. Even from all the way up here, kissing looks way too intimate for my comfort zone.

The new moneymaker Dad has going involves a royal family and mind control.

For some time now I have been entertained by the exploits and accidental one-liners of a man Dad calls the Blowhard. The author of various books on mental training and memory improvement and an accomplished speaker, the Blowhard has an IQ of 160—*tested and proven!*—and my father has been doing marketing for him. Like all my father's business ideas, it seems fun. I never imagine it will accidentally cause my father to be banned from reentering Israel—that we will be separated.

Dad has somehow managed to get the Blowhard hired by a European noble family, teaching high-powered executives and government bigwigs how to have minds like steel traps. Now they can remember the names, hobbies, and preferences of all their business acquaintances, the main points of all the books they read, important historical dates, and mistresses' phone numbers.

Long before Dad met the Blowhard, he was already training us in memorization methods. It's not really that people don't see things, he says, it's that they aren't truly *looking*. I've always recognized people and faces, and I remember my life as a series of clear mental photographs. But with the addition of the Blowhard's methods, we can all march up to someone we met for a minute, months ago, and remember their name, their kid's names, and what they do. It has the effect, in my experience, of deeply flattering someone, or just as often, totally freaking them out.

The method is based on association. Upon on hearing a person's name, you pair it with a characteristic or a similar-sounding word and invent a little story. Aharon just goes on and on, whereas Javier has great hair, and Chris will forever be stuck under a Christmas tree in our minds. In the same way, a long string of numbers is actually an exciting adventure, because 4 is a sailboat, 7 a cliff, 9 a man with a fat belly, and 6 a cherry. Sometimes Mr. Belly (9) is off sailing, enjoying the day with his snowman friend (8) savoring a nice bowl of cherries (6), as his pet swan, also known as 2, swims alongside, when *BAM!* he crashes right into the cliff (7). I enjoy some of my mental stories so much that I still remember the phone number of a random vegetarian restaurant in Hamburg.

It's all part of Dad's unusual method of educating me. Some weeks we don't even do any schoolwork, or at least it doesn't seem like it. But he has a way of sneaking up on you with knowledge. He likes to present me with elaborately wrapped books exploding with ribbons—his trademark—and lately besides the Blowhard's memory games, much of the reading material centers on mind control. Everything from getting a beautiful woman into bed to programming the perfect assassin. It's fascinating, but something about it makes me uncomfortable.

"Why are you frowning?" He regards me with interest as we lie on the couch together, discussing my current volume.

"I'm not sure I like the idea of leading people on subliminally." Actually I *am* sure—I don't like it at all—but I'm too timid to openly disagree with him. "I'd rather get people do what I want because I'm really good at something, and not have to trick them."

His eyes meet mine and hold. "Who says this is about controlling them?"

I feel myself getting even more confused.

His smile is slow, even cold. "It's so no one can ever trick you."

DURING THE ISRAELI summer, everyone flocks to the beach, admirably bronzed and highlighted by the sun. The waves are huge and crashing this evening as I kick out to sea on my foam bodyboard.

"Roy! Ey!"

Frank looks around, water dripping down his face, as two muscular guys paddle toward us, grinning.

"Mah nishmah?"

"All good." Frank nods to them as we lie on our boards, rising and falling with the swells. "This is my sister Crystal."

Tucking wild strands of hair behind my ear, I don't need to be told these guys are on the Israeli national swim team—their shoulders are a dead giveaway.

"You're the one who's a gymnast, right?"

I smile, flattered at having been talked about.

"She's our great Olympic hope." Frank splashes some of the Mediterranean Sea playfully at me.

"You know," the one with the sharp eyes observes me, "you don't look Jewish."

"It's the German-Jewish side," Frank and I say simultaneously.

Back on solid ground, salty and sand-covered, we rejoin Chiara, and the three of us amble home along the boardwalk, hitting each other with our boards. Two dark-haired and tanned, in their early twenties, and their blonde eleven-year-old sister. For a moment, the tension between them seems to dissipate. To all the people passing by we must look normal. But Frank and Chiara are over twenty and still not allowed to date or have outside friends. All our fake passports are hidden by our father for safekeeping. And yet, walking in the evening light, the three of us still think we are more clever than the rest. Because carrying so many secrets always makes you feel like you know more. Like you are a step ahead.

We stop off at the corner store to buy bananas, and I peel one as we near our hotel. We're approaching the glass doors when Frank whispers urgently, "No, *no*, straight. Keep going!"

Jerkily, we adjust our course and I see the problem reflected in the glass. Across the street are his wave surfing teammates, trying to hide behind other pedestrians.

"Shit!" Frank hisses.

They must realize we've seen them, because they come jogging across the street.

"Is this where you live? You never tell us where you're staying." The sharp-eyed one from earlier is in the lead.

"C'mon, who *lives* in a hotel?" Frank's voice is neutral, but to me he is clearly tense.

Behind him, I see our favorite front desk clerk spot us and raise her hand in a familiar eager wave. I studiously ignore her, and the three of us move on down the street. "Go home, dumbass," Frank calls over his shoulder to his teammates, managing to produce an amazingly natural laugh. His hair is perfectly messy, teeth so white in that careless smile. He couldn't possibly be hiding anything.

We walk fast, through nearly empty streets. An hour later we double back cautiously, splitting up to make sure they're not around, and meet at the elevator, near the hurt expression of the front desk clerk. Back in our apartment, full of relief and triumph, I'm proudly recounting how we lost the tail when I notice my father looking at us in fury. Frank and Chiara have already gone motionless. I see Dad's hands clench into fists and my own start to tremble. He will never hit Frank, who is taller and made of muscle; for my brother he still uses the silent treatment, the punishment of pretending he doesn't exist.

"Am I supposed to be impressed that you lost a tail right outside our hotel? Why did you have one in the first place?"

I avoid his eyes, trying not to provoke. Dad's moods are so difficult to predict. They rarely seem based on actual events but instead on some delicate inner switch that one day makes him laugh off the worst of risks and on another lash at you for the smallest of mistakes.

"They did the best they could—" Mom is obviously forcing herself to speak above a whisper.

"Shut up." He doesn't bother looking at her. When he starts to scream, it's terrifying and unstoppable, the veins on his neck standing out, words tumbling over each other. All of us stare at the carpet, my hands still shaking. Then he steps forward. "Next time I'm not going to let something like this go. You had a tail because you lost focus, because you think it's all right to go play on the beach like idiots! Don't ever put us at risk again." He turns, slamming the door to their interconnecting suite. As always, we stand mute, adrenaline pulsing in our blood. And then I make it into a joke.

Turning up the Israeli music on the radio, I start to dance, and soon Frank and Chiara follow. We fling ourselves around to work off the panic-induced energy, and Mom starts to smile despite herself. With a twirl Frank drops to his knees dramatically. "From now on, we will be like ninjas!"

Giggling, I stagger toward the kitchen counter where the big glass plate holds our oranges. One by one, I take them off. Picking up the plate with both hands, I turn, and smash it down on Frank's head with all my strength.

The glass shatters, sending shards in all directions. Frank falls forward, flat against the carpet. There is a horrible silence except for the music playing on. Slowly he turns to look up at me in shock, touching the top of his head.

"Bhajan! Why did you do that?" Mom rushes over the broken glass in her thin Japanese slippers.

"I . . . I don't know," I answer honestly. Rarely, if ever, do I do something without thinking it through at least ten times. I hunch my shoulders in shame.

"You could have really injured him!"

Chiara is watching with an odd expression. Like she enjoys watching me take him down.

"Is there blood?" Mom reaches for his forehead.

"No," Frank stands gradually, carefully, and leans a hand against the counter. We look directly at each other. The way we haven't for a long time. "It's fine," he tells them. "Let's forget it."

They frown; normally in these situations one of us would be braying for retribution. He walks to the freezer for an icepack. I stare at the shattered glass around my feet.

From this day on, he never gets into bed with me again.

17: Tel Aviv, age 11

THE BLOWHARD IS treading on thin ice indeed. He's begun bickering about paying the agreed-upon commission on stock market investments he asked Dad to make on his behalf. It seems to have slipped his mind that Dad is the one who chose the investments that doubled his money. So my father's suitcase is by the door, packed for a week in Hong Kong.

"Are you worried about being able to get your money out?" I say, reviewing his sock collection to find matching pairs for the voyage. Of course I will miss him very much; he has never been away for more than a couple days before. Yet, I know our family dynamic always becomes more relaxed, less careful, as soon as he leaves. And anyway, he'll be back in time for the Maccabiah Games.

Dad sips Earl Grey on the window sofa and shrugs good-naturedly, "I made sure the investment account is in my name. So if the memory guru insists on being a nincompoop and doesn't give me my share, I'm just going to clean the whole thing out." This can apparently be done only in person, and only in Hong Kong.

I nod approvingly. "He'll *remember* that."

He laughs in his wild way, head thrown back, before gathering me in a bear hug, "Ah, China will be no fun without you, my Bhajan."

Sure enough, when the plane has taken off, everyone seems to unconsciously exhale and let their shoulders drop. In the coming days, the interconnecting door between our suites is left open all the time, which has never happened before. Mom eats dinner with us, and everyone is a bit louder, more themselves. I wish we could be this way all the time, but I'm beginning to see that will probably never happen. You have to all want it for a campaign like that to succeed.

For the Blowhard, things don't go as smoothly. In the middle of a routine weekday, Dad cleans out the entire investment account. The Blowhard was asking for it, really—trying to shortchange my father on the agreed-upon commission. We may be outlaws, but a deal is a deal.

Over the long-distance line, Dad tells me that this'll be a priceless lesson on the ways of the real world for the Blowhard; a man who, frankly, spends too much time pontificating.

"But is everything going to be okay?" The phone cord is twisted tight around my finger.

"Of course, sweetheart. I'm coming back tomorrow and bringing you a surprise, seaweed chips and two kimonos."

The phone rings late at night in our silent apartment. It's Dad, calling from Paris where he tried to board his connecting flight and was blocked by Israeli security from entering Tel Aviv. Our first reaction is to go on high alert, considering what could have caused him to be barred. It's impossible that it's the doing of the Blowhard: he knows Dad under an entirely different name. After mulling over every possible angle, we come to the conclusion that it's because of us.

Surrounded by a seemingly nice family, Dad simply looks unusual. Alone, he stands out like a highly trained, sharp-eyed operator. I've watched him stroll toward me through airports, eyes alert, a slightly naughty set to his mouth, and that precise, martial-arts way of moving that conveys a force to be reckoned with. Even I would mark him, and I'm just a sweet, wide-eyed member of a Brazilian family that enjoys traveling.

Since there is no way he's getting back on Israeli soil now, he has decided to wait for us in Paris. In one month, the games will be over and our visas will expire anyway. I can't wrap my mind around the concept of him being gone for such a long stretch. What are we going to do with ourselves?

The answer, bizarrely, is carry on as usual. I train, Frank trains, Chiara is moody, we go to the beach. Repeat. Mom, though, changes. She signs herself up for a dance class in a nearby studio. This is a first. Mom does not engage in recreational activities; she just organizes ours.

We all go by the studio one day to collect her and observe this anomaly in person. Through the glass window, I can't take my eyes off her. Without any training or experience, she can *move*. I find myself smiling. Her hair is coming loose in soft, dark curls and her cheeks are flushed; the other women look heavy and ponderous in comparison to our dancing queen. Even Chiara and Frank, totally unimpressed by anything Mom does, watch with raised brows.

Often when I'm training, I'll look over to the observation area, and ponder how bored Mom must be. Once I asked if she ever glances up from her book, sees me on the gym floor, and thinks, *oh no, not another backflip*. With an expression that was sweet and a little sad, she said watching her daughter be able to spin through the air with so much freedom is one of the great pleasures of her life. I didn't believe it.

But now, as she sashays lightly into the end of the song, I feel the sheer joy of being a spectator. I could stand here in a stuffy waiting area all afternoon and watch her be completely herself. Full of life, a little mischievous, with a damn good sense of rhythm. She looks happy. Really happy. And it occurs to me that this shouldn't be such a shock.

TEL AVIV IS abuzz with the Maccabiah Games. The third largest sporting event in the world is finally here, with five thousand athletes from thirty-three countries competing. Ramat Gan Stadium is filled with pulsing energy and the sound of thousands cheering. I sit in the stands with Mom and Chiara, jiggling my knee excitedly, as we wait for the opening ceremony to begin. The competitors have all been taken to a secret location, away from the open-air stadium, for security reasons. All Frank was told is that they will walk from there to the stadium in a heavily guarded procession.

An important-looking man in a suit strides across the field, causing a wave of excited whispers to spread through the spectators as he enters the dignitaries' box. It's partitioned from the rest of the audience, and I lean forward, trying to get a better look. The recent arrival, who can only be Prime Minister Benjamin Netanyahu, settles into his seat, fine white hair neatly parted, face pink.

We wait and wait. I start to fidget impatiently. Looking around the stands where colorful flags from around the world are flying, I see people checking their watches impatiently. *Bring out the athletes. Let's get some torches lit.* There's a slight commotion in Netanyahu's box as a man in black slips past the guards and whispers in the prime minister's ear. I strain forward, even though I'm too far away to hear. When the man leaves, Netanyahu sits very still.

Something changes behind us. Powerful lights flood the outside of the stadium. When I look back at the box, another man is speaking urgently to the prime minister. The ceremony should have begun ages ago.

Whap, whap, whap. The sound of heavy-duty helicopter blades make us look up searching the sky. Faraway, a siren wails.

"Something's wrong." Mom stands abruptly and heads for the aisle. An official with an earpiece is moving by swiftly, descending the stairs. Mom manages to get his attention and ask why there is such a delay.

"Everything is fine. Please just stay in your seats." He doesn't even pause in his rapid descent. Familiar as we are with spin, we know when we're being lied to. In the dignitaries' box, people frown, discuss, whisper into earpieces. But we're already on our feet, jogging down the concrete steps, spectators a colorful blur on either side of my tunnel vision. There's a sick feeling in my stomach and I want out of this stadium to where we have room to maneuver.

When my sneakers hit the gravel outside, a deafening roar makes me look up, wind whipping hair into my face; a military helicopter, like a dark beast with guns, is flying low above us, powerful spotlight trained ahead. An ambulance screams by. Something is definitely wrong. There are too many military operatives, too many unholstered guns.

Our eyes follow the helicopter. In the distance it joins others, circling in the night sky like dangerous insects, spotlights combing the earth. Mom weaves through the crowd and walks up to the nearest soldier.

"What's going on?" I can hear the restrained panic in her voice.

"I have no information," he says blankly, his automatic weapon pointing at the ground, finger on the trigger guard.

"My son is one of the athletes, please tell me!"

"Everything is fine. Stay calm." He moves away.

"WE'RE NOT GOING to find out anything here," Mom says. "We need to get home so he can reach us on the landline. He has no idea where we are." As we hurry toward the street, her hand clasping mine, Chiara following closely, I keep glancing back at the helicopters, hovering low to the ground.

In the lobby of our hotel, we accost the night concierge. "Have you seen my son?" Mom lifts her hand above her head to indicate a tall person. This is unnecessary. The concierge is a woman; of course she knows who he is. She probably reapplies lipstick before he comes home from swim practice every day. But she knows nothing. Helpless, we stand in the lobby.

Then mom blurts out, "Cab drivers." Between the radio they always have on, and the constant communication between taxis, it's like an honest news channel. I'm relieved to have a plan. "There's a stand nearby, let's go." Mom instructs Chiara to go up to the suite in case he calls, and then we're out onto the street. We find the drivers standing all together, at attention, instead of smoking and chatting in small groups as usual. Mom walks up without hesitation.

"A bridge collapsed," one of the cabbies answers her in English. "They think it's been blown up by terrorists."

"Which bridge?" we ask simultaneously.

"A small one." He draws on his cigarette, cheeks shadowed with dark stubble.

Mom and I stare at each other. "So the athletes are fine?"

He stops mid-exhale and frowns at us, the smoke spreading lazily in the still air. "No. The athletes were walking across the bridge when it was blown up."

Mom steps back as if punched, a hand pressing her heart. The world narrows and focuses the way it does when I am very scared, so much that I feel no fear, only an icy clear calm. "What else do you know?" I ask.

"That's it, they aren't giving information out."

"Was anyone hurt?"

"Someone said two have died already."

"From which team?" My voice must be hard because he moves away slightly.

"Do you know one of the competitors?"

"Just tell us!" Mom is still pressing her chest. "Do you know which team?"

"No. They were just beginning to march toward the stadium."

She makes a small sound, like breath leaving her body. I put my arm through hers and draw it to me. My knees almost buckle and I realize why Mom is so pale, why she's clinging to me as if to life itself.

The athletes had just begun to walk.

The march of the athletes is country by country, in alphabetical order.

Which country is stamped on our passports, the ones we got from Our Friend in Frankfurt Airport?

Frank is competing for Brazil.

18: Tel Aviv, age 11

BACK AT THE hotel we don't dare call Dad for fear of blocking the phone line. Instead, we stare at the walls, alone with our thoughts. Chiara is immobile on a chair, her shoulders hunched, and I find myself wondering how she would feel if he didn't come home. If she would truly be sad. I think of the pencil in his leg, the punch through the wall, his hand bloody. Even when they are tolerating each other, play-fighting with foam wave boards on a boardwalk, I know there is hatred between them. It flows more easily from her toward him. Ever present, but seeming to intensify with each passing year, each passing chapter in our existence. He is so handsome and charming, everything seems to come easily for him; she is the opposite, awkward and angry. People hardly ever feel comfortable around her, whereas they flock to him. So maybe she'll be glad if he's gone, crushed beneath the heavy stones of a bombed bridge. Guiltily, I shake the thought away.

My own emotions should be complicated—he has done things to me, with me, that violate all the trust I had. Maybe I should hate him. But I just want him back.

I pace the room, needing to move even if I'm not getting anywhere. *Couldn't we have gotten fake passports from somewhere else? Panama, or better yet, Zambia.* As I walk past our kitchenette, the phone shrills. Heart beating, I snatch it up immediately. "Yes?"

"I'm alive."

ON THAT NIGHT, some of the world's best athletes walked toward Ramat Gan Stadium and waited in formation, with Australia near the lead, to traverse a slender pedestrian bridge spanning the Yarkon River. Then, they started across.

When fully loaded, the bridge collapsed under their weight, plunging the young competitors into the river, infamous for its dangerous levels of pollution. People and chunks of wood churned in the poisonous water, as those still conscious struggled to climb onto the river bank.

Four members of the Australian team died, three of them from infections after being pulled out. Another team member survived, but only after twenty-eight brain operations. Sixty other athletes were injured in the tragedy, which was kept secret for hours from the family members, friends, and fans sitting in the stadium. The torch was even lit after officials already knew of the disaster.

What sticks forever in my mind about this night is the terrible randomness of life. Just because you are in the wrong part of the alphabet you could fall to your death, while *B* watches from solid ground.

When Frank comes home, his official tracksuit rumpled, shadows under his eyes, it's as if he's back from the dead. I am half-asleep on the couch, and it all seems like a misty dream. Mom holds him tight for the longest time; Chiara actually appears to be relieved, which will undoubtedly pass soon. They go off to the kitchen to prepare something to eat and Frank and I are left alone.

I heave myself into a sitting position, my head too heavy for my tired neck. He sinks down beside me, elbows on knees, the competitor's badge still dangling from a cord around his neck. He stares at the standard hotel carpet we have seen a thousand times, all over the world. Frank seems older, so serious, his cheekbones sharp in the dark. Slowly, I lean my head on his Brazil-colored shoulder and he turns to hug me. Just the way it used to be.

19: Virginia, USA, age 12

I'VE LIED ABOUT being from this country so often, it should feel more familiar. Standing on the back deck of our new house in Virginia, overlooking the pool, I rest one hand on the rough wood of the railing and listen to a soft wind sigh through the trees. The forest seems endless, mysterious, as evening gathers in the shadows.

Our house is picture perfect, like an old-time photo of where the lucky few live.

"Goddammit, stop getting in the way," Dad snaps from the driveway, where he and Mom are unloading the car. I move toward them, ready to distract or resolve, but as I round the corner he grabs her arm, shoving her roughly to the side. Quickly, I start carrying bags up the path, out of his way, while scanning our surroundings. There is nothing but oaks and evergreens shielding us with their branches. Neighbors, if any, are too far away to see. My stomach relaxes; there is no one to hear our dysfunction. It's only when my hand touches the front door that I turn, looking across the lawn, the complete isolation, and realize: This may not be a good thing.

WE'RE RIGHT NEAR Washington D.C., and this, of course, is the reason we relocated. To be close to political power. When we joined Dad in Paris, he felt the time had come to move to a country with a good amount of hiding places, and the most potential avenues for profit: the United States of America.

Dad flips through a synagogue newsletter as we sit side by side on our rented couch in what I've learned Americans call the "family room." Nearly all of Washington's power players live in the beautiful suburbs of Virginia, and some of them go to our small future place of godly worship. "What's your plan?" I pull my mass of hair into a ponytail.

"We'll see. Just go in and do PR for now."

In my room, I close the door and stand in front of the mirror, squaring my shoulders.

It's more obvious lately, in my eyes. A kind of darkening or wariness. The good news is no one I meet seems to notice. Not even at gymnastics, where I train five hours every day. Because the unpleasant things are put in little boxes, I close them, and they stay here, hidden in my mind. I've become so skilled at appearing cheerful that I can even convince myself. And it scares me sometimes, how good I've become at ignoring my heart.

THE FIRST TIME there is blood on the walls of our Virginia house, it shocks me. Chiara is supposed to be on a diet, to better represent the family when she applies for political internships in the upcoming presidential campaign. Dad is helping her apply to both parties, of course. It's good to keep your options open and not let politics get in the way of getting ahead in politics. Chiara doesn't seem to appreciate the importance of appearing perfect and keeps sneaking chocolates and white bread and then claiming there is something wrong with her metabolism.

"No, it's because you lie and eat junk food on the side." Dad stares her down in the entrance hall as I wander down the stairs. Anything with sugar is, as always, strictly forbidden to us all. It may seem bizarre, now that Frank is twenty-two years old, and Chiara, twenty-four. But Dad's hold is like iron.

"I don't!" she protests unconvincingly.

Suddenly there's the odd and horrible sound of a body slamming into an immovable object, and Chiara hits the wall near the door. On the stairs, I want to gasp but seem unable to work my lungs. He is hauling her up by her arms when an strange expression passes over her face—a calculation—and she kicks out at his leg. *No!* I think. I know before he even reacts that it will only provoke him further. The fits of rage have become more common; and when he's like this, you have to ride it out stoically without showing weakness—or worse, challenging him.

He punches her in the face, hard. There's a spray of blood, and part of the white wall is speckled red with terrifying graffiti. It's a sharp uppercut to the stomach next and she doubles over, legs giving out as she slides down the wall to the floor. He stands above her, hands in fists. I can hear him breathing heavily through his nose, the veins in his neck bulging. "Don't ever lie to me."

She raises her head, blood tricking from her mouth, but what I see in her face turns my stomach. It's . . . a kind of open adoration.

"No, Papa." Her voice is sweet. "I won't."

Dad turns and spots me, standing frozen on the stairs. "Go to your room," he snaps.

I concentrate on moving my legs, bending the knees, going up. When I glance back, they are hugging.

I'M VOTED BEST Smile in the weekend Hebrew class at our synagogue, and Most Likely to Succeed. For my own sake, I hope both are true. I've got under six months to learn to read and sing Hebrew in time for my bat mitzvah, the Jewish coming-of-age ritual timed to occur when you are thirteen, at the peak of your awkwardness, and which involves leading a service in front of the entire congregation.

At home, there is never a moment for me to analyze a new development before another one knocks me off balance. Our parents fight nearly constantly now; and when Dad isn't yelling, the terrible strained silences are even worse. Mom seems to fade under the pressure of all the things she leaves unsaid, and I know Frank looks down on her for never really standing up to our father. It's been almost five years since Dad spoke a word to him. They live in the same house, but my brother has no voice. Frank is pacing one day in the hallway outside our rooms, when he stops abruptly and drives his fist through the wall—on purpose this time—splitting his knuckles wide open. He wants desperately to go away to college, but Dad is determined to keep watch on him and Frank remains stuck at home.

"I want out of here"—Frank's dark eyes flash inches from mine—"or I'm going to bring this whole thing down. I'm going to go to the police." We are in the hall, blood on his fist. I glance at Chiara and see the smallest of smirks curve her lips.

This is his first threat against—us? My dad? Our family? I can't be quite sure, but it's the first. She didn't even have to bait him this time, he's hitting out at himself. Quickly I reach for Frank's shoulder, but he pulls away, voice harsh. "I'm not joking."

"It's going to be okay," I look up at him. "We'll fix the wall."

"It's not about a fucking wall." He pushes past me in frustration, slamming the door of his room.

I know he's not joking. That's what scares me.

To my surprise, Dad writes off the hole in the wall as a simple lack of self-control on Frank's part. Even more shockingly, plans are set in motion to get Frank an interview at Yeshiva University, the Orthodox Jewish college in New York City. Definitely not the normal university experience Frank was hoping for. And then, Dad discovers there's also an Orthodox girls' middle and high school here in Virginia.

I'm told to dress in an extremely modest outfit and be ready for duty on Monday. We are going to meet the head rabbi about getting admitted. Since I've always wanted to go to an actual school, it's difficult to wrap my mind around the fact that it might happen for both Frank and me. Passing the recently repaired hole in the wall, I tap on Frank's door. "You actually got your way," I say, taking a seat on the floor of his room.

With a cool stare, he abandons the desk where he's been sorting natural energy pills, a recent business idea of his, and sinks down across from me. "Is that the way you see it?"

I pick at the carpet. "I guess so?" I offer doubtfully.

"This is still part of Dad's plan. Doesn't matter if it makes any sense, we all have to shut up and follow along. I go infiltrate the Jewish community in New York, where there are even more powerful people. Sister psycho gets into politics here, as far as it's possible for her to go. And you're sent to this school to get in position and keep doing what you do best."

I frown. "What's that?"

"Smile, work, be perfect. Be the little queen."

"I'm not playing some role, Frank." I feel color rising to my face. "I'm trying to keep everything going. Mom's barely surviving. Don't you get that?"

He looks away. "That's not my problem."

I realize my hands are clenched. "What do you mean? Of *course* it is! We have to—"

"Look," he interrupts, a hardness in his voice. "I know you're trying to hold it all together, but it's not going to work."

No. No, I'm not going to give up; there is no reason why this family could not work. *Of course*, I'm exhausted, too. But I hang on, because the basic principles seem sound: loyalty, dedication, believing in tomorrow. Why can't they all just cooperate with me in glossing over the rest?

I watch Frank, his cold expression, and worry about what he might pull once he's in New York. "You're going to behave, right? Don't get into trouble at the school for partying or something, okay?" I've never been to New York but can imagine that his natural charm and beauty will open all sorts of doors, including some risky ones.

"Bhajan, you should spend your energy looking out for yourself." He stands dismissively. Even I have to admit when I'm not getting anywhere, but as I move toward the door, something makes me stop.

"I'm going to write you, okay?" I say it over my shoulder, opening the door slowly, waiting. I stand for a long moment, my fingers on the handle.

"Bhajan," he shakes his head tiredly. "Knowing you, you're going to do exactly what you want anyway." But I think I catch the ghost of a smile on his lips as we both turn away.

For my admissions interview I'm attired like a nineteenth-century country lass, every inch of skin covered except my hands, neck, and perspiring face. Dad looks over and grins at me as we wait on a bench outside the rabbi's office. I tug at my high collar, going over the story in my head. I have no school record, or really any record of my existence, so today we must rely only on charm, gymnastics accomplishments, and the fact that I've lived in Israel.

"Shalom!" I was expecting a small, scholarly fellow, but the rabbi fills the doorway, a big bear of a man with wild copper hair.

"We've never had a famous athlete at our school before!" he booms as we take a seat in his office, hemmed in by high stacks of papers.

I sigh inwardly. *Famous* is a massive exaggeration and based on the fact that every time I win a gym competition, Dad proudly informs a newspaper or three of the occurrence. At first I loved the attention, but that was before I started to lose. With each passing month, I'm growing taller and height is the enemy of any gymnast. My long limbs seem to tangle, sending me crashing to the ground. I'm no longer winning. I'm not even close. And as for my father's habit of courting attention, even while we're on the run, I just force myself not to think about it.

The rabbi claps his hands jovially, startling me. "We'll just give you a math test now to see if you'll be in the advanced or regular class. And welcome to our school, Crystal!" An exam? At a school? Now? Dad usually just throws out verbal pop quizzes while we are cruising around purchasing stylish matching socks at the mall, or laundering money at a gold buyer.

The fluorescent overhead light makes the black print stand out threateningly. I'm supposed to be all right at math, this will be fine, it will be fine. I take a cleansing breath and roll my shoulders back.

Question #1 . . . With gradual dread, I realize I don't even understand what they are asking me to do. *Quotient*, what does that mean? The product of two numbers? I must look appalled, because the teacher checks on me and asks if I am okay. My abacus didn't have quotients.

"Yes!" I say brightly. Family rule #236: Never admit to being out of your depth. Radiate competence until it becomes a reality.

Despite my best guesses, I score less than 30 percent on the test and will be thought to be mildly intellectually disabled by the faculty. But I'm still in!

Brimming with curiosity, I show up early for my first day of school. Chiara is by my side. To make sure things go smoothly, she is actually going to be a teacher's assistant at the school. Not sure how Dad swung that one. I think we both wish I could be left to fend for myself. In the morning light, we give each other a look. The look of two people stuck with each other.

A kindly older woman appears at my elbow, leading me off to my first class, and assuring me—for some reason—that math skills do not matter as much as being a good person. I'm about to get me an education!

Soon enough, I discover something I would never have suspected: School is not that hard. Or this one isn't. Most of it involves showing up, memorizing formulas, and knowing when to shut up. I am encouraged enough to dip my toe into dangerous territory with Dad. We're on the highway, cutting through the night in our new Corvette—bought in cash, silver-gray, and rumbling with power. Working up my courage, I go for it. "I was thinking, maybe I could go to a normal public school next year . . . There are lots of good ones here."

Dad looks at me sharply. "Sweetheart, you think I haven't considered that?"

Actually, I don't think he has. Sending me to a school with regular kids seems far too direct and simple for our family. "Those places are like factories teaching propaganda, preparing people to settle into a life of being scared and doing what they are told."

"What if I just try it out for a while?"

"Bhajan, you would be going in as a freshman, into a mass of hundreds of older people raised on MTV and without discipline. You have no idea what you would encounter."

I want to groan. It's frustrating to be thought of as naive or breakable. This innocence of mine is mostly a figment of other people's imaginations. Dad covers my hand, somehow always cold, with his, always warm, and squeezes comfortingly. "D'you remember the war museum we went to, during our layover in England?"

I nod slowly. It was on a blustery winter day when I was nine, dodging puddles in my boots. The museum walls were hung with black-and-white photographs of young men in uniform, standing tall. I looked over the rows and rows of handsome faces, probably barely eighteen. It wasn't until Dad pointed at one photo and explained that all the boys in it died during the WWII that the significance sunk in. This was more memorial than museum.

I stayed there a long time, studying the photo. There was one young man, in the second row, looking straight at the camera with a big mischievous grin. Just like mine.

"Yeah," I say now, quietly, "I remember."

"Just because a few people in power decide to start a war, millions of young people on both sides are slaughtered or starved. Do you see where I'm going with this?"

"Not really . . ."

"You are precious and it's my job to guard you. Do you think the children of the powerful were sent to the front lines? When I do what I do, I'm not trying to complicate your life. I'm thinking ahead." We pull off the highway, the sharp curve pressing me into the door and releasing new car smell. "Life is not always like this, shopping malls and safety. That can vanish in an instant. I don't want you to be cannon fodder. That's all most people become, war or not. Working nine to five, doing something they hate. I don't want that for you. I want you to have the connections to operate as you please. That doesn't involve going to Penn State and partying for four years like your brother would like, or living on her own and being directionless like your sister would enjoy. It's my job to maneuver you into position . . kicking and screaming if necessary." He pauses, voice softening. "Do you know . . . you are the most important thing I have ever done? Most people spend their life running into walls because they don't have someone to guide them. . . . I want to save you all from that. I know it's difficult, but it's hard now so it can be easy later."

When I look at him, so sincere, I think I do understand. He wants to create a legacy for us, not a flash in the pan. And now that I actually interact with my peers, I see how unusual that kind of forethought is. Of course, the expectations placed on my shoulders are hard to carry, but I'm not sure I would change it to be just a normal kid, who no one takes seriously.

CONVENTIONAL WISDOM SAYS you need a high school diploma before you can be accepted into college. But that is why it is called conventional—it lacks imagination.

Frank and Dad drive to New York, not speaking the whole way, and meet with the head rabbi of Yeshiva University in Manhattan. Although Frank got his GED while we were in Vancouver, we had to destroy it since we were all using different names then. Just like Chiara's studies at the herbal college and the records of my sports competitions, it's been wiped out. We have all emerged from a fog a couple years ago, fully formed, yet lacking any history.

But Frank is Frank. When they come back from New York, he's been accepted to college, and even Dad has to acknowledge: Frank has a formidable talent for charming people. My father can get people to follow him because he is brilliant and makes them feel all things are possible. But I've noticed that sooner or later they begin to sense the truth: He thinks they are stupid sheep. It's different with Frank, who genuinely likes people and *wants* to be liked. It makes him more persuasive but, as Dad often to point out, also vulnerable to being led astray, like a lamb, to the slaughterhouse of peer approval.

"You should have seen the meeting," Dad tells me with a hint of wonder. "Your brother kept smiling and asking the Rabbi about the school's goals and values, and by the end he couldn't have cared less about a lost high school diploma. I think Frank has a future in politics." Dad looks thoughtful. "If he can keep his focus."

Now that Frank is set, a hefty donation to the Democratic presidential campaign secures Chiara an internship working to put Al Gore in the White House. We ended up choosing the Democrats, not because of any party's beliefs—we have as much faith in politicians as we do in McDonald's—but because we want her to work for a winner. The Republicans have set their hopes on George W. Bush, who my father has nicknamed the Nincompoop after watching an interview. Given these facts, Dad is nearly certain it's going to go to the Democrats, but just to be safe, he also makes a generous donation to the Republicans. In life, you have to prepare for the impossible.

I stand at a table at Kinko's, preparing to keep up our family tradition of smoothing over obstacles with creativity. My table is equipped with white-out, an industrial-size guillotine-style paper cutter, glue, fresh paper, rulers, and an X-ACTO knife. Looking down, I sigh. My hands are ugly. Red and dry from chalk, palms calloused like a bricklayer's from the constant friction of bar routines, and topped off by ragged bitten nails. But my fingers are slim and extremely steady, and that's why I'm in charge of adjusting documents. Dates that need changing, letters of recommendation from Fortune 500 companies to which I must add Chiara's name. You imagine it, I've rearranged it.

With the knife I trace the logo of a famous company, printed out from their website, and carefully glue it to the upper left hand corner of a letter Dad wants to send. Then, copying their font, I open Microsoft Word to create new contact details to go beneath the logo. If someone calls the company to check, they'll really be calling Mom's cell phone. After pasting on the new numbers, I take the letter to the copier and run one off to make sure it prints without shadows. I press on the lid until the paper is completely flat and the copy comes out seemingly pristine. Hunched over the paper, I check every detail for any tells. Logo alignment, matching contact info structure, font size and spacing—

"Vegetarian pizza?" Dad asks, startling me.

"Hell yeah." I massage my stiff neck, then hand him the letter.

He studies it under the Kinko's fluorescents before we step out into the evening. The parking lot is nearly empty now; we walk across in a peach-colored twilight, holding hands, a spring in our step. "Princess, what you can do with an X-ACTO knife and a little white-out would put most forgers to shame."

20: Virginia, age 12

GLOW-IN-THE-DARK STARS TWINKLE on my ceiling in this peaceful stolen time between the end of night and getting up to face another day. As so often happens, my mind spoils it all by frantically going through my to-do list. I groan and roll out of bed, considering what can be outsourced.

Recently, Chiara has been cast as my part-time secretary. I don't recall there being a discussion; maybe it just seemed like the logical way to keep the cause moving forward. After all, my day starts at sunup and finishes when I stagger in from training all evening, while Chiara is only working part-time at my school until her presidential campaign internship begins. In the unforgiving stakes of our family, I'm more productive.

Opening my door, I see Chiara heading sleepily into the bathroom. Why does she insist on wearing such ugly clothes? Even her pajamas! "Hey." I lean out of my room. "Can you do my science homework? I'll handle the English essay."

She nods resignedly. The upstairs feels deserted since Frank left for college, and I glance at his door, which he keeps padlocked. He shared the hiding place of the key only with me, and when I am especially lonely, I slip in silently and sit in my spot on the carpet where we used to talk. It may not be logical, but despite what happened, he is still the one who knows me best. The secret place where I could voice the doubts in my head.

I set my homework down outside Chiara's door. Sometimes I feel sorry for her, especially since both she and Frank have been banned from the living room and kitchen area of the house by Dad. He sleeps on the couch in the living room, never upstairs with Mom anymore, and that makes downstairs *his* space. He refuses to have the slightest whiff of neurosis or negative thinking pollute his environment. Mom now takes all Chiara's meals to her upstairs.

I'm trying to be nicer to her, I really am. It's just that Chiara makes it so *challenging*. Some mornings we go for a short run through the Virginia forest to assist in her weight-loss protocol and to work on my endurance. I follow her tiny backpack, bobbing along with her as she jogs ahead. My heart rate accelerates and a pleasant warmth spreads through my limbs. She always sets a good pace. Ironically, for someone who trains constantly, I tire easily, while both my siblings shine at long distances.

Today, Chiara comes to a stop in a small clearing where we often take a water break and motions me to one side, digging in her backpack. She is saying something, but I tune her out, catching my breath. Looking up at the leaves, heavy with dew, I reach out my hand for the water bottle.

The gunshot freezes me in place, my arm extended, as it echoes in the emptiness. Whipping around I see Chiara standing, feet apart, a black handgun aimed at a tree.

"What the hell!" I yell.

She looks both surprised and innocent. "I told you to block your ears, weren't you listening? Did I startle you?"

I shift uneasily on my feet. "Where did you get a gun?"

"Papa bought it for me." Her voice takes on the odd, babyish quality it always does when talking about him. "I'll be walking alone in the city when I start on the campaign, and I'll have to be able to defend myself. Stand way back there, Bhajan." Aiming in the opposite direction, she fires again. The sharp, unfamiliar scent of gunpowder fills my nose as a piece of bark explodes off the tree.

She regards her aim with satisfaction and lets out a little staccato laugh.

All the sympathy I felt this morning vanishes. It's always like this between us; as soon as I vow to be nicer and more considerate, she does something that makes me pull away from her. "Let's run," I say, starting off. But what I really want is to get away from that eerie laugh, from everything I can't understand.

OUR OTHER BRAND-NEW car, a Lincoln, creamy white and bought, of course, in cash, purrs along the empty road from our house. Every weekday morning, Dad makes the thirty-minute drive from our remote area to the nearest stop serviced by the Orthodox girls school bus. Once Chiara and I are on the yellow clunker, it still takes over an hour to reach school in time for first period.

"How's the research going?" Dad asks Chiara over his shoulder.

"Good, Papa," she responds quickly, in a way that I immediately identify as a lie. He pauses, eyes sharp in the rearview mirror.

"Have you found the best options?"

"I still have to look more, but I've found a few similar names."

I know Chiara and the way she rearranges the truth well enough to sense she's not researching but probably going out to eat forbidden foods instead. Carefully, I keep my expression blank. Usually I wouldn't mind, but her assignment is a vital one: to look through the archives of Jewish family lines in D.C. and trace names similar to the one we're using. Many immigrants changed the spelling of names to make them more easily pronounceable in the new world, and this will work in our favor as we falsify a Jewish family tree. Her assignment is to find a family with a name similar to the ones in our fake passports, preferably with as few living members as possible who could discover and contradict our being relatives. Dad seems determined to legitimize this new identity, and I like the idea of actually putting down roots and sticking to a name. In a way it saddens me, though. Our religion is no longer about truth and beauty, but business. We have switched faiths like so many names, and now I have trouble taking anything seriously.

As we near the large parking area where the school bus stops, Dad drops the interrogation and fixates on the road. We're early and our car comes to a stop in the empty lot. Sitting silently, we wait for the bus in the gray morning light.

Suddenly, in one seamless move, Dad turns in his seat and plunges a pen into Chiara's thigh. She screams in shock and pain. His fist moves once, twice, three times in a blur, plunging the uncapped pen through the long skirt she's wearing. "Don't. Ever. Lie to me." Eyes like ice, his face flushed, he raises the pen again.

Without thinking, I shoot my hand out to cover her thigh and hear myself say, *"Please."*

Very calmly he turns to me and moves the pen so that it is poised directly above my right knee. "Do you want to be next?"

Wordlessly, I shake my head.

"She's supposed to be doing something important. Instead she's putting us all in danger. Don't interfere again, Bhajan." The pen is still there, inches from my leg. I cannot take my eyes off his hand, sparse blond hairs just above the white knuckles. "Get out. Both of you."

We scramble for the doors and are out in seconds. The bus has arrived without my noticing, standing there, yellow against the gray. I gasp in air and force my legs to walk toward the bus; a few pale faces are already inside, looking sleepily through the windows. The driver cranks open the doors with a wheeze, and my numb foot advances automatically onto the first step.

"Morning!" I smile more than usual.

"Hey Sunshine!" He waves us on board.

I ignore Chiara, who sits alone.

Leaning my forehead against the cool glass of the window, I wish I could just stop. Give up the constant adjusting and improving of myself and just be. Walk up to someone and simply say: Help, my family is falling apart. My mother is detaching from life, my father treats her like a servant, I miss my brother and yet am scared to have him come back to this. And Chiara. That last day in the forest . . . and the bold lying to someone she knows will hurt her—her beloved *Papa*. What is happening in her mind?

But I stay silent, and every morning the school bus moves on, looking like any other: bright yellow and empty of secrets.

21: Virginia, age 13

I AM ARRESTED and taken to jail on an average evening in the supermarket. That's when life always sneaks in and slaps you upside the head: on normal days when you are thinking mainly of what to have for dinner. I'm walking the cosmetics aisle when a mascara display catches my pale-lashed eye. A quick scan of my surroundings and I palm one of the tubes as I've been taught, slipping it casually into my pocket.

I'm a few aisles over, looking longingly at the potato chips, when I sense someone behind me. Before the tall, sour-faced man says a word, I feel my stomach drop. The security guard stands so close I can smell cigarettes and orders me to take everything out of my pockets.

My mind is working furiously, powered by panic. "I have to talk to my mom."

"No, you have to come with me." He towers over me, eclipsing the exits.

I'm thinking frantically, hands sweating, the mascara wand in my pocket feeling hot as fire. If I can get out of this, I promise God—whichever One we believe in—to never try to make myself look hot again. Some things weren't meant to be.

We exit the Chips and Dips aisle while I search for Mom's cart, my heart pounding, every step taking us closer to the security office door. At the last moment, I turn desperately and call over my shoulder, "Mom!" praying my voice can be heard in the crowded store. Almost instantly I see her powering out of the health food aisle, cart abandoned. She marches over, eyes blazing.

"Who are you?" she asks the guard, moving in front of me.

He explains that I am a criminal. But I'm more struck by the fact that although he is twice the size of my mother, she looks tougher. The quiet, hesitant person she is around my father has vanished. There is something unshakable about the way she holds her slim body.

If only I could sidle away for long enough to toss the mascara, they wouldn't really have anything on me. But he's watching me. I'm taken up cold, fluorescent-lit stairs, the walls so white they hurt my eyes, and into a stark room for questioning—alone. Now I have to empty my pockets onto the Formica table and there it is, the evidence. As I take a closer look at the mascara tube, the word "blue" stares out at me. Is that even the color I should be using? Holy cow, all this and I was probably stealing the wrong—

"What's your name?" He uncaps a pen.

I look up from my fidgety hands and make my second mistake. I give a completely false name, one we've never used before. But just because we don't have a computer at home, doesn't mean the rest of the world follows suit. They have store surveillance cameras, databases, instant name and address checks. And suddenly, I'm in far more trouble than an ordinary shoplifter.

Heavy boots climb the stairs and stalk down the hall. Two cops enter, their uniforms and gun belts blocking the door, motioning for me to stand. My legs are numb, frozen, and for a moment I wonder if I can.

Downstairs I'm loaded into a police car. The sight of mom's Lincoln determinedly following is the only thing that keeps me from bursting into tears. At the station, from my single chair in a bulletproof-glass-windowed holding cell, I can see Mom outside, calling for backup. I try to steady my breathing. Honestly, I'm not scared of jail as much as I am of how Dad will react. The pen? The punch? The cord?

What if they check my story and I've blown everything for my family? I should have remembered—it's not a high-speed car chase, or a helicopter spotlight pinning you in the darkness that gets you caught. *It's the simple mistakes . . .*

A plump woman cop opens the door and tells me it's time to go to a real cell. She pats me down thoroughly and leads me through doors that snap shut and lock behind us. The halls are endless, cold. Near the cells, I give everything left in my pockets—lip balm, some coins, a snotty Kleenex—to a man and woman in a glass box, who bag and label it.

I'm sitting on the hard bench of my two-person cell, avoiding the stare of a rangy, tattooed fellow criminal in her teens who is inspecting me through her eyeliner, when the irony occurs to me. We've been worrying about Frank's threat to "bring the whole thing down" and destroy us by going to the cops. But now? Now it's me, ol' angel face, who has run straight into a brick wall and put us all in danger.

"Hey, girls." An officer unlocks the door and she and her partner step in, assessing me for damage. I must look frail in comparison to my cellmate. But it's okay, if the girl gets aggressive I'll just punch her in the trachea the way Dad taught me.

"Would you like a drink?" The male cop is holding a couple cans of Coke.

"That's nice," I say. "But I can't drink soda."

"Oh really, why not?" His brows draw together, deepening the worry lines.

"Very high sugar content."

"I'll take 'em both." My cellmate speaks for the first time, in a low, raspy voice. He hands the sodas over to her and turns back to me. "If you need anything, just knock on the glass, all right?"

"Okay. Well, actually there is something . . ." I lean forward on the bench, elbows on my knees. I'm craving the Coke; I can see myself drinking it in great, thirsty gulps, imagining the taste to be powerful and bubbly, strong enough to wash the taste of fear from my throat. They pause, the door open, looking expectant. "I want a lawyer, please."

A few hours later, the court-appointed lawyer, a clever-looking guy in his late forties, looks up from a table in the consult room. The cop who escorts me in slams the door on his way out, leaving us alone. The lawyer seems puzzled to see me here, skinny in my loose T-shirt with a butterfly on the front, hair in a high ponytail. "How are you?" he asks, unpocketing a pen.

"Good." I sit down across from him.

"You mean apart from being in jail?" His eyes twinkle, and I know we'll get along.

"Sure." Folding my hands and swallowing my nervousness, I grin. "But we can fix that, right?" As I try to get my story straight in my head, a strange feeling steals through me. I am not relaxed really . . . but pleasantly focused. Unlike dealing with life on the *outside*—a few hours in jail and, look, I'm already talking to myself like an inmate—I sense that I have more freedom here. More opportunity to use my skills.

The lawyer arranges it so I'm not put back in my cell. The cops from property-claim agree that I'm more suited to the conference room, where I can sip water and discuss the failings of the juvenile court system with my lawyer while he waits for his calls to have an effect. "It's so rare that I can have a real conversation while at work," he sighs.

I nod my head understandingly. "I saw some of the boy prisoners on the way in here." We are rolling our eyes in sympathetic agreement when the door clicks and a female cop motions at me. "Okay. You can go home until your court date."

She escorts me out of the room, her face a series of sharp angles as she assesses me. "You must be relieved," she says. But as we walk the antiseptic hallway, doors locking in reverse behind me, on my way to being free . . . I am more scared than ever. I'm sure jail is a dangerous place, but there are parameters here, some rules, and maybe that's what gave me the feeling of a kind of safety. Now I'm heading home—where anything can happen.

How angry will my parents be? The fact that our identities may be blown worries me less than the fact that I might have lost their trust. We can always run again. I will go anywhere, do anything, to keep us together; I only care what they think of me.

At home I lie in bed, eyes raw from crying, pondering my glow-in-the-dark stars, when I hear my father's heavy step outside my door. My body stiffens, viscerally afraid of his mood. He stands for a moment above me, a dark silhouette. Instinctively, I search his outline for an electrical cord.

I can smell his spicy cologne as he sits on my bed. "I'm going to tell you something which I think will help give you a new perspective on life," he declares, gently taking my cold hand in his.

The fear leaving my system makes me so weak that I lie still.

"You haven't lived, until you've been indicted."

"What's indicted?" I turn my head on the pillow.

"Arrested. Charged with a major crime . . . Look, it doesn't have to happen again, but this can be a strengthening experience for you."

I stare openmouthed.

"Bhajan, people spend lifetimes fearing the unknown, the things they haven't overcome. You've been to jail. It's done. And"—as he leans forward, his eyes twinkle in the light of the moon—"welcome to the big leagues."

22: Virginia, age 13

Dear Frank,

Chiara says I'm a classic overachiever, but if George W. Bush isn't letting his former DUI get in the way of running for office, I don't see why I should let my juvie record hold me back from anything.

The judge didn't buy a word of the story we came up with and I'm stuck with hours of community service cleaning a local middle school, and group counseling sessions with other juvenile delinquents. So I guess one of us finally made it into a public school, even if it is with the cleaning crew, after all the kids have left for the day.

I'm impressed that you're a bouncer in a nightclub, deciding who gets in or has to leave, how did you land that job?

Of course my lips are sealed; I don't tell anyone what you write.

Oh wait, I know how you got the job. Did they put you at the door to get girls to come in? Haha, I know I'm right! Mom told me you got scouted by a big modeling agency in New York and that they are taking photos of you to send to clothes designers. Give up the bouncing and do that, man! Sounds way more fun.

Mom is worried about me becoming too serious about everything, and came up with the idea to have the Israeli gym team that I used to train with come to America for a competition and visit. Only Mom would go to extreme measures like that, but it's actually happening. Your nemesis Chiara turns out to be really good at organizing things . . . The upside of bossy? Anyway, she called all these rich people in the Jewish community and got the whole trip funded: food, accommodation, sightseeing around D.C. and in Ohio.

You remember the Buckeye Classic? It may be fresher in your mind as the gymnastics competition last year where I ran so hard at the vault that my feet missed the springboard, smashing my chest into the vault, flipping me over, and knocking me senseless on the mat in front of top judges, cameras, and a thousand spectators. Don't smirk. It wasn't funny and it hurt like hell.

So I'm going back to Cleveland this year for the same competition. I know it's really far, but maybe you could come visit?

I'll be straight with you; I'm not looking forward to being compared to an Olympic team, along with the rest of the competitors. This is one of those family projects that start out as a sweet idea and then turns into a big, exhausting deal.

But the real reason is, I miss you, and I wonder if you are OK. If you want to feel more at home in Ohio maybe you can stand near the arena door and decide who gets in.

Love,
Bhajan

On the day of my bat mitzvah, the day I'm supposed to become a woman, I'm not feeling much like one. It's still me, flat-chested in a new poofy white dress. Standing alone on the synagogue podium in front of the whole congregation, I bow my head and start to sing the Hebrew words from my section of the Torah.

A section of pews in the center is reserved for my family, and it looks sadly sparse with just my parents and Chiara, all dressed formally and looking encouraging. I've already sat through a fair number of bar and bat mitzvahs where the pews were overflowing with aunts, uncles, annoying cousins, and grandparents dabbing away tears. We really should've hired some people from central casting.

At the end of the service the rabbi, a tall, jovial young man, drops his hand on my father's shoulder. "You must be very happy today." He smiles. "A small family, but much to be proud of." The rabbi looks between Chiara and me, and I'm about to take a breath and remind him that I have a brother as well, when a sharp glance from Chiara silences me. As I watch my parents chat with some congregation members, the feeling of unease, always with me, intensifies. They told me they'd offered to buy Frank a ticket to come. Did they? Or was it simpler, safer, to let it slide by?

I say nothing, and by the time the party arrives that night I've convinced myself that I am overdramatizing. He was probably just busy. He has better things to do.

As with most bat mitzvah celebrations, we are holding it in a hotel ballroom and the whole congregation is invited. Mine is not as lavish as some. I like the fact that my parents resisted the temptation to show off and opted to put a lot of personal effort into it instead. It's here in the amazing young magician they found, my favorite pizza, and the silhouette of dancers in my signature gymnastics leap on each balloon. I watch as they float up toward the lights and think how very different each birthday has been. New countries, new faces. Only one thing stayed the same, even in India: They pulled the car over at the stroke of midnight in the last days of July—air so soft—and lifted me out into the night. On an empty plateau, my song, Spandau Ballet's "Gold," still clicked into place, unwinding in the dashboard cassette player, and we danced together in the light of two flickering headlights.

Now I hear the first haunting chords, that familiar melody, and in a dark silk suit, his beard short, my father places his hand on my waist.

After the rush has gone I hope you find a little more time
Remember . . . we were partners in crime

Unable to resist, I smile up at him and we begin to move, his steps guiding me. I rest my head on his broad shoulder and despite all that's happened, all the pain, we are back under a blanket of stars, my hands banana-sticky, dancing like we can count on tomorrow.

Gold, always believe in your soul . . .
You're indestructible

As the final chords melt away, I find I don't want to open my eyes. Because then we will be here, in a hotel ballroom—minus one of us. With yet another fake name on a white cake.

A COLD, STORMY sky presses toward the asphalt, but the mood around the Buckeye competition venue in Cleveland is so electric that no one notices. It is nice to spend time with the Israeli team again, to see their friendly faces. But I wish they hadn't come; I prefer my life to remain compartmentalized. Seeing people from a few years ago, seeing our family through their eyes, is to see how much things have changed.

I can already sense Dad's patience fraying. Today, while driving the team van, he screamed terrifyingly at the Israeli coach, Zahava, for interrupting him and suggesting a different route. He's not used to spending extended periods of time with people who have not been trained directly by him.

While the team members collect their badges, I peek into the massive arena, already filling with spectators. Music echoes off the concrete walls as vendors work busily, selling fresh lemonade and popcorn. Over three thousand gymnasts are here, but today is the Elite competition. The best are in action, injuries taped, game faces on. I stand next to the Israeli team wearing my old Israeli tracksuit, relieved to be here only to cheer them on because of my recently fractured ribs. The terrible fall occurred at my last competition, and crash landings happen so often these days; it's as if my coordination is coming undone.

Scanning the rows of roaring spectators, I see a sprinkling of Israeli flags, blue and white among the jumble of colors. As the team chants echo, I think I hear someone call my name but my family is all the way on the other side of the arena, faces blurry in the distance.

Frank walks out in front of the seated spectators and waves. My brain stalls for a long moment. I stare at the apparition in jeans and a black tee, a few day's stubble peppering his jaw. It can't be. He's in New York, and it's been so long since I've seen—

"Bhajan!"

My real name jolts me and I rush past gymnasts, past coaches and medics, until I'm off the competition floor and standing in front of my brother.

"Bhajan, hi." His smile is happy, but up close I can see he looks different. "What are you doing here!?"

He hesitates, studying my face. "Nice to see you too, squirt."

"No, I didn't mean it like that!" But I'm thrown off, guarded. "It's just such a surprise, I didn't know—" Uncertainly, I step toward him, and he sets down the dark duffel bag he's carrying to hug me.

"Watch the ribs on my left side," I say. Accustomed to years of sports injuries—both his and mine—he doesn't even ask. I smile up at him; he smells exactly the same, like his favorite blue soap, and like my friend. "When did you get here? Are you staying at our hotel?"

He shakes his head. "I just arrived. No one knew I was coming."

"Mom and Dad don't know?" It seems impossible that something of this magnitude would escape their surveillance.

"You asked me to come, remember? In your letter. So I took a bus and came to surprise you."

When I wrote those words I never thought someone with such an interesting life in New York would actually listen, read between the lines, and show up for me. I just look at him, taking it all in. Holding out his arm, he measures my ever-increasing height against his constant six feet two inches.

"Sure you're not on 'roids, Bhajan?"

" 'Roids stunt your growth." I bat his arm away, absorbing the changes a year has made. The anger that I saw in his last days with us seems to have gone, replaced with something older, more wary. He has filled out some since he's no longer training every day. He's less lean and hungry and more solid. "You look more . . . mature," I say.

"I've been on a bus for twenty hours, that would age anyone. And you, kiddo, are looking tired."

I nod in silent agreement.

"Do you want some lemonade?" He reaches into his pocket, counting out crumpled dollar bills.

"It has sugar in it."

"You're a teenager, I think you can handle a few tablespoons."

"Do you eat sugar in New York?"

"Ah, I missed you." He is laughing, head tilted back, when Mom appears at our side.

The last time they spoke, he was leaving for the city; now they share an awkward hug. Reality starts to filter back into my world, and I see Dad watching from the stands, his face made of stone.

"Let's go talk outside, Frank." Mom points to the hallway. "Bhajan, why don't you go back to the team?" From the automatic way she speaks, I can tell she's gotten her marching orders from Dad. Not to be argued with, by any of us. But something is different. Frank came across the country on a bus with his own money, and I can see it now in his expression, the change I've been trying to identify: He's hopeful, hopeful that a gesture like this could mend things.

"Can't he hang out here for a while?" I say, but I'm backing away from my question even while asking. There is no way Dad will come over here to break years of silence. Chiara is at Dad's side, not budging, looking serious and watchful, clutching her day planner. He beats her, stabs her with a pen, and yet she stands proudly—even defiantly—by his side.

"Another time, honey." Mom touches my shoulder, and I'm filled with confusion. What should I do?

They are turning toward the exit when Frank looks directly at Dad. I can't remember the last time that happened; they've avoided eye contact for years. There is something brave about it, Frank's face open, waiting . . .

Across the floor Dad marks it, holds his gaze for the first time, and turns away.

I can see a barrier shutter down over Frank's face, trying to hide the hurt. Reaching up, I hug him quickly, ignoring the pain on my left side. Vivaldi begins to play for a floor routine and I rest my hands on his shoulders, unwilling to let go. I should do something, I should take a stand . . .

I look between Mom, Dad, Chiara, Frank, and slowly I move aside.

Frank starts to follow Mom without another glance to the stands. Hoisting the duffel, he smiles sadly over his shoulder. "See you, Bhajan."

I manage to wave, my other hand cradling my ribs through the tracksuit, where the bruise spreads, yellow and purple, under my heart.

THE NEXT MORNING, by the time I've yawned myself awake and started asking questions, Frank has been sent away from his separate hotel with a return bus ticket in his pocket. "But . . ." I sit on my bed, head heavy, and force myself to look up at Chiara.

"We didn't have a choice, Bhajan, you know how he can be. He could have started saying all sorts of things, or punching walls."

"You should have told me! I never get to see him."

"We decided it was best."

"I'm sure you did." I lie back, arms limp at my sides, the fight drained out of me before I've even gotten dressed.

"Bhajan, I know you and Frank were always close, but he's threatening to put us all in danger and go to the police if Dad doesn't give him his passport."

"What? Still?"

"He was angry this morning when we told him to leave. He threatened to tell them about Dad, about his businesses, about our fake IDs—everything."

I mull it over in my head. "But why shouldn't he have his documents and just be able to do what he want—"

"Watch what you're saying."

I feel blood rushing to my cheeks and sit up. "I don't get what the big deal is. Dad should have talked to him. Frank obviously wanted to fix things. You can't just ignore people until they collapse in on themselves."

"There's no point reasoning with someone who is angry and violent like your brother."

"He punched a *wall*, Chiara. Get over it!" The thought that our father, and sometimes Chiara, can be far more violent passes through the periphery of my consciousness.

They make it seem like Frank is demanding something outrageous, but I've noticed normal people all get to carry their own ID cards. They aren't hidden away by their parents.

I stand and start to turn away, when an idea dawns.

"If Dad doesn't want to give him his passport, why not just buy Frank a new one with a different name from ours? Then he can be free and there's no connection."

Chiara hesitates. "It's not that simple."

"Of course it is." I wave a hand dismissively. We've burned identities and changed tracks so often it seems like the most natural of options.

"It's not a game. You remember Our Friend, the one from Brazil?"

I nod. The woman we met at the Frankfurt airport when I was nine. Our source of fresh documents.

"Do you know what she told Mom that day? About why the money we sent went missing?" Vaguely I recall that a contact of Our Friend had fallen through, and that she needed more money to bribe someone new. "Her contact at the embassy," Chiara continues, "the one who was her key to registering passports, to making our documents real . . . Anyway, he was a nice man, Mom and Dad met with him when we were in Brazil. This was before you were born . . ." She seems to waver.

"Tell me."

"Some people found out what he was doing, went over to his apartment in Rio, robbed him of all the cash he had hidden, our money as well—and beat him to death. Then they found Our Friend and beat her, too, as a warning. You wanted to know why she had a limp. That's why."

I am silent, a shiver traveling across my skin. I imagine those hard men, faces cruel and devoid of emotion, coming for us.

"*Every* time is a risk. It's no joke, Bhajan."

23: Virginia, age 13

DEAR FRANK,

Are you OK? Sorry I haven't written in so long . . .

What I didn't expect is how much I like, even need, to write these letters. They started because I hoped to keep Frank from spinning even further away from us. But it's become the only place either of us can be honest. Sitting on the back deck, I hold my pen tight, wanting to write the truth, even though I am forbidden. Wanting to warn him about what is already happening.

He is going to be expelled from school. He just doesn't know it yet.

One of the students told the head rabbi that Frank moved out of the dorm and is living with a woman and working at a nightclub, two actions that are against the rules. I'd like to have a few minutes alone with the guy who informed on my brother and is probably jealous of him having a life outside their walls.

The truth just feels too heavy and I stop writing, leaning my head against the railing, legs stretched out on the pale wood deck. Of course we haven't gotten any chairs for out here. I look up at a soft sound and see Tigger walking toward me determinedly, a little clumsy on his big paws. Spontaneously, I smile, because the moment I saw my kitten shivering in the rain without a home, I fell in love. After years of stuffed animals bought to compensate for not having a pet, Tigger's little gray-and-white body, so tiny and soft, is the best thing I have ever held. Lifting him to my chest, I feel him purr against me.

From inside the house, I hear raised voices and frown. For once, Mom seems to be talking back to Dad in daylight hours, not at midnight when darkness, tears, and the mistaken assumption that I can't hear seem to give her courage. When I open the door, she's holding the phone.

It's Frank. After months of silence, *finally*.

Dad is in his bathrobe, shaking his head and directing Mom, sotto voce, on what to say. From her flushed cheeks and teary eyes, I can guess she's deviating from the script.

"Can I talk to him?" My voice comes out too high.

Mom waves me away, trying to hide her tears.

"No," Dad says, loudly. "Let Frank talk to her. He's threatening the family; Bhajan's the one who will be the most affected, let him realize what he's destroying."

I can hear Frank's voice, shouting something; Mom is undecided, her body still shielding me from the phone. But I see my window of opportunity, step around her, and take it.

"—identity! I need some sort of paper—"

"It's me." I interrupt Frank mid-yell.

"Bhajan, don't let them involve you in this. Get off the phone."

I grip it tighter, my stubborn streak coming out to play. "No, I want to say hi."

He sighs mightily, but I can hear some of the rage in his breathing ebb. Dad motions Mom away, his voice low. "Let them talk, she always calms him down." Reluctantly, Mom follows my father to the living room.

"What's going on?" I ask Frank worriedly.

"They're sabotaging me, refusing to give me any kind of ID and not backing me up with the rabbi. I got kicked out of university here, all that studying gone to waste. I *had* to go work at the nightclub, Dad stopped sending money and they pay in cash under the table, I had no other . . ." He pauses. "No, never mind, it's got nothing to do with you."

"Yes it does! I'm sick of hearing that! No one ever tells me anything. I live here! I'm part of this family, and I want to . . ." I stop, unable to articulate the fire in my belly.

His voice is flat. "You want to fix things."

"Yes, exactly."

"Our family isn't fixable. It wasn't functioning in the first place."

The last vestiges of my positive attitude drain away. He, who knows me so well, senses it, many miles away.

"Look." I can picture him rubbing his brow, head bowed. "Maybe it will be fine. Maybe it will all go back to normal."

"Don't treat me like a child," I snap, surprising myself.

"Huh. Well, then, don't waste your life in a disaster zone." I stare at the floor, trying to sort my thoughts out.

"Listen, Bhajan, you'll be fine. Out of all of us, you were always the strong one."

"Me?" Growing up with so many warring personalities, the thought of me being the tough one is hard to wrap my mind around.

"Of course." He speaks as if it should be obvious. "Even with all the names, you're always you."

Fear touches my heart, an icy finger. "You won't leave, though?"

He takes a deep breath and says nothing at all.

24: Virginia, age 13

WE ARE DRIVING Dad's Corvette with the top down, my hand stretched out to ride the wind, tall trees casting fleeting shadows on my skin. I love these weekend escapes, no plan, just us, the open road, a whole day and sometimes most of the night. We discover little Virginia towns nestled along surging rivers, with old-fashioned general stores, soda fountains and local artists, historic battlefields and oceanside amusement parks. As before, as always, we are perfect companions. Laughing about our travels, flying high, our arms flung wide to grasp life.

This is my world: One day there is unspeakable tension in the house, my father's rages and beatings are escalating, and the next, we are a happy family. Or at least half of one.

Today, we've driven all the way out to the beach. Stepping out of the car, I steady myself and our feet crunch over crushed seashells as we inhale deep lungfuls of salty air. A beautiful wood-shingled restaurant overlooks the waves. Delicious smells greet us just inside the door, and we slide into one of the comfortable booths lining the windows.

"Ah! See this?" He is scanning the menu. "Root beer float. That used to be my favorite when I was your age." He smiles at a passing waitress. "A tea with cream for me and a root beer float." She nods and heads toward the kitchen.

"Isn't root beer a kind of soda?"

"Yes, and then they put ice cream in it."

I'm shocked. "But doesn't that have sugar in it?"

He winks. "I won't tell if you don't."

When the float arrives I still haven't adjusted. I regard the apparition with awe, bubbling midnight-black soda, vanilla bean ice cream floating on top, swirls of whipped cream and an artificially red cherry. I don't even know how to begin my approach.

"Try to get a little of everything on your spoon," he suggests.

The soda foams over, spilling down the frosty mug. Finally maneuvering it all into place, I close my lips around the full spoon.

It tastes like so much: summer, sweetness, chemicals, fifties music, everything manufactured and delicious—like doing whatever you want, and putting things together that you wouldn't think belong. It tastes, I realize, like America.

My first brush with sugar is not my only one with the outside world. At our synagogue, I've managed to befriend a girl named Sandra and am now getting a rare glimpse into the life of normal teenagers. The first big public school dance she invites me to is like most social events in my teenage life: horrible, terrifying, and magnificently fascinating. Clutching my woven straw purse with a seashell clasp, I follow Sandra, who is threading easily through the crowd toward the soda bar. They're out of root beer so I order Sprite, all natural-like.

Since that day by the ocean I've tried chocolate cake, saltwater taffy, caramel apples, clam chowder, and countless of my new favorite: hamburgers with extra mustard. It still feels bizarre to have this suddenly sanctioned, without any discussion. A jeans-clad group of boys jostle each other loudly out of the way, fighting over the last of the Coke. They've probably been around all along, but we have only recently begun to *consider* them. Although we've only been friends for a few months, Sandra and I are in agreement that, as a whole, boys are ridiculous and annoying, not on our level at all. Except, of course, for the ones who are indescribably beautiful.

In my own mind, I have skimmed over what started with Frank when I was nine, but the older I get, the harder it becomes to ignore. I wonder if other guys can sense something off about me. Something dirty and used. Whenever I see a boy I like, the paranoia worsens, the worry that Frank's touch has somehow branded me. I turn away from Sandra, as if she, too, may see, and focus my attention on the crowd.

So this is it: Life. A room, people bobbing to pop music, lights low, Chex Mix bowl running close to empty. Shouldn't having some street smarts put me ahead, help me to not feel so awkward? If a terrible crisis were to occur right now, I'd feel in my element, capable of handling the situation, whereas they would all panic. And yet here they stand, relaxed and unaware, heads tilted back with laughter. I suppose what it all boils down to, is this: I know how to survive, and they know how to live.

A FEW WEEKS after my first normal teenage party, I'm reminded how far away I am from normal. It's a rainy Sunday, and when both Mom and Chiara are out, Dad tells me to follow him into the den. He opens his closet, lifts a board at the bottom, and shows me the nondescript black backpack hidden there. Only I am to know about the $10,000 in cash, $5,000 in gold Krugerrand coins, and all our passports and birth certificates except Frank's. He must have hidden that one somewhere else, where even I won't be able to find it. Also in the bag is a water bottle, flashlight, and a burner cell phone. I'm being put in charge of our family's escape plan when I'm barely thirteen.

If everything goes to hell, I'm supposed to take the bag and run: run through the woods I know so well, watching the roads for cops and unmarked cars, and get as far as I can before taking a cab into the city center and breaking the trail. The rest is the same protocol we've had in every city I can remember; a prearranged meeting place in a busy area. Here, it's a corner near Dupont Circle. Noon and 6 p.m. every day.

If we don't find each other, we'll run an ad in the classifieds of the *International Herald Tribune* under the heading *Lost Ring Engraved Platinum* with the new contact or meeting place below.

"I know I can trust you." His beard tickles as he plants a soft kiss on my forehead.

"Always," I say.

GIVING TIGGER A final cuddle, I close the door on the darkening front lawn and glimpse Chiara upstairs, chatting on her cell phone. She paces, just outside her room, probably sweet-talking someone at the Jewish women's organization where she is rising fast. Not such a loser after all. The girl is going to get job offers soon, probably in public relations or event coordination. I try to convince myself to be happy for her, but can't. What if I am falling behind? There is only so much approval to go around in this family, only so much love. And what have I done lately?

"I totally understand where you're coming from." Chiara's voice travels down the stairs. "It must be a complicated situation, but you're handling it so well now."

I roll my eyes, but even as hunger moves me toward the kitchen, I'm still listening.

"Mmhmm. I felt I just had to call last week and tell you about how violent he can be. For your daughter's safety."

Partway through the kitchen door, I freeze as she continues to describe our brother punching through walls and threatening our mother for money.

We never, ever, talk about such things. With anyone, let alone outsiders. What is happening?

And then suddenly, I get it. Don't know how—intuition, or experience—but Chiara is talking to the mother of Frank's girlfriend. Taking away the roof over his head. The last safe haven he has in New York.

I make a hard left through the kitchen, past the windows with their beautiful view of the forest, to the living room, where Dad is drinking tea and reading Balzac. As I approach him, my pace slows, and I almost reconsider.

Instead of a question, I go for a statement of fact, something I learned from him. "Chiara's upstairs on the phone with the mom of Frank's girlfriend."

"Who told you that?" He watches me calmly with his intelligent eyes.

"No one." I push my hair out of my face nervously. "I figured it out."

"How?"

"I dunno. Elimination?"

He laughs with genuine pleasure. "This is why I miss doing school together. Teach you one concept in math and you can apply it to life."

Somehow, this conversation already seems to be getting away from me.

"Why is Chiara doing this?" My voice is desperate. But I think I am understanding one thing about my sister—finally. It's almost as if she can't help herself. In a life where we've never had a say in what happens, she needs to control *something*. And the people closest to her, the only people actually, are us. Like the day—a decade ago—when we played cards in Srinagar: an empty pool, the soldiers, and the three of us. When I took my eyes off the game for a moment, she stacked the deck against me. She may even have loved me, but she still fixed it so I would lose.

Dad stands, and I swallow hard, trying to hold back emotion. Feelings only annoy him—they get in the way of logic. "Bhajan, pull yourself together, all right? You've had a very charmed life so far. A very protected life."

I'm about to object, but think better of it.

"But that's not reality." He reaches out and raises my chin firmly with his thumb and forefinger. I've always disliked this gesture, the feeling of being repositioned. "Life is not shopping malls and root beer floats. It's dangerous—one wrong step and your chance is gone. You disgrace yourself, choose the wrong man, lose control, and it's over. Second chances are an invention of people who have failed. Do you understand?"

I've heard this before, I know I have to plan all my steps carefully, but this time I want to shout. You're the one who takes me to the mall, says to buy three outfits instead of one! You're the one who tries to make me feel life is limitless! Instead, I free my chin. "I don't see why we can't all sit down and talk about it. He's your son, your flesh and blood." I read that in a book and it sounds persuasive.

"That doesn't mean anything." He shrugs.

"He's your son! He's my brother!" Blood is rushing to my face. "I don't . . . I'm looking at this clearly! I am!" My voice rises and breaks. "It doesn't seem right . . ."

He moves forward, blocking the lamp, framed by light, and I stop.

"Let's talk about right and wrong," he says. "Right is being loyal to your family and protecting them, no matter the stakes. Do you think it has been easy keeping all of you safe, all around the world for twenty years?"

"But—" I say.

"But what?" The question is a challenge. I'm silent but I don't budge. When he speaks, his voice is calm, so factual that I know it's going to be the truth. "You want to know what will happen if we're found."

Suddenly, I'm not so sure I do.

"You will be taken away from us and one of two things will occur. You're a minor, so you'll be put in foster care with strangers who are in it to get money from the state. You will get raped there, someone like you. It will happen. Or they'll send you to live with your mother's crazy father who has been trying to destroy us for the last twenty years. And you can see what he has in store for you. Is that what you want?"

The sobs choke my throat, rushing up from a place of pure panic and making it hard to breathe.

"Hey!" His voice softens slightly. "Stop that and look at me."

I wipe at my cheeks, hot tears streaking my face.

"You cannot have it both ways, Bhajan. If you want to have a say, you can't resort to acting like a hysterical child. Understand?"

Trying to hold it in, I nod.

"You have to be strong in life. This will work out, and I will keep you safe, but you have to learn."

Safe. I manage to get myself under control. Our family, safe.

"All right. Go up to your room now."

Wanting more reassurance, I waver, and he shakes his head.

"I'm going to come up there soon and if you're crying," he says, matter-of-fact, "I'm going to hit you."

Unsteadily I turn and head for the stairs.

Chiara is still talking on the phone as I start to climb, but I realize it's a different conversation. She's speaking to my brother now. My feet soundless on the carpet, I pause just out of sight.

". . . I know, it must be difficult in New York. Frank listen, I don't know where this all came from, but I'm on your side."

My hand grips the bannister.

"No really, I want to help. . . yeah, of course I'm serious, I already talked to Dad and he agreed. Just come home and we'll give you your documents. . . . Yes we're exhausted, too! I get it."

Even though my mind is racing, I can't understand what she's doing. She's ahead of me again, playing a game I don't even know exists. Why tell Frank he can have his documents? Does she also want our brother to come home so we can all talk? Will they actually compromise? I rub my forehead.

"Look, just promise us you won't go to the cops, and we'll give you the passport and everything. It's better this way. Bhajan will stay safe, and you can go live your life however you want—"

Without hesitation, I step into view. I have no idea what's going on, but I don't like her involving me.

Chiara watches me climbing toward her.

"I've got to go now Frank, let's talk soon." She hangs up.

We stare at each, our eyes level.

In my room, sitting on my white lace bedspread, I have such an urge to cry. To let my rigid shoulders shake and the pent-up tears flow. *Swallow it down, swallow it down.* The minutes stretch past.

My door bursts open without warning. He never knocks, no matter how often Mom tells him I'm too old for this. Dry-eyed and composed, I look up. I have not cried; I will ask no questions. "Good girl." Dad nods and leaves.

25: Virginia, age 13

IN THE DARKNESS, the leaves are just shapes, drifting in the chill wind, when suddenly they are illuminated, gold, red, and deep purple in our headlights. "Are you going to make one of those collages?" I ask, turning the heater up in our Lincoln as Mom drives me away from ballet practice. She can look at a pile of leaves and turn it into art, pressing the colors into permanence between the pages of a thick book and then surrounding them with watercolors on paper.

Mom watches them float, telling the story of winter to come, and nods. "If you help me collect them."

"It's a deal."

"So do you like the new class?" she asks. This easy ballet school, with nonprofessional dancers, is part of her decade-long Socialize Bhajan plan.

"Yes," I say, deadpan. "I feel myself becoming more socially integrated with every sashay."

"Oh, Bhajan! It isn't for communication skills, you get along easily—"

"—now!" I interrupt, laughing.

She waves a hand. "Bof, that was when you were little and only used to spending time with adults."

"Remember when I would make you take me over to other kids on the playground and introduce me formally? As if we were at a UN conference."

She tilts her head tenderly as if she can see a little-me in the darkness outside the windshield, hair rumpled, peeking out from behind her with infinite caution. We drive in silence, headlights flashing past, until her cell phone rings. I can tell it's my father from the way she picks up.

"But we already have things for breakfast," she replies.

On the other end of the line, he raises his voice impatiently.

"Okay, sure. We'll stop and get it." She hands the phone to me to end the call and switches lanes. "We have to go back to Whole Foods and get the cereal he likes."

Thirty minutes later, loaded down with the ten-grain cereal and a bag of things we don't need, we drive homeward again, as I munch through an entire packet of rosemary breadsticks. The roads become quieter as we drive farther from town until we are the only lights on the narrow road. I lean back in the warm cocoon, closing my eyes, rocked by the familiar turns and curves of our forest. The sharp incline of our driveway jostles me out of a pleasant doze and I blink awake.

The automatic-timed outdoor lights aren't on, and every window is black. We feel our way up the path to the front door, my gym bag on my shoulder, Mom lopsided with the eco-friendly grocery bag. "If Chiara flicked the outside lights off just because she's home, when we're still on our way, I'm going to yell at her." My toe hits the front stoop.

"Honey, the power is just out."

Fumbling the key into the lock, I step inside, letting my gym bag fall to the floor. The foyer lights flare on suddenly and I squint, disoriented.

Chiara stands inside the open door to the kitchen, her hand on the switch, staring at me. What's she doing in there? She's not allowed in that part of the house. "Bhajan, go straight upstairs."

Now I'm aware, now I'm awake. Chiara doesn't talk to me like that. She's not supposed to. Behind her in the dim kitchen I see Dad.

Chiara's face is white, her expression strained, as she steps into the foyer. Dad's whole expression is set in hard lines as he comes forward. All their movements are off, jerky.

I falter. Have we been found? Should I run for the escape bag?

"Go to your room." Dad walks toward me, measured and controlled. I look between them and don't move an inch. He grabs my arm, his grip like steel, and throws me onto the stairs. My feet scramble, searching for solid ground as I fall hard against the steps, and then the instinct to flee takes over. Somehow I'm in my room, the door closed, chest heaving. I put my hand against my bicep, still feeling the heat and power of his hand. From downstairs, I can hear hushed voices and don't dare to turn on a light. I have no idea what is happening . . .

Then I hear a wail so primal and raw that when I recognize it's my mother's voice, my heart stops. I'm at the top of the stairs in an instant. Mom is lying on the wooden floor, gasping, but now she is making no sound at all. Dad crouches, trying to calm her.

I blink. They are in a pool of light below, watching me. Chiara exchanges a look with Dad, and starts to climb the stairs. Her small, deep-set eyes are fixed on me, coming up into the shadow. For a moment, we are back in India, children again. I'm sitting on the window ledge, watching colorful turbans below, and Chiara is baiting Frank, teasing him forward . . . making him forget caution, forget to watch her. In the second he rushed forward, arm swinging, she dodged cleverly, and it's him that got hurt. I will not make the same mistake.

I turn and run. My numb hands struggle to wedge the bedroom door shut, before my knees give out.

". . . Bhajan . . . Bhajan, wake up."

I swim upwards, my limbs like lead weights. Dad is looking down at me with concern. "It's two p.m."

I sit up and see myself in the vanity mirror. Someone has dressed me in pajamas and combed my hair . . . It was me, I realize. The memory is more of a dream, scrubbing myself in the shower before dawn, skin turning pink.

"Chiara already called and canceled your workout for today. She checked and you were sleeping so deeply."

"Where's Mom?"

"Resting in bed." He pauses at my door. "I'll start breakfast for you."

In my mother's room, I stare hard at her under the covers. The rise and fall of her chest is a thing of beauty. Gathering my clothes, I go downstairs, put them in the washer, pour in extra soap, and sit at the kitchen counter. My hands folded, I watch as Dad ladles ten-grain cereal into my bowl.

WE NEVER TALK about that night, or my brother, again, and I know better than to ask. Some secrets are unspeakable. The gymnastics meet, back in February, when I was twelve, is the last time I will ever see Frank.

I DO NOT belong to the world.

I stand in the gym, like every day, but my body is heavy and exhausted. All I feel is numb. I'm staring at the empty runway in front of me, preparing to sprint and hurl myself into the air, when I realize I can't anymore. I just can't. The decisions that change your life seem to come from a place you didn't know existed, where instinct rather than logic rules. I'm not meant for this. I don't know what I'm meant for—but in a desperate instant I don't care, and an instant is all it takes.

Instead of launching into a run, I start to walk. The coach's confused voice echoing behind me. Each step I take, I care less. Olympics, no Olympics. It just seems so far away. Chiara looks up in surprise from her book in the observation area, as I stand before her, hating her. "Call Dad to pick us up."

"Did you hurt yourself?" She scans my muscled body worriedly.

"No." I turn, heading for my locker. "I'm quitting."

MOM IS SOBBING when we get home. I can hear it all the way from downstairs, even though she's shut up in her room. The sound grates on my nerves. Why can't anyone here keep themselves under control? I swear it's like living with a passel of dysfunctional children. Am I the only one who can remain appropriately detached? I sit at the unused dining table, rest my face against the cool wood, and close my eyes for a long time. *Please* stop crying, *please, please stop.*

When I finally climb the stairs, I see Chiara at her desk crushing pills on a white dinner plate. I'm hesitating outside, when Mom opens the door to her room. She looks terrible. Her eyes swollen like a boxer's, self-inflicted scratches are ribbons of red all over her porcelain skin. Chiara freezes guilt-ily, the spoon in her hand clicking against the plate, and we both look at her. "I won't take them, I told you!" My mother sounds like a cornered animal. Only now do I notice Mom's favorite teacup, full of steaming liquid, next to the plate Chiara is working on. Chiara doesn't move. Our mother stares at her for a moment, almost as if trying to recognize her own child. Then, slowly, she heads back to bed, closing her door softly, like an old woman.

WHEN MOM LEAVES, I'm across the hall in three paces. Viciously, I dash the hot tea over the mound of powdered pills. "Bhajan!" Chiara gasps, some liquid scalding her hand.

My disgust is so strong that it is almost pleasure. I can feel blood pounding in my head as I pick up the pill bottle and inspect it.

"Bhajan, these are to calm her down and let her sleep. I'm trying to *help*."

"Don't ever try to drug my mother again." I shove Chiara aside, taking the bottle of pills.

In the bathroom, the little white tablets spill into the toilet bowl and I flush them with satisfaction. Deliberately, I brush my teeth and comb my hair.

On the pillow my head seems to swim, a kind of weak, floating haze. . . .

I WAKE ABLAZE with energy, the moon still a sliver of ice in the sky. My numbness has vanished, and instead, a pulsing feeling of power and strength seems to pull me to my feet. It's like the feeling I get in dangerous situations when adrenaline kicks in, but this is bigger; I am on fire. I could lift the house. Every nerve, every sinew, is screaming *fight, fight, fight*. I want to surge out of my room and make this right.

On my feet, I clench my fists, something in me is building, hot and ugly. They are right out there—the people who have torn my mom apart. Right out there. I open my door and am nearing the stairs when my legs waver. I stop. What should I do? What should I say? What will happen to my already destroyed mother? What if the cops find out about our family? She may have to go back to the parents who have tried to hurt us for as long as

I can remember. I'll probably get raped in foster care. I want to sob, attack, flee. But they are my family . . . they are all I have.

Despair floods through me, and my legs give out. Sinking down against the wall under the repaired fist-hole, I look at the door to the room of the sister I despise. And just steps away, the door to the mother I must protect. Below is the father I adore and fear. And outside is a world I don't really know or understand. What normal people do, and what they might do to me, is beyond my range of experience. I only know how to wow them or con them.

My head feels so heavy that it lolls back, hitting the wall behind me. I can't move, shivering in my T-shirt, the carpet rough under my bare thighs. There is nowhere to go. Nowhere to run. No one to fight. There is only surviving. I want to run away and I need them to hug me close.

Help, I pray, staring at the blank white ceiling, *help me.* But of course nothing happens. I realize I didn't even expect it to. In a cold hall, carpet flattened by all our feet, I sense this will be my final prayer.

26: Virginia, age 14

Twelve months since I've done any school. Funny, how one day you do something for the very last time, see someone for the last moment, without having any idea it's the end. Like the love in my family, my schooling was sporadic at first and then gone altogether. I'm left stranded with just an eighth-grade education. But I've got more important things to do anyway.

I never considered a career as a psychologist or counselor, yet for the last year it has been my job to take care of my mother. No one tries to stop me, except maybe her, begging me to go back to sleep when I come downstairs, sometimes holding her while she sobs, my father looking on, his face empty of sympathy. We never talk about anything, not a word, he simply says that she has lost her mind. And maybe she has, maybe they all have—somehow convincing themselves I'm too young to comprehend what's happened. Of course, I play along, because I've learned my lesson. Be the one to yell, cry, express what you feel, and you'll be branded as crazy. I'm above all that now. No matter how many times my mother begs me to leave her alone, to not get involved, I ignore it. Because: she needs me.

I sense it every time I go to her, sometimes rushing in, sometimes hesitating, steeling myself. Never knowing how bad it will be, fearing the worst. The horrible sound of her voice screaming in the night, his always icily calm, in total control. That beautiful face unrecognizable from crying, the scratches on her arms and chest where her nails have scraped the flesh away. Almost every night she slams her emotions against an iceberg, destroying herself, taking herself down, *I can't survive it, I can't . . .*

Don't blame me because you're weak.

You play everyone, you play us off each other . . .

Until she falls like a broken doll to the floor, and looks up to see it all reflected in my frightened eyes.

On those endless nights, she shrieks BHAJAN, GO AWAY!, saying it has nothing to do with me. As if that isn't the most ridiculous statement ever made. My family has everything to do with me. So I sit resolute on the bottom stair, as if my presence will stop anything worse from happening, clutching the wooden balustrade, watching as my family tears itself apart.

Much later, lying next to my mother on her big bed with her shaky hand held tight in my steady forger's one, I watch the rise and fall of her chest, timing my breathing to hers, hoping our being in sync will keep her going. My breaths filling her lungs with air. Interlacing our fingers, I whisper my new mantra, *It's going to be okay Mom. I promise, it's going to be okay.*

That's probably what a mantra is anyway. A lie.

I sit on the couch in Sandra's basement, observing my peers, at her birthday party. Will it always be like this for me? I have the sensation that I am watching all this unfold from a distance, both pointedly interested and yet somehow detached. I arrange a smile on my face; I can still do it quite easily. Because now I have more little boxes in my head. The worst of which I never acknowledge. Little boxes made of iron.

I'm trying to lose the feeling of being immeasurably old when the tall boy sits next to me and says he's running for president. "Of course I'm serious! The main platform of my campaign is that I'll build a water slide and wave pool at our high school."

"Can you do that?" My puzzled voice is drowned out by the combined power of 'NSync on the basement stereo and a dozen teenagers trying to be understood.

"Pardon?" He leans forward to hear better, and my question flies out of my head. I'm aware of his closeness, his face touching-distance from mine. I haven't been able to worry properly since he sat down next to me, and that worries me. I'm preoccupied with his skin, tanned from the summer, the way he moves, and a particular curl of dark blond hair brushing his forehead. So this is who goes to public school.

I wrestle myself back on track. "Can you really build the slide and wave pool?" It seems ambitious, even to me.

He shrugs good-naturedly. "Well, running with the slogan 'Will improve cafeteria food' just seemed too *normal*."

"What are you guys talking about? Why are you laughing?" Liz, a friend of Sandra, is standing above us, arms akimbo. Lately she's been saying I stole Sandra's friendship away from her with my adventurous outings and fancy house. Now I realize I'm moving in on territory I'm usually excluded from: their dating pool.

"Is laughing illegal?" he retorts with easy confidence.

"We were talking about Tyler's campaign," I add, feeling the need to explain.

"Oh, I see. So you're still calling yourself Tyler." Liz turns to me. "His real name is John, and one day he just decided he didn't like it."

"Why can't I change my name?" He grins provocatively.

Liz throws her hands up, bracelets jingling. "Because you can't! It's probably illegal."

I look down and almost smile.

"It's not funny, Crystal!"

"Oh, Liz, leave her alone." His voice has gotten deeper, and I hope I'm not blushing.

A shadow of hurt passes over her face. "Fine, you two stick together Tyler. But one day you're going to go to jail."

"Well, Liz," I say sweetly, raising my face. "You haven't lived, until you've been indicted."

We sit together, behind the pool table, on the sagging couch from the eighties, unaware of the rest. Our bare knees are almost touching while everyone else dances, and I'm moving my hands as I speak, drawing dreams in the air as I used to.

All the cake has been eaten, only the broken pretzels are left, but we are still where we started, alone on the couch. Tyler stops speaking, serious for a moment, then leans forward slowly to kiss me. I flinch, pulling back abruptly.

He tries to hide the hurt on his face and a hopelessness spreads through me. Why, when I want so much to go forward, do I shy backward, and get all tangled up in myself? This gap, between my life and theirs, seems too wide to bridge. An impossible chasm filled with terrible secrets—all the things that make me strange, different. Yet I also feel something else—guilt. I do not hear the music or the chatter of teenagers, but instead, my father's voice. *Give in to a man and you will be worthless, no one else will ever want you.* It must have started so young that by now it's a simple fact in my mind: to let go would be to surrender my worth.

But worse than any of that, and what really stops me, is so simple. Going forward would mean losing my father's approval. And what he thinks is still far more important than anything I feel.

THE FORM-FITTING EVENING dress just skims my shoulders, leaving my arms and collarbone bare, before plunging in a column of dark silk to the floor. I carefully layer mascara over my lashes, black not blue, bought not stolen. Learned my lesson on that one.

"Yoo hoo . . ." His voice travels up the stairs.

Nervously, I wrestle with the unfamiliar tube of rosy lipstick and dab it on.

"I'm downstairs and dateless!"

I cautiously descend the stairs in my heels, focusing on balance. Turning in his custom-made tuxedo, he throws out a hand, then stops. His beard is shorter now, so it's easy to see his grin vanish. When I step down in the silver shoes I'm as tall as him.

"What?" I fidget with my purse.

"I'm speechless." Dad is almost frowning. Then his face clears and he steps forward, taking my shoulders in his warm hands. "That hasn't happened since 1974."

The sound of my laughter brings Mom out of the kitchen, walking with this new wariness, as if planning her steps.

"Can you believe it?" He keeps his eyes on me. "Look at the beautiful daughter I created."

Expertly, she takes the dig in stride and stares up at me, almost a head taller now. The way we regard each other is peculiarly similar: motherly concern. "You're wearing makeup," she says nervously.

"Dad and I got it at the mall."

"Oh." She can put so much worry into that one sound.

I feel impatience building inside me. Here's the thing about being a mother, you can't take a hiatus, can't let me be the parent and then switch back. I feel strangled. Loving her, worrying every moment, drains me in ways that anger never does. It's been more than a year of my hardly leaving the house, watching over her. I can't soothe her about me wearing makeup, too. I need to get out of here, even just for the evening—anywhere.

The gala is at one of those hotels I know so well from our travels. Uniformed doormen, everything polished to a perfect shine, flowers spilling out of giant vases in a creamy marble lobby. I know I'm out of my depth as soon as Dad hands the keys of our Lincoln to an attendant. The men and women climbing the red-carpeted stairs, in tuxedos and flowing gowns, are all about thirty years older than me. This is not their first time wearing high heels or mascara.

Just as I'm hesitating, Dad places my hand gently on his arm. He gives me a conspiratorial look, and we climb the stairs and walk through the doors to find out what a hefty donation to a presidential campaign buys in the way of parties. There is money in this ballroom; in the expensive tailored clothes and the sculpted faces of the women. I sip soda water with lemon and admire the way Dad has simply walked up to the most interesting-looking group and captivated them. I can't remember what each of them does except that everything sounds important—broadcasting, speech writing, campaign managing. I consider my own title. Failed gymnast? No, retired gymnast sounds much better.

"And who is your date?" A beautiful blonde in her forties with the look of a former cheerleader tilts her head at Dad. He's sipping red wine. I've never seen him drink before; things are moving fast.

"This"—he looks at me seriously—"is my favorite person." As the faces smile at me, I recognize some of them from TV. "My daughter." He positions his arm around my shoulders, and I start to feel like I matter enough to be here.

Looking harried, Chiara comes over from where she and the other interns have been helping the organizers. Dad's donation is paying off as expected for Chiara, providing work experience for this piece of work. I give her a distant nod before walking away, keeping myself under control. I'm no longer scrawling hate messages and taping them to her bedroom door, but I still find it hard to speak with her. She blamed the notes and slammed doors on my hormones—they all did, in keeping with the family tradition of ignoring unpleasantness and marching obstinately forward.

I cut across the dance floor, trying to slip away. But as I wander close to the stage, I nearly run into Chiara again. She's hovering at the edge with three colleagues: two women and a small, intense man, who stands very close to her. Niall. Something about the man puts me on guard. It's a combination of his eyes, constantly shifting, and the almost proprietary way he looks at Chiara.

"So she tells us you're her little sister," Niall says, scanning me up and down. "But you two look nothing alike."

There it is: a brief lowering of Chiara's eyes, the tiniest wince.

I smile down at each of them. "We're not alike. We are very different."

"Isn't that the way it is so often with sisters? Even ones who don't have such a big age gap . . ." One of the women carries on, but I see my words have hit their intended target. Chiara hunches her shoulders, fidgeting with her ill-fitting black dress. For a moment I feel guilty . . . and then I remember. I remember she deserves it.

It's a new ability of mine, to inflict pain and almost relish it. From the outside no one would guess, but it's here, pointed and angry, ready to slice at someone's weakest point if they threaten me. It makes me feel safer, no longer a kid playing an adult game but a cold, disillusioned adult, cleverly disguised as a teenager. The perfect cover.

When I go find Dad in the crowd, he is still talking to the former cheerleader and has moved far too close. His beard nearly touches her face as he talks. She seems to be somewhere between enjoying herself and wondering if it's too much; alternately leaning in with a giggle and then pulling back. The other people are still here, but all I see are vague outlines. I approach them awkwardly, as if I'm intruding.

"Crystal!" Dad touches my cheek softly. The woman—previously so friendly, moves to one side, stirring her martini with exaggerated concentration. But Dad, at least, seems genuinely happy to see me. Maybe I was misinterpreting things? But the hand that takes my empty glass for a refill is not wearing his wedding ring.

I've always loved my parents matching rings. Pure gold, pebbled with tiny nuggets, and a story worth remembering. He was just getting into the gold bullion business and took Mom for an adventure, prospecting at a wild mountain stream. In a moment when she wasn't looking, he sprinkled the creek with gold nuggets, sparkling as they fell, for her to find. She figured it out pretty fast, staring at a sieve full of gold, and playfully tried to push him in the water; but those nuggets became part of their wedding rings.

Now, Dad goes to refill our drinks and I'm left making conversation. A sudden tiredness comes out of nowhere; I need to be alone, to breathe. In the bright lights and cool air of the lobby, I find a corner of empty couches and sink down, staring at the silk stretched across my knees. Is this what life is? You have three kids with a man, never say a word against him—even now, Mom refuses to criticize him in front of me—and he cozies up to some blonde with none of the class you were born with. Men are idiots. No, people are idiots. Selfish brats dressed in diamonds and silk, doing whatever the hell they feel like. Obviously nothing can stop them. But why do I have to witness it? Why do I have to be the keeper of their secrets?

The back of my head feels heavy and I close my eyes tight against the fragments, jagged photos that still splay themselves out in front of me, overpowering my defenses. It's not just the woman, she is only someone at a party, it's . . . The memory comes back, sharp and clear. Almost a year ago, when I was still numb.

DAD AND ME, walking after dinner at a cozy restaurant, hidden away in a postcard town of the Occoquan Valley. I've hardly left the house for a month, since it happened. I am too busy caring for Mom. Even now—when my father is probably rewarding me for my work with a dinner like we used to have—I'm worrying about her, alone in the house with Chiara. It feels wrong that the world has carried on so normally. Lights are strung like stars along the streets and a cold wind sneaks into my thick coat making the hair on my arms stand up. I am suspended in darkness, at the center of a bridge, watching the river roil and froth far below, when I notice Dad is no longer by my side.

Where . . . ?

I stop myself from turning around abruptly; everything I do lately is with caution, watching from the corner of my eye. . . . He glances over his shoulder at me. The black water churns below him.

"HONEY." DAD IS standing tall above me, his face concerned. I almost flinch, but compose myself. If Mom can pass for normal now, we all can. He sits beside me, making the cushions on my end rise. I almost say, *It's okay*, he doesn't have to explain what happened tonight. The woman. None of us have been ourselves lately. "Bhajan, are you all right?"

I become conscious of the fact that my arms are crossed tight in front of my cramping stomach. "I feel sick."

He stands in one swift motion. "Let's go home darling."

"Don't you have to say goodbye?"

"No. They don't matter."

MUCH LATER, WHEN Mom comes into my room, I sit up gingerly in the dark. My lipstick is all worn away, my dress a puddle on the floor. Her face is in shadow when she takes me in her arms. It's strange that the only person I can cry with is the one I often feel is trying to drag me down with her out-of-control emotions. I can't stand feelings. They are messy and frightening, trying to cling to me like slime. I brush that shit off.

But here, in secret, it feels so, so good to cry. Huge gulping sobs, my head buried in her shoulder. For a moment, I can still be a desperate child, as she lies and tells me it's going to be all right.

27: Virginia, age 15

I'VE NOTICED PEOPLE often complain about the monotony of life. How sometimes every day is just like the last and they all blend together. Do they know how *lucky* they are? But maybe that's the problem with a smooth, pleasant routine, you begin taking it for granted.

Every Sunday morning, I hop into the Corvette with Dad and we drive to our favorite Silver Diner. Walking through the parking lot now, I'm inhaling the sweet familiar scent of pancakes, looking forward to my usual breakfast, when his phone rings. It's Mom. Her voice so urgent and high-pitched, I can make out the words even as Dad paces. Chiara has stolen away with a suitcase, leaving a note for each of us. Dad's face hardens. After all those years of Chiara docilely saying "yes Papa," he is shocked. Covering the phone, he turns to me, "Do you have any idea where she could have gone?"

I try to think fast. "It has to be that guy—Niall, the other intern who was hovering around her at the political party." I remember his shifty eyes. It must be a double slap in Dad's face. Not only has Chiara has bolted, but she's taken with her the contacts she was gathering in politics, the contacts she was supposed to share. All the potential investors he could tap for his next big idea.

"Holy cow . . . That guy? She must have been pretty desperate."

I shrug, and he fixes me with a look. "You're taking this pretty well."

I lift my shoulders again as if to say, *Well, what are you gonna do?* I'm used to moving, used to people dropping away.

I can imagine what her letter to me will say, if they let me read it. Nice words about missing me and hoping we can see each other again one day. Maybe an email address. I'm sick of words that mean nothing, the things people say just to make themselves feel better. I'm sitting on the curb, arms folded across my stomach, the day oddly warm and pleasant, when I realize half of my family is gone.

We go inside, sit in our regular booth, and order the usual. French toast for me, Cajun steak for him. I stare quietly out the window until our breakfast arrives. Dad ignores his plate and leans forward. "So, we're not going to be able to go back to the house."

I drag a piece of my toast through a golden ocean of syrup making a little wave. "Not till later?"

"No, honey, never."

My fork clatters down, "Why?"

The people at the next booth look over. "Shh, you're talking loudly. In one of the letters, your sister wrote—" I note how now she is only related to me, nothing to do with him—"she said she's going to get in touch with her grandparents."

My stomach drops. "The crazy guy who chases us?" When I imagine my grandfather, he is always larger than life, more monster than man. In my mind's eye I'm always running, small but fast, as his arms, his legions of secret police, reach for me in the dark.

Dad leans across the table. "Yes. Chiara is going to give them everything, do you understand? Our names, our address, the synagogue, the names of people we know."

I thought we would just carry on as normal, minus Chiara. The syrup, the powdered sugar, are suddenly cloying in my throat.

"Bhajan," he says, asking me to keep myself together with just a look.

"Hey, sweethearts, how's the food this morning?" It's our favorite waitress, the one with the tattoos and fascinating love life.

I smile brightly.

"Everything's fan-tas-tic." Dad commends her new hairdo, which is in fact very nice; it defies gravity, and you can't say that about a lot of things. We wait until she is definitely out of earshot. "All right." He rubs his beard. "We can't use these passports again. No more contact with people we know here, makes it too easy to find us. Your mom will pack up everything; we'll stay at a hotel and then move on."

I think of the huge house, full of all our possessions, scattered on tables, disorganized in closets. "But that will take her so long."

"No, she thinks she can clear it out, wipe prints, and take the important things in three days. She's very good in a crisis. Why do you look so surprised?"

"You complimented her." That hasn't happened in ages.

"She's good at a lot of things, an intelligent woman. But then she decided to have a nervous breakdown."

"Well, I don't think she *decided* . . ."

"Of course it's a choice. You watched your mother go nuts and you're still fine."

I knew my calmness would come back to bite me.

"I suppose she's not entirely to blame. She was emotionally damaged when I met her."

"How so?" I ask cautiously, the way I always approach the past, my curiosity tempered by fear.

"Well, her father was abusive, hitting her, telling her she would never be able to succeed in life. Who knows? With someone like that, he may have even touched her sexually."

I am struck mute.

"After something like that, it's all over for a person."

"Why?" My voice is more like a breath, not really wanting the answer.

"She's damaged goods. That sort of experience weakens you."

Damaged goods. It runs through my mind on repeat. *Am I . . . ?*

"Then why did you marry her? If she's so messed up?"

He raises his eyebrows at my tone. "At that time the positives outweighed the negatives. We were in love. She has amazing genetics, just look at you—"

I grit my teeth, but then something vital occurs to me. "Wait! If it's dangerous for us to go back to the house, she can't stay there packing."

"She'll be fine. It has to be done, and she's very efficient."

"Shouldn't we go and help?"

"*No.*" He's firm, batting the suggestion away before I can get any ideas. "She doesn't want you at risk, and she'll be fine."

That statement doesn't make sense, but it's probably better not to press it.

"What about Sandra, my friends—" I stop again, the answer obvious.

"Your sister has destroyed everything we've built here. You can't see any of them again, Bhajan." He holds my hand briefly across the table.

What was the point, then, of any of it?

He squeezes my hand a last time. "We have to make a clean break. You understand."

And, logically, I do. But inside I'm screaming and kicking the walls. Another clean break, another part of me erased.

28: North Carolina, age 15

THESE PARKING LOTS all look the same. A little patch of wilting grass framed on two sides by the L-shaped motel. The always present, mostly-broken snack and soda machines. The air of standardized defeat. We're somewhere in North Carolina, I think, bounced down here to see a gold dealer about selling our Krugerrand coins.

The Corvette is already gone, sold to a ferret of a man with a knowing smirk for thirty percent of its value. You pay for the lack of questions. You pay for cash. Our Lincoln followed a few weeks later.

The only shade here is in the shadow of the motel sign, blaring false promises in neon. That guy in room 17 is playing the Grateful Dead again with the door thrown wide. Why do people living in these places so often leave their doors open? It's as if they're hoping someone wandering by will see them drinking beer in an undershirt, watching the Daytona 500, and think, *That looks fun, I think I'll join.*

I follow the outside walkway, one floor above the parking lot, passing numbered identical doorways, till the path dead-ends into a small section invisible from the hallway, almost like a private balcony. Given its proximity to the coin-fed washer/dryer room, it always smells of fresh laundry and Summer Breeze fabric softener.

I sit on the concrete and lean back against the rough wall, staring through the bars of the railing. Our former life in Virginia has been packed by Mom into cardboard boxes that now huddle like short, square refugees in a storage compartment. I can still hear the metal door rolling downward, picking up speed and hitting the floor with a final shudder.

The story is that we moved to Colorado for my father's work, as though the gold market is somehow richer there, closer to the mountain streams where prospectors panned for nuggets. It's not great, but we needed a story.

Mom called the synagogue, some of my friends' mothers, and apologized for the abrupt move. She ventured that I should, perhaps, call Sandra, my best friend, personally. I pulled myself together and handled it maturely by ignoring it completely—right up to the point where so much time had passed that it would have been more awkward to call than not. In the end, I solved the problem with an email: an upbeat, chirpy missive so dishonest that it makes me cringe every time it crosses my mind.

From my balcony, I can hear raised voices in the motel parking lot. Those teenagers are back. I think of them as, *those teenagers*, as if I'm a forty-year-old economics professor with a briefcase full of papers to grade, rather than one of them, with jack-all to do the whole day. I observe the trio of girls with a couple inches of bare flesh between their tight tank tops and low-rise Mudd jeans, and the two boys who are along to see if they can widen that gap. There must be a school near here—though I would never know—because they come by regularly to shove each other with barely suppressed sexual tension and sneak an occasional cigarette on the curb. I am offended not by their loudness, their obvious wasting of time, but by the fact that they don't seem to want me to participate in it.

Whatever. I'm just waiting for someone to recognize my uniqueness. At this point, even my weirdness would be fine. Lately, everyone just looks through me. My one-liners are falling flat in this joint. There is no concierge, and the only person in the motel to befriend is the woman at the front desk, near the drooping potted plant, who looks exhausted by life in general and by me in particular. I inhale the scent of just-washed laundry from the machines and sigh mightily.

Every day I find myself pacing, full of energy, skinny legs eating up the pavement. But it's far more than frustration that keeps me moving. It's like a fire, this burning in my core. I walk wherever—across the highway to the strip mall, to the dollar store, picking up random things and putting them back. Is it ambition or anger? I have trouble telling them apart. This need to rise up, do amazing things, to be the youngest, the first, to be *somebody*. Not just a girl from nowhere. A girl without a name—and nowhere to go but back to that room.

The wind has turned chill by the time I hurry along the hallway, unlocking our door. As soon as I step inside, my parents turn from their conversation at the little standard-issue motel table, focusing on me, and I know something is wrong.

"Come here, Bhajan," Mom says sympathetically. "We want to talk to you."

I don't move, my eyes darting around the room.

"What are you looking for?"

"Is Tigger dead?"

"No!" She seems shocked. "He's under the bed."

I bend down, checking to be sure. Relieved, I sit on the edge of the bed and face them. "Okay, what's up?"

Dad leans forward, elbows on his knees. "We have always tried to protect you. To do what we thought would be best for you, so you could grow up in a complete family environment . . ."

It's bizarre the places my mind goes when I know something game-changing is about to happen but . . . why is it that no matter how skinny my limbs are, my stomach still seems to stick out? Like a little Buddha belly over the top of my jeans. Or maybe it's just the way I'm sitting? Nope, still here.

"If we told you certain things . . ." Mom looks at her hands. "We—"

"Just tell me."

She looks up. "Frank and Chiara are not your full siblings."

"They aren't your brother and sister," he cuts in.

I tilt my head, confused.

"They're your half-siblings," Mom clarifies. "I was married once before."

"What?"

By far the most surprising piece of information is that Dad would allow such a thing to happen. That she had a life before this one, our one, began. As for the rest, the signs were probably there. I think about it: the age gap, their dark hair and olive skin. I sit up straighter. The fact that Dad never loved my siblings as much as me. Why didn't I see it? I look between my parents as the puzzle starts to take form.

Wait!

"Are you my real mother?"

"Yes!" She is bolt upright in an instant, cheeks flushed. I haven't seen this much certainty from her in years, it's as if I've hit at the last thing she has. "You are *our* daughter."

"Okay," I say.

They seem to be waiting for something more, some kind of reaction. But part of me is hovering above, detached, regarding the situation with academic interest. It must have been hard for Frank and Chiara. Hard in a different way than it ever was for me. Approval must have seemed completely impossible to attain. Then something else comes to mind, and a sensation of relief washes over me. Cool rain on a summer day. Chiara isn't my "real" sister. There doesn't have to be something of her in me.

Although by some misshapen logic, he still feels like my brother. Slowly, I raise my chin and look straight at them. "What really happened before I was born? Why did we have to run?"

Their eyes find each other, and Dad takes over. "I don't think that's necessary to discuss."

"I'm old enough." I stay calm, hardly moving, walking a tightrope. While I'd much rather remain comfortably in the dark, I need to know what we're up against. I need to get us out of this.

"She has a right to know." Mom ventures.

Rights and feelings, two things he sees as flexible entities. Even her vocabulary has always been opposite to his. How they ever got together is a mystery to me. But he leans back, running his hand over his short beard. "All right."

She looks at me, "Are you cold, do you want your hoodie?"

"No, Mom."

"It's drafty—"

"I'm *fine*."

"Just let me . . ." She has found it, rumpled and black, thrown over a chair.

Resignedly I pull on my sweatshirt. The really annoying part is, only now do I realize I was cold.

"You sure you don't want a scarf?"

"Mom!"

She holds up her hands in surrender and begins to tell the story that shaped my life. A daring gamble and the greatest of stakes—

A family.

PART TWO

29: Luxembourg, Fall, 1979

IT WAS A cool, cloudy day in a city run by money. A tax haven for the wealthy, Luxembourg was one of the richest countries in Europe, with winding cobblestone streets leading past countless private banks, housed discreetly in beautiful historic buildings.

She was born there. It was only a matter of time before he arrived.

Inside Banque du Sud, a woman sat behind the credit manager's desk. At thirty-two, she was unusually beautiful but had never believed it. The front doorbell buzzed, and Anne looked up.

One instant was about to change everything, and to understand why, you have to know a few things about Anne. She was the daughter of a secret-police operative. Controlling and obsessive, Konrad was born for the job, and fighting in WWII cemented his natural tendency to crave authority. Square-thinking and a strict disciplinarian, he loved his child and occasionally said so, but these declarations often followed an outburst of his unpredictable temper, or a beating. Her mother was dutiful and detached. Ostracized in Luxembourg—a straight-laced, largely uniform country—for being an Italian immigrant, she seemed to always have her mind on some faraway home. She had never held—or spanked—Anne, and never said "I love you" to anyone.

Secondly, Anne had been married once. She met Max, handsome and intelligent, at university in France. They married soon after, and she moved with him to Paris, where he continued his studies. At twenty-six she had their first child, a daughter. Within a year of the birth, he began having affairs with women he met while playing guitar to make extra money.

When Anne found out she was pregnant again, they tried unsuccessfully to make things work. But by the time their son was born, Max had moved in with a girlfriend, and Anne gave birth alone. As soon as she was released from the hospital, she took the children and left. Six weeks later, Max taped all the windows in the kitchen of his Paris apartment shut and gassed himself to death. At the age of twenty-nine Anne became a widow, with a toddler and an infant. She moved into her parents' attic.

The third thing is a product of the other two: Anne did not want her children to grow up absorbing all the doubts and fears she had internalized from her parents. She didn't trust that she alone could give them the knowledge and experience they needed to truly thrive.

In the bank, the doorbell buzzed again. "The receptionist is still at lunch, d'you mind getting it?" Anne's supervisor, a jovial Scotsman, poked his large head around the corner of his office door.

Walking through the main area of the private bank, Anne prepared her polite face. She was used to dealing with businessmen and could run through the paces of a typical conversation on asset management in a near coma. Unlocking the heavy carved wood door, she pulled it open and inquired on automatic, "Good afternoon, how are you?"

A massive smile, the likes of which she had never encountered before, lit the face of a blond man on the doorstep. "Fan-tas-tic!" he boomed.

This was a country where people were fine—anything more was considered extravagant. Anne started to laugh. It was a deep, unreserved laugh. And that was the beginning.

A year and a half later, just after dawn, Anne's small apartment in town was bare except for its furniture and four suitcases stacked by the wooden door. She had only spent two months in total with George since they met, always when he traveled through town, trying to get his gold bullion business financed. But it was enough. Enough time for him to introduce her to yoga, Sikhism, health food, and the joys of thinking outside the box, something he did with particular skill and comic timing. Enough time for her to fall in love with the mind of this very different man.

Forty-two years old, Canadian by birth, with Russian and Scottish ancestry, George had an inquisitive, restless mind and traveled as much as possible, often leaving confusion in his wake. Educated, charming, and utterly confident, he briefly taught philosophy at a university, then started a company manufacturing health supplements. Quickly, though, he decided to stop all the heavy lifting and find his way into high finance. It would be the gold rush of the 1980s that lit his path.

Anne's and the children's passports lay on the table. Now aged five and seven, Frank and Chiara stood zipped into their jackets, occasionally shoving each other.

Anne and George were in love, but two months of time together is only two months. None of this might have happened if it weren't for her father, Konrad, now a high-ranking secret-police agent. He was furious when Anne dared to get her own apartment in town after being promoted at the bank. She was having chronic migraine headaches that affected her vision and knew she needed to be free. He demanded that she return with the children to the attic.

But Anne held her ground. Even though she was only twenty minutes away, and visited weekly, Konrad refused to compromise. After a month of the stalemate, Konrad called Anne in a fury, threatening to use his influence, declare her an unfit mother, and take the children away. There was no doubt he was serious; he even outlined which connections he would use to fast-track the procedure without the necessity of evidence. Anne knew he could do it. She became terrified of even letting the children go to school, since her father could easily snatch them there.

In that moment, George came to town for some meetings and, discovering her predicament, suggested they leave together—as a family.

Three days later, the bags were packed. George's gold bullion business was still new and he was low on funds. After much agonizing, Anne emptied the bank account she shared with her father; a good deal of the cash was Konrad's. Walking away from the bank with the money, Anne knew there was no going back. She took a last look around the apartment— at George chatting to the children, even though they didn't understand English yet—and said, "Allons-y." *Let's go.*

That first year in California was all sunshine and fresh oranges from the backyard tree, the endless possibilities of America, and trying to adjust to George's high expectations. He could be alternately charming and demanding with the children, but there was no doubt they were learning and experiencing life as never before. Anne's health problems, the terrible stomach pains and chronic migraine headaches, vanished into the clear San Jose sky.

George methodically promoted himself in the press as a gold bullion expert and was soon hired as a consultant to investment companies. After six months, he started his own successful bullion investment fund.

Chiara, now eight, was excelling at school, top of her class, and ringleader of a clique of third-grade alpha girls. Frank, skinny and tall with huge feet and hands, was already being watched by scouts from rival swim teams as he cut through the water like a miniature torpedo aimed for team Mission Viejo. Everything was just about perfect.

"I think we have to leave." George stood in the spacious living room of their hillside house, just back from a business trip in Vancouver. Anne stopped her progress across the room as he heaved his travel bag off his shoulder and onto the floor.

"What happened?"

"I think your father is putting out international alerts on me. I was stopped at the airport, coming back into the States, and questioned about how much tax I'm paying."

"International? Are you sure?" Anne still spoke with her mother and, occasionally, with her father. The conversations always started with a quiet *click*, prompting Anne to ask if she was being recorded, a fact Konrad vehemently denied. From this auspicious start, the calls usually devolved into him screaming, "I'm going to find you!" while Anne lapsed into stubborn silence. She had phoned him immediately after leaving to explain that she would let him see the children any time if he signed a lawyer's document promising not to use his influence to take them from her.

He refused, and from there, things only got worse. As a secret-police agent, no one had ever outsmarted him. The fact that Anne and some foreign man had slipped away—with a pile of his money, no less—seemed to push his mind to the breaking point.

"Well, why else would I get stopped?" George headed into the kitchen for an orange juice.

"*Have* you been paying taxes?"

"That's beside the point." He put the glass down with his characteristic *thunk*. "He's drawing attention to us here. We should go to Canada where I can do business more easily."

Anne still didn't want to believe her father would use the authorities to try to hunt them down, despite his threats. Accepting it would mean also accepting that Konrad was mentally unbalanced. That he had found a job where his particular paranoia was an advantage, rather than something to be diagnosed and treated.

Reluctantly, Anne packed their bags again. Standing on the back balcony, her vision blurred with tears just thinking about leaving. She had been hoping to expand the family here. But George was set against the idea. "How can you think of having a child? There aren't even curtains on the windows." Anne tried to point out that the reason for the absence of curtains was not knowing how long they were going to stay.

"Exactly," George replied.

THE PLANE TAXIED to a halt at Vancouver International Airport at 11 p.m. Bleary-eyed, they trudged toward customs. George went through easily with his Canadian passport, while Anne waited with the children. Frank, overtired and antsy, hopped from foot to foot as their passports were checked.

"Come back here," Anne sighed as he bounced further away.

"Ma'am, you're going to have to come with us."

A uniformed border officer appeared beside the passport control booth.

"Why?" The kids became quiet, sensing something going wrong.

"Just come with me."

As Anne and the kids were led swiftly away, she caught a glimpse of George trying without success to get back through customs. She was taken through a metal door, which clicked shut, obscuring her view of George and the exit. Another border guard appeared between Anne and the kids, taking their hands and beginning to lead them away. Anne snapped out of her fear-induced trance. "What are you doing?"

"Don't worry," the stone-faced officer assured her. "Your children will be in the office just next to you."

"No, I want them with me."

"I'm afraid that's not possible. Please, come in here." With coordinated efficiency, the two officers split, one taking the frightened kids away while the other escorted Anne into a small, windowless office.

"What's this about?" Anne felt her heart beating in panic.

"We just want to ask you some questions." He cleared his throat before folding his hands on the desk. "There has been a report filed with Interpol concerning the welfare of your children and whether you are a fit mother. It also states that your companion, George, may be a criminal."

Anne went silent for a moment. "Who filed this with Interpol?"

"Konrad Schmidt."

Anne registered it gradually, like a person operating in slow motion. George had been right. They were being framed. By her father.

After hours of hammering questions, the officer made a note on the open file in front of him and conferred with his colleague, the one who had taken the kids. "I'm sorry," he seemed almost ashamed. "Everything you've told me checks out and the children seem to be happy and healthy, so you can go for now. But if you want to stay in Canada, you will have to apply for permission in court." He gave a small apologetic smile.

Anne was lead out to retrieve Frank and Chiara from an interrogation room down the hall, where they had spent the last three hours being asked if Mommy and New Daddy were nice to them. Teary and upset, they walked with Anne back out through customs to where George was waiting.

That one night would change many things. Anne would never again doubt George's opinion about her father, and how far he was willing to go. If Konrad could orchestrate having his own grandchildren interrogated, anything was possible. She would not speak to him for ten years.

WHEN HE FIRST met Anne, George had hardly any capital, but now his ideas were paying off and money flowed in steadily. In addition to consulting, George's bullion fund, incorporated in the Bahamas, catered to American investors looking to avoid taxes. He settled the family on Paradise Island, where clear Caribbean water and powder-white sand surrounded their apartment complex.

George spent his days lying on the beach or meeting with investors who flew in from the States to work on their tan while hiding some money. Anne homeschooled the kids, the only real option in what was quickly becoming a vagabond lifestyle.

One cloud darkened the clear, tropical horizon: Anne's passport was about to expire, and after the interrogation at Vancouver Airport, there was no telling how far her father's influence could reach. Anne called the Luxembourg embassy in Miami while George happened to be away on business in Bermuda. By then he was almost always traveling on tiny charter flights—"puddle jumpers," as he called them—since they didn't keep passenger logs or check passengers with Interpol. At hotels he registered under one of his favored aliases, Mr. Cash, Sterling, or Gold.

The Miami embassy told Anne she had to get in touch directly with Luxembourg to renew her passport. She did. After taking down all her information the man in her home country's passport office put Anne on hold.

Click.

"Bonjour." He was back. "We will not renew your passport. You must return here."

"But how can that be? I am a citizen; I was born there. My passport should be renewable from anywhere."

"I know," he said pointedly. "I worked with your father. . . . He has his issues, but if you want to renew it, you must return first." Anne could feel herself go cold as she hung up. In a small country like Luxembourg, even though his colleagues apparently knew Konrad was unstable and volatile, they were sticking together.

The next morning, George called to say he had been stopped at the border from reentering the Bahamas. He suspected a conspiracy. Voice tense, George informed Anne he'd taken a commercial flight to Panama City. Anne and the kids were to pack up again and join him. Their trail was getting too hot. "But my passport is expiring soon, they'll never let me on a plane—"

"I'll take care of it. I've met someone here who can help."

Days later, Anne stood nervously at the tiny, open-air Nassau airport, with the kids sitting on the luggage and her nearly useless passport zipped in a shoulder bag. *How was George going to pull this one off?*

A tall, good-looking Bahamian lawyer arrived, shook her hand firmly, and reassured her that all was arranged. He walked them onto the airfield and ushered them aboard a puddle jumper bound for Turks and Caicos. It all happened so fast and seamlessly, under the glorious Bahamian sky, that Anne was up in the air before any worry or concern had time to register.

They touched down in Turks and Caicos, where a young man on the runway, wearing a reflective vest, told her to wait for a private flight outside the terminal. It was deeply disorienting to have no idea what the plan was, when the stakes were so high. They waited on the tarmac, empty except for a crowd of rough-looking men loitering outside the fence. The gate wobbled as the men leaned closer, fingers threading through the thin metal barrier. Feeling spooked, the kids reached for her hands and the three of them stood, waiting. Anne realized that if George couldn't create something like a miracle, they would be stranded.

A rumble came from above and they all looked up simultaneously. Like an angel, a beautiful white plane was gliding toward them through the pure blue sky. "Is that for us?" Chiara asked disbelievingly.

"I . . . think so," Anne said, watching the private Learjet touch down and taxi forward.

"Are we famous?" Frank marveled, as the plane came to a halt.

Moments later, high above the thin clouds, the friendly pilots even let Frank hold the steering controls as they made record time. One hour later, the private jet came to a halt and they stepped onto Panamanian soil. A young man in uniform stood ready at the base of the steps, squinting his eyes against the wind from the still spinning engines. He loaded them and their luggage into his jeep, blaring Calypso music, and drove to the customs building. Behind the checkpoint, they saw George waiting for them with his mischievous grin. Already fluent in five languages, Anne had been reinforcing her basic Spanish with the help of a book, preparing for a possible crisis at the border. She tensed as the guards looked up.

George gave them a nod.

"Bienvenida." Both men in uniform stepped aside, letting Anne and the children walk straight through into George's waiting arms.

A few days later at an outdoor café, George introduced Anne to the man who helped arrange for the rescue Learjet. Resplendent in an all-white linen suit, still crisp even as he wiped droplets of sweat from his forehead with an immaculate hankie, John was a massively obese, thoroughly jovial criminal from Canada. He had originally arrived in Panama to hide out and ended up making it his permanent base of operations. He knew every politician, cop, and gangster in the country, and kept the important ones on his payroll.

Anne, George, and the kids settled into Panama while they figured out what to do about the expired passport. On the surface, George's bullion business appeared to be proceeding smoothly, but in reality he had been forced to siphon off investors' money for the expenses of moving the family to safety. He had his eye, though, on one big client in the United States whom he had been courting for some time. An investor big enough to repay the money he'd withdrawn from the original clients' accounts and give George capital to make lucrative investments as well.

Everything hinged on the American.

30: 3 a.m., Panama City, 1985

A LOUD RAPPING sound startled Anne out of a deep sleep. The motel bedroom was dark, lit only by the colored glow of streetlights and neon signs coming through the open window. George was already awake and standing at their bedroom door, looking cautiously out into the small living room. Anne tied her robe and joined him as the pounding from outside continued, making the wooden entrance door vibrate.

Checking through the peephole, George frowned and then opened the door, keeping one shoulder braced against it. He was forced back immediately as three men in dark clothes pushed their way in.

"Policía!" One of the men, tall and slender, stepped forward, flashing a badge. "Jenes que venir con nosotros." *You must come with us*, Anne translated for George, who was watching the men intently. It was obvious they were not regular police—more likely special forces.

Two small heads appeared at the door of the second bedroom, blinking sleepily.

"What is this about?" Anne asked in Spanish.

"It's about him." The man pointed to George. "You must come with us."

"We can't leave the children." Anne glanced toward Frank and Chiara's frightened faces.

"You'll bring the children. Get dressed now and come."

They were rushed into an unmarked car. Doors slammed and their convoy took off, speeding recklessly through deserted streets until they pulled to a halt in front of a long stone building. Two of the officers pulled George up the steps, and he vanished within.

Two hours later, the first light of dawn began to spread outside the narrow windows, but Anne and the children still waited in the entrance hall. They had photocopied her passport alongside George's, and she sat very still, thinking of her father, of Interpol. The kids had finally stopped fidgeting and were passed out on the hard bench, but Anne kept a watchful eye on the men inside the glass-walled office. At last, the door opened. "Come with me to talk to him." The officer was bushy-browed and authoritative.

"I want a lawyer."

"Just come with me." He pointed over his shoulder down the corridor.

"I'm not leaving my children here alone!" She was a petite woman, but could give the impression of mule-headed determination when the occasion called for it.

George was brought out into the main room. "I don't know what's going on," he whispered urgently to Anne, his long hair wild. "Call Eduardo." Anne vaguely remembered Eduardo as a local lawyer George had hired to incorporate a company for him.

"How will I pay him?"

"There's still some money on his retainer." He surreptitiously pressed a roll of cash into her hand as they kissed. The officers were advancing again, taking George's elbows to lead him away. "The motel is paid until the end of the month," he called over his shoulder. "And you have the insurance."

The "insurance" was in a black makeup pouch Anne carried everywhere with her. The pouch contained her one and only cosmetic, a tube of soft pink drugstore lipstick; the rest of the space was filled with gold Krugerrand coins, and a dozen one-ounce bars of pure bullion.

Anne and the kids were driven back to the motel in the early morning, and as soon as businesses opened, she contacted George's lawyer.

"Here's the thing," Eduardo said as they sat down. "They're denying they have him. None of the branches of the police force admit knowing what you're talking about."

Anne started to protest, but the lawyer held up a hand. "I believe you, but at this point I think there is only one option. I will file a habeas corpus petition, which means—"

"I know." Anne gripped the chair. "Make them bring him before a judge."

They sat silently, the worst left unsaid—*if he's still alive.*

How do you prove a person has disappeared, when he spent most of his time covering his tracks? George was in a South American jail, everyone was acting as if he didn't exist, and all Anne had were a couple kids, some gold coins, and an expired passport. They were two weeks into the mess before the lawyer called with any real news. "I think he's alive. They're admitting they have him. They gave me the name of a jail," he said wearily.

Anne's heart leapt. "So we know where he is!"

"Not exactly. As soon as I got the information, they seem to have relocated him." Eduardo began to worry the case was getting too big for him when another week passed and the authorities continued to stonewall, no matter how high up their ranks he went. Then a peculiar coincidence occurred. One day, while on a routine visit to one of his other clients in jail, Eduardo was shocked to see a tall blond man and a flash of watchful blue eyes.

"Did he say anything to you?" Anne asked eagerly.

"No, George was in a large cell with other prisoners and I wasn't allowed to get close."

"So you don't have any message from him?"

Eduardo hesitated. "No . . . but . . ."

"What!?"

Eduardo hesitated, as if what he had to relate was just too preposterous. Finally, he spoke disbelievingly. "George was teaching yoga. More than half the prisoners sharing his cell block are now part of his class. Apparently, they do it twice a day."

Encouraged by the sighting, Anne took matters into her own hands and got an appointment with the Consul General of Canada, George's home country. The Consul General, a calm woman in her fifties, listened as Anne gave her the story. "No charges have been filed and they just keep moving him to different jails every time we get close. Can you help?'

"I'll do everything in my power. But . . ." The Consul looked down regretfully. "You're not married, and the children are not his, so you have no legal rights to him. I can't even file anything in your name. The most you can be is a witness—nothing more."

It was well past midnight when Anne, lying sleepless on their bed and watching the overhead fan stir hot air, had an idea. Something so outrageous it just might fly. At 8 a.m. she got a number from information and dialed.

"Buenos días. Oficina del Presidente," answered a young woman.

"Buenos días," Anne said. "Quiero hablar con Presidente Noriega." *I want to speak to President Noriega.*

There was a pause and then, "Can you tell me what this is about?"

Anne explained the situation, making it seem like the Canadian Consulate was more involved than they actually were.

The woman called back two hours later. The president was out of the country on an official visit and his deputy, Colonel Roberto Diaz Herrera, was in charge during his absence. "You can meet him tomorrow, at nine in the morning."

Carefully groomed, the children and Anne appeared at 9 a.m. and entered an elegant waiting area. Around the edges of the room stood wall-to-wall glass display cases, filled with menacing guns, rifles, and an AK-47. An attractive woman in her late twenties appeared after several minutes and led them through a heavy wood door and into President Noriega's private office.

Colonel Díaz Herrera was seated behind a large ornate desk, clad in a khaki off-duty uniform, framed on either side by a guard standing watch over two additional closed doors. Anne deposited the kids on one of the plush sofas and whispered, "Don't you dare move."

Sitting across from the colonel, she steeled herself for what might be her last chance to save George. In a calm voice, hopefully not betraying exhaustion or panic, she laid it out, in Spanish. Five minutes later she took a deep shaking breath to conclude, "I won't give up, there must be some resolution. We—"

He held up a hand, interrupting, and looked at Chiara, sitting frozen on the couch. Switching to English, Herrera leaned forward. "Do you want to see your father?"

Chiara's eyes opened wide and she nodded vigorously.

He gestured to the guard at the door behind his desk. Within seconds, the heavy door swung open and George stepped into the room.

Two more guards flanked him but remained by the wall, letting George advance alone. He was dramatically skinny and still wearing the same clothes as when he was taken, six weeks ago. Anne jumped to her feet but stayed rooted to the floor, assessing the situation. "There. You can go say hello to your father," Herrera encouraged Chiara, his face surprisingly soft, obviously deeply moved. Chiara rushed forward. Anne still hadn't budged when the voice from behind the desk said, "You are all free to go."

Hailing a taxi outside, Anne took in the specter of George as he smiled wanly at her, his cheekbones standing out in a gaunt face, clothes hanging in loose folds.

"You smell funny," Frank observed.

That night, Anne finally got a chance to talk to him in private as George sat on the edge of their bed, sleepy-eyed, after a much-needed shower.

Anne touched his thin shoulder. "Why did they hide you for so long?!"

A wry grin tugged at one corner of his wet beard. "They thought I was the Jackal."

"The Jackal?"

"Yeah, they thought they had made the capture of the century and were going to be famous."

Carlos the Jackal was one of the world's most wanted men, an international terrorist, responsible for the armed takeover of the OPEC headquarters in Vienna and many deaths in other attacks across Europe. Apart from their full lips and strong noses, George and Carlos the Jackal didn't look much alike. But if you compared pictures, there was something, a certain rebel glint, that was eerily similar. When someone observed George's meeting with the local Canadian crime-lord, arranging for a private Lear jet, and always paying cash, they made assumptions.

George stared contemplatively at the floor, his face serious, periodically flushed red by the blinking neon sign from across the street. "You know . . . if you want to have another child," he said, looking up at Anne. "We can."

Anne watched him sprawled against the pillows later, dark shadows under his closed eyes, and thought, *All it took was breaking him out of a South American jail.*

THE NEXT DAY, George bailed his entire yoga class out of prison. They were in for medium-level offenses and all eligible for release, but didn't have family members with enough money to pay bond. He was delighted by the spectacle of the convicts marching past the guards and out of jail—all displaying impeccable posture.

But something haunted George and Anne. With both their identities now in the arrest records in Panama, Anne's father would find out precisely where they were. The trap could already be closing in on their family. They needed a lot of money, and fast. George's big American client hadn't come though yet. There seemed to be only one option left. . . . George sat by the window for a long time, trying to think of another way, any other way. Precious time ticked by, and he turned to watch Frank and Chiara. A seemingly peaceful afternoon, punctuated with the children's laughter and a gentle rattle of dice as they played.

Then George stood decisively; and in that moment, he became the criminal Anne's father had framed him as. Early the next morning, George took all his investors' money from the fund—emptying the account—and they started to run. With almost two million dollars.

Everything depended on speed. They caught the first available flight from Panama to Ecuador, where George had an embassy contact in Quito who might be able to get Anne's passport renewed under the table. The object was getting to a country where the authorities were known to be *flexible*—but where they could also settle permanently should leaving South America prove to be too dangerous. That pointed to Brazil. From Quito, they would break the trail, traveling by bus under assumed identities to Lima. Then they would just need to find a way out of Peru, to cross the Amazon to Brazil—traversing the greatest forest on earth, all while avoiding all major airports or transport hubs.

Upon arriving in Quito, though, the embassy contact fell through, leaving Anne with no valid passport. It was a hard blow. But facing a twenty-eight-hour ride to Lima, they couldn't afford to stop. On a rickety bus, crowded with people and a few squawking chickens, they tried to catch some sleep, before continuing via puddle-jumper past Cusco to the last Peruvian outpost on the edge of the jungle.

The town had one dirt road, a little inn where they were staying, an airport runway without any planes, and hundreds of incorrigible monkeys. The only prepared food they could find was garnished with flies and a sprinkle of gravel dust. George tried to view it as an opportunity for a cleansing fast.

On the first morning, awakening on scratchy sheets, Anne crossed the street to the man selling bananas from his cart, and bought the only food any of them would be eating for the next days. There were a few other problems. The town had two payphones, standing next to each other in the blazing sun. Whether or not they worked seemed to change on an hourly basis. Also, the pilot they'd contacted to come collect them at the town's makeshift airport runway only spoke Brazilian Portuguese. Because of her language skills, Anne was put in charge. She managed to reach him after several attempts and a few hours in the heat, yelling through a crackling phone line in Spanish and deciphering what she could of the pilot's answers in Portuguese.

Eventually, though, they came to an agreement. A day later, at 3 p.m., a motor whirred overhead. Fully briefed and eager for rescue, the kids lunged for the door and George carried their suitcases outside. Anne ran across the street to the banana stand to mobilize its owner, the only person in town with a functioning car. "Please hurry!" Anne begged as he leisurely left the stand in the care of a teenager.

They piled in and sped toward the airport. Pulling to a stop twenty minutes later on the packed dirt surrounding the runway, they were greeted by an eerie silence. "Where's the plane?" Frank looked at the empty runway in confusion.

A few locals were reclining against a hut, smoking and taking in the scene unfolding before them like a rare and baffling play. "Did you see a plane?" Anne asked the audience in Spanish.

"Yes, miss, it landed here."

"Great! Where is it?"

"It flew away again."

Weakened from a combination of hunger and heat, Anne looked at George and tried not to collapse on the spot.

"Did you see the pilot?"

"Yes, he was angry because Mrs. Cash wasn't here and he got back in the plane and went away."

Mrs. Cash was back in action the next morning, trying over and over to reach the pilot by phone, when she noticed a line forming. It seemed like the whole town was gathering behind her, mostly strong-looking men, with bulging muscles and calloused hands from working in the jungle. After overhearing a few emotional greetings and tender farewells from the neighboring phone, Anne realized it must be Mother's Day.

Frank trundled out of the motel, hollow-eyed, and tugged on Anne's long cotton skirt.

"There are only two bananas left, are we going to starve?"

Just then, the line crackled to life and the pilot's tired voice snapped, "Sim." *Yes.*

She began the process of calming down an irate Brazilian who thought he had been stood up, while glancing nervously over her shoulder at an ever-increasing line of men waiting in the unrelenting heat to call their distant mothers. By then, she had been monopolizing the phone for almost an hour. Seeing her frazzled expression, the man behind her patted her shoulder. "Não se preocupe, Mãezinha!" *Don't worry, mum.* He smiled sympathetically and moved without complaint to the back of the second line. One by one, the others followed.

THIS TIME, THEY were already waiting at the airstrip when the small two-engine plane taxied to a stop. "We can't fly," the pilot said after a quick look at their passports.

Anne translated and George reached for his wallet.

"It's not that," the pilot said, picking up on the movement. "You need a stamp from this place in order to get through the check in Brazil."

Anne returned to consult the same locals sitting near the customs hut. "No, the man with the stamp isn't here."

Anne drew a deep breath. "Where is he?"

"In town," supplied the youngest, about sixteen. "He runs the shoe repair store."

"Zut!" Anne fell back into her French while massaging her temples.

"I have a motorbike." The teenager smiled, showing three missing front teeth. "I can help."

Anne, the kids, and the pilot watched as George climbed onto the back of the bike with the boy and zoomed away in a cloud of dust, all four passports tucked into his khaki shirt pocket.

An hour later they returned, having woken the cobbler/customs agent from his siesta and gotten the passports stamped.

Looking out the oval window of the six-seater, as they sped up for take-off, Anne saw something racing alongside the plane. The teenager on his rickety motorbike was keeping pace and waving at them, showing his missing front teeth in a beautiful smile. As the plane lifted into the air, Anne leaned forward and burst into tears.

They landed at a small airport, not far from São Paolo. Everyone tensed as they entered the airport's single room holding two customs officers. Time to see if the rumors about Brazilian leniency were true.

George and the children went first. Then the officer opened Anne's passport, saw the expired date, and smiled gently at the kids as he stamped her into the country.

THE DISCOVERY THAT enabled their escape happened in a photocopy shop. George was by the machine, watching it print, when he noticed photocopies of various local work permits scotch taped to the wall. After turning his trademark charm on the proprietor—with Anne translating into the basic Portuguese she had taught herself in the last month—George discovered that there were a huge number of Chileans who wanted to work in Brazil but didn't have proper permits. A lively forgery business had sprung up to accommodate them. George listened, paused, and then went for it: "How difficult is it to get a Brazilian passport?"

Within thirty minutes, a friend of the proprietor's arrived. "I can help you," he said quietly. "There is someone who can do this. After I speak to her, I'll leave word here about when we can all meet."

Before the meeting was even set, Anne was having second thoughts about going as far as actually changing identities. It was a big leap from just using fake names at hotels. But George had already made up his mind. "There's no way you can get your real passport fixed now. Your father is sabotaging everything. Look how much trouble he's caused already, and that was with nothing to go on."

Anne shook her head, trying to think of a solution, a way out. George lowered his voice so the kids in the adjoining room wouldn't hear, and fixed his intense eyes on her, "I just stole two million dollars. Now he has a reason to take the children away from us."

They met the forger at a busy outdoor restaurant. A woman was sitting with the young man they had already met, and she gave them a dazzling smile as they approached. Her thick jet-black hair framed a pleasant-featured face with sharp black eyes.

Our Friend.

She efficiently took down the information George had invented to construct their new identities. The woman had a contact in the registrar's office, so she would be able to backdate, insert the whole family in the real birth registry of Brazil, and have actual passports issued. After all, the best "fake" passport is one the government unwittingly prints itself.

"Dá-me um mês," she said. *Give me a month.* George passed her an envelope with $3,000, half of her total fee.

Two months later, operating on her own perception of time, she finished the documents: new passports and birth certificates for everyone, with additional driver's licenses and voter registration cards for Anne and George. One afternoon, the forger's inside contact—the same slight, kind-faced man who would later be beaten to death in Rio—guided the family through a side door into the basement of a federal building. One by one, he dipped their fingertips in ink and sealed their fate.

The whole family passed through customs without question and boarded a flight to South Africa for a stopover—always breaking the trail—before arriving in Singapore. The kids were coached to respond to their new names and remember they were Brazilian. To celebrate having made it, they lay in a row of four by the pool and sipped fresh-squeezed pineapple juice.

In the morning George disappeared with a big black shoulder bag and headed to the Singapore investment company he'd tasked with transferring the stolen money overseas from South America. The normally legitimate firm had been seduced into laundering the cash for a percentage of the total. There was a chance they'd take all the money and run, but that was a risk George was forced to take. Fortunately, the investment firm did not possess the same entrepreneurial spirit as George; they handed over all the cash, minus commission.

He staggered out, $1.5 million richer. For the risky business of depositing the funds in a bank the next day, he selected Anne. She walked into Hong Kong International Bank in a long, lightweight peasant skirt, a string of South American beads around her wrist, and $750,000 in a bag slung over her shoulder. An immaculate man in a suit approached. "How may I help you?"

"I would like to open an account and make a deposit."

"Of course." He made a small bow. "How much would you like to deposit?"

She told him. He only looked dumbfounded for a moment before collecting himself. "Please, follow me to a private room."

Inside was a money-counting machine. Anne sat at the polished table, filling out forms to the whir of the counter as an assistant fed in the crisp bills. After showing her Brazilian passport and opening the account under the new name, she returned the next day to deposit the rest of the cash. No one ever asked where the money came from; clearly it was not the first time someone had walked in with a bag full of bills. Such were the perks of private banking in the eighties.

Goal accomplished, George decided they should to get out of town while the going was good and head for the anonymous coast of New Zealand. Leaning across the aisle after takeoff, George started up a poker game with the kids, betting each other with a mixture of coins from their intercontinental escape. Anne looked at them, resting her head against the airplane seat, and finally let the tension drain away.

They didn't know it yet, but she was pregnant.

THE ARRIVAL OF the "third guy," as the kids dubbed the newcomer, did not disappoint on the drama scale. After ten hours of painful labor, Anne finally convinced George to give up on the idea of a homeopathic Ayurvedic home birth and drive full speed to the hospital in the middle of the night. Frank and Chiara were in the room when the third guy appeared, red-faced and kicking off any attempt by the nurse to be wrapped in a blanket.

His eyes moist, George immediately took the baby into his arms and refused to let a nurse even weigh the child. He seemed mesmerized by the nearly identical little face looking back at him. Ever after, George ignored the pram and carried the baby everywhere, cradled against his heartbeat.

So it happened that on the 27th of July, in a New Zealand hospital, a real baby was born but registered under a fake identity.

The child should have been a New Zealand citizen by birthright, but because the parents wrote their false Brazilian names on the birth certificate, they had just committed fraud.

The first rule of changing identities is to destroy all proof of your real ones. Anne and George adhered to it— burning their real passports to ash in the metal wastebasket of a hotel during the escape. As a consequence, though, their child would have no haven in her parents' home countries, which they had abandoned. If the child would try, as an adult, to claim citizenship in any country, she would become a criminal. She would be punished for continuing the fraud—and held accountable for what her parents had done before she was born. In case the flimsy papers of the forged documents were ever to be lost or destroyed, there would be no proof of life at all. The third guy did not, technically, exist.

Some believe that a person's character is formed based on the events leading up to their birth. This was the baby of two renegades; dreamt of in a Panamanian prison, conceived on a money-laundering run, and grown in her mother's belly during a transcontinental escape.

Unaware, the baby hummed musically while sleeping, one leg kicked defiantly outside of the blanket. Frank and Chiara leaned in close, trying to hum in tune with the newest family member. With a unanimous four votes, the baby's name was decided: "Song of God" in Sanskrit.

Harbhajan.

PART THREE

31: North Carolina, age 15

CRACKS RUN LIKE fault lines through the asphalt, sprouting tiny weeds. I've never noticed it before, but—sitting here on the motel curb with my elbows on my knees—they are everywhere. An orderly line of ants, probably of German descent, march toward a crevice.

"Bhajan . . ." Mom must have followed my meandering path from the room, and now sits hesitantly beside me. This alone is an indicator of her worry. We don't sit on curbs in our family—it isn't dignified.

I cross my arms, "So, I'm not part French."

She frowns, confused. "Well, no, I'm actually half Italian and half Luxembourgish."

"You said you were French."

"Yes, but—"

"I really liked that part of the story, Mom!"

"I'm so sorry, dear, I didn't realize . . ."

My whole body feels heavy but I force myself to ask. "So . . . we're in a lot of trouble, right?"

"Well . . ."

"You can be straight with me." I look my mother in her uncertain eyes.

"Yes, Bhajan, we are." She seems to want to touch my shoulder, then second-guesses herself.

I take a breath—in, out—and nod. All this time, I assumed Interpol was chasing us for some unfair, invented reason. But my father stole millions from his investors. And yet, he did it because he needed money to keep us safe from my grandfather . . .

"You're taking this so calmly." Mom says.

A small smile curves my lips, the triumph of irony over good sense.

"Mom, at this point if you guys told me my real name was Fukiyama Nagasaki and we were moving to Tokyo to start a unicycle business, I'd just ask, *when*?"

Instead of laughing, her face falls. "I've been a bad mother."

"Don't take it that way," I sigh, irritation fighting sympathy. "At least I'm adaptable."

Her hands pull at each other. "I was trying to do the right thing. I . . ."

Observing her from the corner of my eye, the ache in my chest is so sharp that I stand abruptly. "Oh well, it's onward or raising chickens by the side of the road, right?" I grin, covering my longing for the way we were. Together and dusted with Kashmir earth. But it's never going to come back. All that's left is figuring out how to survive. And, looking at her slumped shoulders, I have the disturbing suspicion that it's up to a fifteen-year-old, standing in a motel parking lot, with a scab on her knee.

WE ARE ON the move again, late summer, only stopping for gas along the interstate, at places where neon signs lure in tired truckers with the promise of coffee. I'm watching my father in the front seat as he counts bills. The multimillion-dollar thief. My breath is shallow, filled with gasoline fumes, a scent I normally like. But I'm uneasy. He's out in a confident sweep, popping the tank lid and fitting the nozzle into our tired rental when I realize I've seen him sort money my whole life . . . but never *count* it. The pump stops on $10. He didn't even fill it up.

Our car is the only one in the storage center lot, parked rebelliously across the yellow lines. We unload our remaining bags onto the asphalt with a tired thump. From now on we are traveling light: just a suitcase each. Leaning against the hood, I focus on the darkening horizon, and listen to them wheel our last bags away.

"Ready?" He's back, hands empty except for the car keys.

I return to reality slowly, with some reluctance, and look to where Mom is arranging suitcases in the ground-level concrete tomb.

"Let's go." He motions me toward the front seat door.

"She still needs to lock up." I roll my neck, trying to loosen the kinks.

"Let's leave her here."

I stop abruptly.

"What?"

"Get in the car. She's just an inconvenience at this point. You're old enough not to need her anymore."

I stare at the puzzle of his face. So matter of fact, as if he is suggesting dinner options. "You're joking, right?" A queasy sort of smile settles on my face.

"Stop being weak. She doesn't care about you, she's involved in her own breakdown. This is serious."

"She does care, she—"

"You know what she told me when I said she had to pull herself together and be a proper mother? She said, 'Bhajan doesn't need someone like me. She's strong.'"

It hits me like a punch.

"So are you weak, Harbhajan, or are you brave? You have to decide."

When Frank called me the strong one, that day on the phone, I was flattered. But hearing it again now, I see the words for what they are. Not a compliment, or a fact, but an excuse. A way to leave me to sort everything out on my own. I've never broken down, because I thought they wouldn't be able to handle the extra stress. But now I wonder—are they coming apart because they know I never will?

The sound of the storage door scrolling down startles me. Her back is to us, trusting.

"Get in," he says.

"No," my voice is almost hesitant, confused at having to explain this. "She's my *mother*."

Something scary, like amusement, crosses his face and he shrugs. "All right."

I can't look away from him, my hand on the still-warm hood of the engine for support. Is this the same man, the good man, who sought out a religion based entirely on Truth, who named his daughter after the kind of life he hoped to lead?

The car doors slam once for each of us: Dad in the driver's seat, Mom in the passenger, and me in the back, with yet another reason to keep my mouth shut.

IT'S GONE, ALL of it. We are down to our last dollars, living out of our overdue rental car in a supermarket parking lot. Three of us, plus Tigger, a five-seater Toyota, and the metal walls closing in around me. It's been sixteen days, sleeping with my long body twisted in the backseat, waiting for morning to lighten the sky.

Walking into the Safeway supermarket as it opens, on my way to try to wash up in the bathroom, I catch a whiff of myself. I smell homeless. Avoiding my own gaze in the mirror, I want to tear the clothes off my body and scrub under a rush of hot water until my skin is raw, until the last two weeks vanish down the drain. Instead, I lean forward in my tank top, trying to wash under my arms. With a loud clang the door opens and a customer enters, narrowing her eyes at me as I flinch away from the sink. Her mouth turns down in a moue of disgust.

We've only been homeless for a couple of weeks and already I feel this desperation within, how my survival depends on other people's moods, their mercy. Will they give us the stale pizza they would normally throw away before closing? Will they turn a blind eye to our car parked overnight in a strip mall lot, or will we be woken by flashlights every few hours, made to move on?

My skin is pasty, a fever I can't quite shake flushing my cheeks. Mom's eyes are bruised from sleeplessness. I can't believe this is us. It's arrogant, I know, I know it is. But how could this happen to us? We are clever. We've evaded every law enforcement agency. How could Dad be so careless as to not budget our money over the years?

It seems so small. *But it's the little things, it's the simple mistakes that take you down. . . .*

At night, sweaty in the humidity, I remember the custom-made tuxes, the luxury cars bought in cash, the mansions, my private dance coaches, and I cringe with frustration and guilt. We used to seize the day, but now we sit in parking lots, barely surviving, killing time. Mom and Dad trying to think of anyone left who might help—but that's the problem with vanishing with such skill for decades. It pisses people off. And then they forget about you.

ALL WE HAVE left are two particular pieces of gold. They've got to be sold. Mom and Dad are off to see a dealer, but I can't face it. Instead, I cross the highway, cars honking angrily at me, my backpack slung over a shoulder, until I am standing in front of an elegant hotel. Taking a deep breath, I stroll in. The desk clerks look up, but I head purposefully for the elevators. Growing up in hotels has imprinted their layouts on my brain.

At the pool level, I look both ways, then quickly slip off my summer dress so I'm wearing just a bikini and sandals. The glass door into the pool area is locked, but there's a couple inside, swimming leisurely and stopping occasionally to kiss. Perfect.

I rap on the door and when they look up I smile apologetically, miming having forgotten my key. He is up and out, trailing droplets of water, and politely holds the door open for me. *Finally.* From my backpack, I take out shampoo and scrub and scrub under a rush of scalding water from the poolside shower until I'm clean and exhausted. I pull on a fresh pair of shorts and tank top in the bathroom, before stealing two cookies from the conference room on my way out.

Across the road, my hair dries slowly in the shopping-mall air conditioning, the cookies a relief in my stomach. But the watchfulness is still here. As I walk past brightly lit stores, I notice one woman has been observing me for a while. For a moment I wonder if she's a cop. But no one could know where we are, somewhere in the Carolinas, halfway between a McDonald's and a hard place. Probably she's watching because I look strange, not made-up and smiling like the other girls, but pared down, rangy. A minimalist version of a teenager.

The woman starts to approach me; she's mid-forties, dressed in black, and I tense. She's too intent, too focused. My feet are flirting with the idea of burning town when she looks up at me and says six words. "Have you ever thought of modeling?"

I'm waiting for my parents outside the gold dealer. A bell tinkles and I look up cautiously from my sneakers. Mom and Dad seem tired, somehow lost. Their marriage, whatever it was, has been dead for a while, but now it's undeniable: Their wedding rings—the last of our gold pieces, the ones I couldn't stand to see sold—are already on display in the dirty pawn shop window. Those whimsical bands of gold embedded with the nuggets she found, their laughter at the creek, sparkling like cold clear water . . .

In a line of three we look at the litter-strewn street. All that binds them now is tragedy. Tragedy and me. I go to her, taking my mother in my arms and feeling the tremble in her back. But in my head, I'm already hundreds of miles away. Because when I heard those six words, I did not see glamor, designer things, or the flash of a camera. I saw a crack, however small, in the impossible. *Have you ever thought of modeling?* I see a way to pull us out.

32: New York City, age 16

THE HEAD OF the New Faces division of Prima Models heaves to her feet at the conference table, Manhattan outlined behind her. Seated around the slab of perfectly polished glass we lean forward—nine faces plucked from thousands, ranging in age from fourteen to seventeen. The lucky ones.

Taking in her expression, I wonder why angry, disappointed women are so often put in the charge of young girls. She regards us new recruits the way you would a stale fast-food burger: with distaste, and a weary acceptance that you're going to devour it anyway.

"If there is one thing you need to remember from today's meeting, it's this."

We gaze up at her, waiting.

"We," she raises a finger, "we don't give a shit about you. And neither does anyone else in this town." There is a quick intake of breath from one of the fourteen-year-olds. I feel my eyes narrow as the head of New Faces levels a final shot. "Everyone wants to be where you are now. Don't forget: The world is full of beautiful girls, and you are always replaceable."

THE CROWDED BUS rumbles away from New Jersey and my cheap motel, following the signs to Manhattan. Eyes outlined in gray, short skirt riding up my thighs, I hold up my new North Carolina state ID card and inspect it carefully in the hot sunlight. My new identity. It's not bad, for the thirty bucks I paid a skinny guy in a copy shop. Travel all around the world, and yet, copy shops are still the place to go. A flash from his camera and for the first time, I saw Cheryl Diamond written next to my photo. Next to those same watchful eyes. An ID this cheap will only fool a doorman and get me into castings, but that's all I need.

My parents have given me everything we have left, $300, for my gamble.

I don't want to think of them, penniless, staying behind in North Carolina to see through a shady deal Dad is trying to make. I've stopped asking for details on the small-time cons he comes up with because it fills me with shame to see him stoop so low.

He was built for the Wild West of the 1980s and '90s, when a maverick idea, and the confidence to make people believe it, was paramount. In the modern arena of savvy investors and computer background checks, he is going to fail. I know it. So when my mother fought him on this—trying to stop me from coming to New York alone—harder than she's fought in years, I stayed out of it. Because I don't care if she's right and modeling is a dirty business. Because I've seen, when the two of them go head to head, she is sure to lose.

My hands fidget with the identity card, and I tell myself this is exactly what I wanted—a new beginning. A chance to make enough money to keep us safe. But every time I look at the name I've chosen, I keep thinking of all the things that came apart when I was Crystal. I don't know if I'm getting worse at compartmentalizing, but no matter where I go, my mind always finds its way back . . . to the last time I saw my brother. And I ask myself over and over, *What would I have done differently, what would I have done if I knew that was our last moment?*

I remember it so clearly—that eternal second. Ohio. The cheering crowd, Vivaldi playing for a gymnast's floor routine, my bare feet on the cold concrete. Frank and me. That instant stretches out in my mind until it is more like a day, a day in which I stepped aside and let others decide, because I was afraid of getting yelled at, afraid of what people would think. I can still see my brother so clearly, the way he smiled sadly as he turned to go. *"See you, Bhajan."*

On the bus, the Manhattan skyline comes into view, a challenge in black and white, and electricity courses along my body. He was here, in this city, only a few years ago, and doing exactly what I'm about to attempt. Yesterday, I even walked past the agency Frank modeled for, on the ground floor, its walls made of sleek glass. Inside agents spoke busily into headsets, and I scoured the room, wishing he were there.

My hand closes around the ID card and through the window of the bus, marred with dust, I make one promise. To a city where anything is supposed to be possible. From now on I will not step aside. From now on, I won't watch as other people decide.

IT'S ONLY BEEN a few days since the head of the New Faces division suggested that no one gives a shit about me, and I'm beginning to see her point. The daily casting circuit is a rush up and down stairs only to be told, over and over, that I'm not good enough. Outsiders watch us models stride by, endless legs, portfolios under an arm, and they think we have it made. But I look at every one of these impossibly lovely girls, and know they are desperate. I know because under every move I make, under every smile, beneath all the deliberate casualness, I am afraid.

It seems I am always *too* something. Too tall, too short, too blonde, not blonde enough, too fat, don't smile you look too young, be serious, no that's too old. It's impossible to figure out what to correct, or what may get me a break tomorrow. All I know for sure is that something about me, maybe about all of us, is disappointing them.

Well you know what? They will regret treating me this way. *They will look back*, I tell myself in my New Jersey motel room as I pour lukewarm tap water into Styrofoam Cup Noodles, *and they will wish they had been nicer to me*. With a plastic spoon I try to break up the cement block of ramen. No dice.

Tigger stares up at me from the bed and I lift a shoulder, smiling wryly. I don't know why I do this, fronting for my cat, trying cover up how desperate things are. As if he could possibly know rent is due tomorrow, know we haven't got it, and see the woman behind the safety glass at the front desk, watching me like she'd love to eject us onto the side of the highway. Mom and Dad call every night, and when they do I hide the worst from them, too. Otherwise they'll rush here spending money we don't have, abandoning some desperate deal Dad is trying to make, and we will be even further screwed.

So when my phone rings with castings, I layer on mascara in the bathroom mirror and go stand across the freeway from the young hookers who work the intersection. Waiting for my bus to the city, it strikes me more, every time, just how little space separates us.

When they dress and undress me in these sleek high-rises, faces hard, words cutting my body apart, I make myself think of Tigger. He is the one completely good thing in my life. Funny that a cat can get you through a day, but I count down the hours until I will unlock a moldy motel room and hold onto something real. The criticism of casting agents shouldn't wound me by now, after everything else, but it does. At least twice a day I want to hide or burst into tears like my six-year-old self. The only difference a decade has made is how very good I've become at turning hurt into ambition.

"Walk for me." My stilettos click as I runway walk, the way I've been taught, and wonder if the hardness in my eyes shows. It may even be what they are looking for. Figuring out what these designers and editors want is a project made more difficult by the fact that they seem to have no firm idea of it themselves. The tastemakers are easily bored, prone to throwing everything out at the drop of a clothespin, and constantly moody without a steady influx of Starbucks. Sometimes it seems to me like the billion-dollar fashion industry is being run by people with the constitution and temperament of naughty toddlers, Xanaxed to their eyeballs, and in charge of deciding how fat the world will feel this month.

But then at a casting like this one, high above Manhattan in a beautiful atelier, someone rakes me with their gaze and I crave their approval. It's amazing how fast civilization vanishes when you are hungry. How quickly everything dark and grabby in me comes out to play. I look around the room wanting to tell these girls, these beautiful, beautiful girls, to leave. Get out! I want this more, I need it more. The money, God. The recognition, a way to prove my worth. I deserve this more. I will work long past exhaustion. Just give it to me. *Please.*

I don't get it. Minutes later, fuming my way down Thirty-forth Street, I hang my head, angry with myself. I must be doing something wrong, maybe it's my wavy hair, or I'm not emaciated enough. . . . Of course it probably went to that lovely Eastern European girl, with the face like a painting and the sweet shy smile. The bitch.

I SENSE SOMETHING is wrong before I turn the motel corner, before I see my gaping door. The harridan from the front desk is hauling my suitcase out, looking smug. She starts to speak but I rush past, dropping to my stomach to search under the bed, flinging open the door to the bathroom.

Empty.

Tigger is gone.

I stand by the roadside. I've had nightmares about this moment: kicked out of my room, no money for another night. But even in the nightmare, he was still with me. Tigger must have bolted for the thicket of trees behind the motel as soon as the manager stomped into our room. He must have learned it from me, to never trust strangers.

The fever starts the very next night. I feel it, along with stiffness, as I wake on a hard chair in the Journal Square bus terminal coffee shop. A cold almost-empty cup of tea sits on the table in front of me. Gradually returning to consciousness, I take stock of the situation. My shoulder bag is still clutched on my lap, the strap wound tight around my arm. Yesterday, I dropped my suitcase in a cheap storage-compartment complex along the highway and spent the afternoon looking for Tigger. Like many things lately, it was a resounding failure. In two days, the only safe place I've thought of to spend the night is here, under the fluorescents of the station cafeteria. For a long time, I stare at the Lipton tea and the Formica table, my feverish brain repeating over and over the promise from my first day. *Things will be different here. I will be different.*

Standing, I walk past the cops in the bus station, feeling them watching me with concern, and out into the rainy night. This is one of the worst areas of New Jersey and I'm homeless, without enough money to rent a room. Warm raindrops mingle with the humidity, slick on my skin. In the corners, dimly lit by sputtering neon signs, eyes follow me, the druggies, the pimps. *Just try,* I dare them with every angry step. Just try.

I wait for a bus. It drops me at the wooded area just beyond the motel

and I press into the trees, rain plastering my shirt to my skin. "Tigger!"
I venture further into the darkness, smelling earth and decay, shoving
branches aside as they cut at my skin. "Tigger!!" An hour later, I'm burning
with fever and have to acknowledge how impossible this is. It's been days.
He could be anywhere. More likely, he is dead. A sob catches in my throat
and I feel like hitting out at the darkness, at the unfairness of it all.

The leaves rustle and my head snaps up hopefully.

A squirrel.

Watching it hop past, I wipe my face roughly and trace my way back
through the trees. On the sidewalk, my flip-flops squish slowly down the
hill, my hands buried in my pockets. The lights of the highway burger joint
sway in the distance, and I realize how weak I am.

Further ahead, I see a solitary hooker, the only girl out along the highway on a night like this—

Meow.

I stop, scared to look. To have the hope taken away.

Meow, meow!

Tigger crashes through the bushes and limps toward me, favoring his
left front paw, a vivid scar across his white nose. I sink to my bare knees,
reaching out. As rain splatters down around us, we sit on the curb, him
purring loudly on my lap. I rest my forehead against his and Tigger gives
a long, contented sigh. For a minute, we are still and then instinct takes
over. With a speed that surprises me, I'm on my feet, jogging down the
hill, Tigger clutched tightly in my arms. I run along the highway, no longer
tired, no longer feeling anything except the urge to get us safe.

We arrive at the imposing gate to the storage place, whipped by the
wind as the storm gathers force. I type my code into the panel beside it. The
light flashes red. I try again, fingers unsteady, focusing on each number,
please open.

Nothing. It must be broken. I scan the darkness before setting Tigger
down in my shoulder bag, and pushing it through the bars of the gate.
Grabbing hold of the slippery metal, I start to climb. Near the top I lose
my grip, but manage to wriggle forward until gravity takes over and I fall

on the other side of the fence, smacking my tailbone. Lifting my bag with Tigger, I run unsteadily for the building.

Inside the dry blackness, rain lashes against the windows of the corridor. I strip naked in our storage compartment, water dripping rhythmically from my hair, and pull on a dry sweatshirt and shorts. Still shivering, I sit on the concrete floor and hold Tigger in my arms. We're cut, bleeding, sick, and my parents' cell phone isn't working—probably out of money. Of course I'm terrified, of course I haven't got a plan, but I've got him back. The warmth of him against my chest fills me with an irrational happiness. *This isn't over.* We've still got a shot.

33: New York City, age 17

SIX MONTHS LATER, a maze of buses and subways rumble beneath me as I lean against a sink in the Port Authority bathroom. Got to get a move on, can't miss a casting. I glare at myself in the mirror. *Focus, Bhajan.* The woman next to me, who I recognize as an addict, washes her hands carefully. It's a kind of education I'm getting; by now I can even tell what kind of drugs people are on.

I've been landing jobs lately, not national campaigns, but enough to rent us a little place in a rough Jersey area. Each morning I wake in our apartment, Tigger nestled against my cheek. A twin mattress on the floor is the only furniture I've bought, and when I stretch my arms out they brush the walls, but to me this place is an oasis. Never again will I take a door I can close and lock for granted.

Of course the heating system doesn't work, so we sleep under a pile of blankets and my winter coat; but my hollow-cheeked look, collar bone protruding like a knife, is apparently quite fetching to designers. As a girl model from Moscow sighed at a casting, "All they want is for us to look as skinny as possible without dying."

Most of my bookings, I find, come when they need a girl who looks innocent, waiflike, and uncorrupted. The irony of it all would make me laugh, if I wasn't coughing. Another fit shakes my body and I grab the edge of the long counter, my mouth strangely warm. Leaning forward, I spit into the bathroom sink, and recoil. My blood is vivid red against the white basin.

"Giiiiiirl, you're coughing up blood."

The woman at my side shakes her head. "That's not a good sign, I'm tellin' ya."

I look at her in the mirror and catch myself smiling tiredly, teeth outlined in red. Because when a crack addict starts worrying about you, you've got to admit things aren't turning out the way you hoped.

The most important thing, I've decided, is to keep up a positive front. When my parents phone, I hide the loneliness that intensifies as Christmas decorations sparkle in windows and people converge on the city to shop. I resent these smiling families, blocking my way with their overflowing shopping bags. Honestly, I prefer not to have my solitude shoved in my face like this. It's much better left in some recess of my brain, studiously ignored and unacknowledged; like a nineteenth-century bastard love child.

By the time spring arrives, I'm used to all of it: the loneliness. The city. The runways. The hunger. When my parents come to stay, it's a relief at first, but I quickly remember what I did not miss: the awful pressure of watching my father slowly break my mother's spirit, belittling her until she hardly speaks, even to me. I find myself leaving my apartment earlier every morning, trying to escape the feeling of suffocation while somehow still wanting to crawl between them and forget the world.

Fortunately, my bronchitis eases as the weather turns, but I force myself to stay as skinny as I was at my sickest. I cannot give them an excuse to get rid of me. The head of the agency likes to pop out at random moments with a tape measure, and once you have attained such a tiny waist . . . well, there's no going back in the modeling industry, either. Even though I have more work now, more money, I have never been more hungry.

During the day, Dad sometimes comes into the city between my castings and jobs to boost my morale, assuring me these nincompoops don't know what they are talking about. We walk across town, his confidence drawing looks. Suddenly, a wave of dizziness comes out of nowhere, rushing up into my head. Leaning against a slash of graffiti, I wait for the world to stabilize.

"What's wrong?" Concerned, he guides me to the stone steps of a building where I sit unsteadily, knees shaking. "Tell me."

"I'm hungry." Putting my head in my hands, I start to cry.

We end up in a little corner diner, sitting side by side in a booth, so reminiscent of the breakfasts we used to have. The sense of loss is made stronger by how old I feel now. A big glass of milk and a slice of blueberry pie appear in front of me; my father's arm rests around my shoulders.

"Tell me what I can do," he says simply, and I look away, feeling choked. There is so much I need it seems impossible, a list with no beginning.

"I'm so tired."

"You don't have to do all these things. Stop modeling. I'll take care of you. I don't care if you want to do nothing for the rest of your life."

Hesitantly, I start to eat, my concave stomach coming alive with a grateful rumble, blueberry filling sticking to the roof of my mouth. His words soothe me and I let them. But it isn't true. Quitting has never been an option, and even less so now. I no longer trust him to be able to pull us out. And yet, I still crave his reassurance. The mess we are in is so convoluted, the shadows that chase us, the new identities we must buy to be safe, those underworld contacts he is so good at finding and managing. I need him. I just have to find a way to supply the money.

My feeling of desperate urgency returns, but I try to cling to this moment. Slowly, I start on a second piece of pie and close my eyes. When I'm out there, fighting for every inch, this memory—his arm warming my tired shoulders—will be something to carry within. Blueberry pie with Dad.

I HAVE NO idea exactly what to do, so I do what I'm supposed to, what the agency advises. I go on every casting, arrive early for each job, and when the day is over—the other part of our job begins. It's important to be on the scene, to be seen. You never know who you'll meet. Who will single you out.

For a while it puzzles me, the way it's so difficult to make doors open during the day—but after dark, velvet ropes just fall away. I have to budget a sandwich for lunch but at night the top restaurants, the most exclusive clubs pay to get us inside. An industry of model-wranglers, people hired to deliver us in groups of five or more, thrives. Most models don't come from much, and so it feels nice. To finally have some power, to hop in the back of a wrangler's Cadillac SUV, my bare legs tangling with the other girls', and to be able to walk in wherever we want, all of us under eighteen, short skirts, stilettos, a smile to the doorman.

It isn't until the police crack down on underage partying in the city that I realize exactly what role we've been playing in the scene. What we're really doing while we stand around thinking we're about to be discovered.

The top club owners band together in the press, promising to keep teenagers out. Except, they still let us straight through the lines, through the back and to the VIP area, making sure we have free champagne, free vodka, free everything. Because when a table reservation in their club costs thousands, they have to give rich men a reason to pay. I only visited Sea World once, but it was clear you need bait for the show to go on. The most powerful men of New York are Shamu, and we're the anchovies.

But tonight, I'm hoping it will be different. My friend Elena has snagged us an invite to a dinner party, the kind with actual movers and shakers, not just sixteen-year-old models and aging millionaires. I think of her as my friend, but really we are more like occasional allies. A street-smart Russian, she knows two blonde models are more powerful infiltrators than one.

I walk through the penthouse door into an apartment that looks like a magazine cutout. Everyone is perfectly poised, dressed in asymmetrical black, most wearing statement glasses that have nothing to do with correcting their eyesight. The only unplanned movement comes from a little curly-haired boy who weaves confidently through the adults.

Elena catches my eye and winks discreetly; she is sensing connections to be made in this room, while I'm still trying to avoid tripping on the designer rug. Somehow, I end up talking to a fellow in what must be a five-thousand-dollar suit and his friend who's seen all the movies but never read the book. "Welcome to New York," Nick the Suit chuckles good-naturedly. "This isn't going to be the comfortable easy life you're used to, walking around like 'la la la.'"

I must look baffled because he continues, gathering steam.

"I can tell just from the way you look, all sweet and innocent, that you haven't been through anything yet. Well, get ready, because this city will eat you alive."

There it is: the ever-seductive lie of modeling. With all the bright lights, you think you're being seen, but in the end you're just a blank canvas for people to project their fantasies onto.

His words become background noise, and I find myself focusing on a man across the room. Strong-looking, steady eyes, not trying to please anyone, just being himself. I feel a pull.

Nick is asking what I'm doing later. This seems to be a very New York technique: Rake someone over the coals and then invite them out for drinks. I want so badly to hit him.

Escaping out onto the deserted windy terrace, I lay my hands flat on the stone balustrade. Looking back inside, I can glimpse Elena, the center of an admiring semicircle of men. I lean forward instead and focus on the snaking lights of traffic far below.

"I know you're just playing hard to get." A voice sounds in the dark behind me. Someone's hand grabs my arm, spinning me around, and I'm facing Nick. Before I can react, the hard press of his mouth is on my lips. It is difficult to breathe and I lose balance, stumbling back. My body is pressed against the railing when I manage to regain my footing and swerve fast, rushing back inside, through all the people, and down a hallway. My hand finds a doorknob, twists, and I blunder into a bedroom.

The self-assured man who caught my attention in the middle of the party is here, leaning back against the pillows, reading a picture book to the curly-haired little boy. This must be his apartment, his child. I stop in place. He raises his handsome tanned face and we stare at each other for a moment. Slowly, I become aware of the way he's looking at me, and it makes my stomach sink. His arm remains around the shoulders of the boy, almost as if guarding him from this girl in stilettos and a short skirt, her ambitious eyes outlined in black.

"Um," I stammer awkwardly. "I was looking for the bathroom."

"Last door on the left." He says dismissively and goes back to the book.

I wobble down the hall in my too-high heels and lock the bathroom door behind me. With liquid soap I start to wash the makeup off, lavender bubbles carrying it down the drain. At once my face looks younger and less alluring. Eyes clear instead of smoky, freckles sprinkled across my nose, the pimple on my forehead now obvious. I'm just a girl, with tired eyes and skin rubbed pink by the towel. But I like myself better.

Out on the street I walk fast, heels in my bag, flip-flops back on my feet. I pass the now-familiar clubs of the meatpacking district, low thudding coming from inside, lines snaking around the block. All those people inside, rebreathing the same air and mentally critiquing each other. It's hell; and there's a three-hour line to get in.

I thought if I got away from the clubs, to the kind of parties you're supposed to be at, that I would fit in. But it's just a different kind of club. The despair takes hold, heavy in my chest, more real than any of the passing lights. It isn't until I am on a nearly empty bus back in Jersey, that my vision blurs with tears and I realize—*that was my first kiss.*

I let myself cry through the endless tunnel. When I'm rushing from one appointment to another, or strutting the runway with a spotlight following my every step, it's easier to pretend that I'm on the right track. But here, slumped in a worn-out seat, reality is no longer something I'm able to push aside. It feels like I am being punished for some mistake, and I can't figure out what it is, what I've done.

The bus winds its way through familiar streets, and I stare out the window, not really seeing anything. Gradually, in my mind, a memory starts to take form. Over a decade old, yet clear as a snapshot . . . a little girl and her father, on the couch of an apartment, nighttime outside the endless windows and the Sydney Opera house aglow. . . . Our two faces were lit by rising stock prices scrolling across the television screen, and I asked him apprehensively if we could stay in Australia, if things could just remain the same. Thirteen years ago, he took a sip of tea and told me no matter how frightened I ever feel, my actions must always be bold. Thirteen years ago, he told me the one position I should never operate from.

But it's exactly what I've been doing here. I've been operating from a position of fear. For more than a year, I have tried to mold myself into the world of modeling. I've played by other peoples' rules—doing what I'm told, hoping to be rewarded for being a good worker. *Think, Bhajan*—I order myself. Do what you've been taught. *Detach. Detach, and go up.* Float up until New York and everything here is Lego size. Until you can see.

Because if I strip it all away, cold as ice, I'm not more beautiful than any other girl they've selected to be here. In fact, most probably outshine me. Why should I hang around, hoping to be noticed, doing the same thing as hundreds of others, and expect a better result? I've been playing one card only: my looks. And now I'm upset because all people see are my looks.

I step off the bus, my legs still shaky, frowning at an idea that is beginning to emerge. Inside my apartment, I open the window so I can climb out, tears dry now. Tigger and I sit on the rusty fire escape, a folded blanket beneath us, my face tilted up to where the stars would be if you could see them on city midnights. He steps carefully onto my lap, making sure not to scratch, and curls so I can rest my hand on his soft, white tummy.

It's taken me seventeen years to understand what's causing this frustration, this burning in my core. In reality, it doesn't have a thing to do with not fitting in, or being different. By now, I'm cool with that. What's really pissing me off, is that no one seems to realize *how* different I am! Here, they box me in as young and stupid, just a body to dress and undress like a mannequin. But they are wrong—and not just about me, but the other models I meet at castings. We're teenagers on our own, tackling a city that frightens most adults, and an industry without rules. None of us have any insurance, a fixed salary, or much of a backup plan. But we've got a story worth hearing.

It's just that, until now, no one has told it. "I've had a revelation tonight, Tigger," I declare. He yawns, and I manage to smile at his sweet face. "I'm serious," I tickle him behind the ears until he squirms. "Now you're listening. Well, from now on, you and me, we're going to branch out in our career."

In the night, a rap song thuds from the corner bar, and I wonder how much time we will spend like this. The two of us, outside our window in the hood, him watching me through half-closed sleepy eyes, as I look up at the darkness. Dreaming on a fire escape.

34: New York City, age 21

"WELCOME TO *GOOD Morning America*. . . Cheryl Diamond came to New York with a dream, and in six short years she has become one of the hottest faces in the modeling business."

Is my stomach sticking out?

"Now her book, *Model*, has just been published by Simon & Schuster."

Cameras surround us; the studio seems too large for just two chairs facing each other. I suppose I should be feeling something big now, but it doesn't seem real. After working in isolation for so long, it's confusing to be around this many people, all this *activity*.

It's been four years since I held Tigger on our fire escape, no parties or friends. I think of all times I wrote through the night, the cold-calls to book agents, all the turn-downs. No one believed my project was worthwhile. None of the people who asked what I was doing, hunched over a notebook in Starbucks between shoots and castings. Except two people. Somehow, despite all the running, and all we've had to leave behind, one thing about my parents never seems to change. They still believe in me. Mom typed up the contents of every notebook while I kept writing; Dad combed through lists of New York's best literary agents.

In the TV studio, a kind of floating sensation spreads through me. One of the cameras pivots toward me, and that's when the nerves hit, in the instant before it all becomes real. "Welcome, Cheryl."

"Thank you." The lights are blinding, but I'm remembering what this was all about. *Everyone looks at models, but no one really sees.* Through the nervousness, I start to smile, and it's genuine. Because this is for us—the ones who were supposed to be eaten alive.

Interview over, I walk out into the early morning traffic of Times Square and wobble in my high heels, afraid of . . . something. Why does this always happen? When the cameras switch off, when I have a moment where I'm not pushing forward, a deep feeling of unease creeps in. It's always hovering close, and that's why I push myself so hard; I will not be like my father leaving things to chance, taking them for granted. We need cash, we need safety. I've got to make even more money, *I've got to, I've got to*.

The amount required to pull us out staggers me. But it's the only solution. I have to buy new passports for all of us, since Chiara blew our identities in Virginia. With each passing year, with increased security checks, it becomes almost impossible to live without a valid ID. It's essential, as well as having a social security number. I'm adept at deflecting questions, but I live in constant fear of being found out. In order to collect the money for my book, I had to have an acquaintance set up an LLC. Even though the money is mine, it's someone else's name on the account. I withdraw it gradually in cash with the ATM card, realizing I don't really have control over my own finances. The money could be transferred away any day and I would be unable to complain. Living off the grid used to sound fun, before I grew up, before I realized it meant having no rights.

We can't manage on the flimsy thirty-dollar fake ID I bought on my way to New York years ago. Good fake documents, the kind you can build on, cost five times as much now. Thirty thousand for me and my parents. Then I'll need to make enough money to rent my parents separate apartments, to save my mom from the way he belittles her daily, calling her stupid, worthless. Now that we all live together in Manhattan, I'm forced to watch it every day, and it drains me; no wonder she hardly speaks anymore. Often I feel a burning impatience. Why doesn't she fight back? This is the woman who challenged fate, who fought so hard to be free. When did she lose sight of her courage?

But ever since that night when I was thirteen, when we drove home to a dark house—I can still hear her desperate wail—she's never been the same. We've been making small talk for almost a decade. I should reach out to her more, should go into her room at the end of my day and tell her about it. But I find, after I've smiled all day, planned the smart thing to say, eaten less than I need, done all I have to, there is just nothing left. I hardly communicate with myself anymore. Even in the book I wrote, I focused only on my years as a model, showing the best of my parents and leaving out all the rest. Just like I do in my own head. I cannot bear to face anything else, because sometimes I still believe we can stitch ourselves back together.

Yet with each good review of *Model*, with each new interview, my underlying fear intensifies. Because what if everything I've worked so methodically to build gets taken away again?

My book publicity tour is dizzying as I give interviews and relentlessly chase more. The trendy Bungalow 8, a place I was only let in as an accessory before, has been reserved for my launch party. In a $20,000 couture dress, the designer who lent it standing beside me, I scan the room and am hit with a realization: The only people I know are the ones I'm doing business with. My publisher, the press. I don't have any close friends—there was never the time; and no boyfriend—there was never the trust. I didn't dare invite my parents. The odds were too high that my dad would mistreat my mother in public, that my whole sordid past would become apparent in their deeply unsettling interactions.

I used to watch people my age while I was writing—university students grouped around a café table, chatting and joking as I worked—and it felt like I was getting ahead of the game, accomplishing something while they wasted time socializing. Now, alone in a room full of people, I wonder if I got it wrong.

Days later, my publisher calls to say they've landed a deal to jointly promote my book with Macy's and are scheduling an event. I've already agreed, when they tell me the last detail. The event will be held in Virginia, near D.C. Even as I hang up the phone, I feel myself shutting down. It's been years since I was in our former home city—since everything shattered. An old motto echoes in my mind. *Never, never go back.*

On the train, I watch Manhattan fade away and try not to remember anything that came before. A driver picks me up from the station in Washington, D.C., and I stare at my phone as the scenery relentlessly scrolls by. I don't even have to look up. Everything about this area is written in my memory: the diner where Dad and I always went for breakfast, the pizza place my brother liked so much . . . and then I'm standing in the same Macy's I used to prowl with Sandra, my best friend, when we were thirteen, gossiping about boys and all our dreams. The only difference is that now I'm six inches taller, named something else, staring at myself on posters of my book, and so, so terribly tired. I feel like a straggler from a war no one else knows about.

I'm on stage when I begin to feel feverish, the audience swimming in front of me. Struggling to stay coherent, I finish the talk and sign my books, the pen unsteady. When I've finally handed the last one back, smile fixed on my face, I don't call a cab but walk out into the night, needing air.

Across the highway I can see the lights of my hotel, and dazed, almost hypnotized, I start toward them. Past the high-end stores of Tysons Galleria, where Frank and I went once, our baseball caps on backward. He was right, wasn't he? Even with all I've done, this relentless campaign of accomplishment, of making my parents proud, I never was able to piece anything back together. Cars shoot by, their lights leaving trails of shimmering amber in the darkness. I blink to clear my vision.

Bracing a hand on the wall of the hotel, I try to gather my strength, then I'm through the revolving door, a feeble smile to the concierge. I can handle this. Can't cancel tomorrow's interviews. *I have to keep going, I've got to—*

As I double-lock the door to my room, my body starts to shake uncontrollably and I sag against the wall until I'm sitting on the carpet, head heavy and burning in my hands. No matter how I try to push the memories away, they're here, insistent. A dark house, my mother's cry. I'm staring at the blank wall of the hotel room, unable to stand, when a terrible thought occurs to me. What if you can't outmaneuver the truth? What if you can't run forever?

35: New York City, age 22

IT'S BEEN ALMOST a year now. Twelve months in my bedroom, too weak to walk a few feet to the living room. I kept thinking this was just a virus, that I would wake up one day, like when I was a kid, and be all better. Even as thirty pounds dropped away from my already slim frame, even as I couldn't sleep from the constant abdominal pain, I was sure my body would make one of its fast recoveries.

But I no longer believe that. Whatever this is has invaded my nervous system, causing me to bleed internally, raising bruises on my legs and locking my left arm in place. It hangs useless now in a sling made from one of my flowered summer scarves. The one that used to float behind me as I rushed along hot sidewalks, stilettos clicking; chin high, dodging taxicabs and discouragement on my way to the next casting.

When I went down to D.C. I was fine, I felt physically invincible. And now I can't walk more than a few steps before collapsing. No one in the publishing or modeling industry knows the truth—Dad thinks it's best this way, lest they discard me forever. But even we don't know what's happening. The hospital tests needed to make a diagnosis are astronomical. All the money I saved, my hope to pull us out, is dwindling with each month that I lie here, with each time I break down and visit a doctor who tells me they can't begin treatment until I'm tested in a hospital. Of course, we have no health insurance.

Finally, I agree with Mom to schedule the most important test, a colonoscopy. I've been bedridden for a year, trying to hold on and save money, but it frightens me to go without treatment any longer. The doctor says she can halve the price if I agree to undergo the procedure without anesthesia. So Dad carries me to the taxi, watching from the sidewalk as we pull away. I keep my eyes on my father in the rearview mirror, remembering him saying this is unnecessary, that I should be strong enough to just snap out of it. That I should write another book fast, before everyone forgets about me. In the backseat, Mom places her hand hesitantly on mine.

When I blink my eyes open, unfamiliar sounds of the hospital mingle with the scent of alcohol and disinfectant. "What happened?" I whisper.

"You went into shock," a woman in a white coat says matter-of-factly. I notice there are quite a few nurses grouped around my bed. All I can remember is being wheeled into the examination room, the hulking coiled machines, and then agony. Here's the thing with anesthesia: Apparently, like insurance, you really need it.

I'm still trembling when they tell me the diagnosis. Crohn's disease. A severe auto-immune disorder. If not genetic, it can be brought on by extreme tension and post-traumatic stress. The doctors warn that due to the amount of weight I've lost in this year without treatment, I'm currently at risk of dying from heart failure. Their words are too much; I turn my head away on the pillow. It can't be happening. Not to me. I don't have *time* for this. I'm twenty-two years old when they tell me there is no cure.

LYING IN MY room later, I think. It's all I can do without medical assistance. I stare down at my limbs. In all my life, I don't think I've ever really noticed my body before. I only considered what it could do for me. How high it could fly as a gymnast, the jobs it could book as a model. It was simply the vehicle that transported my mind toward the goal. And now, when I look down at the skeleton that is me, I've got to admit I lived my whole life without ever appreciating my body; I've just been using it.

As soon as I start on the prescribed cortical-steroid therapy, my system rejects it, the agony in my stomach worsening and my long blonde hair falling out in thick clumps. In bed, Tigger rests his forehead against my cheek, sometimes drawing back to watch me. I lie as still as possible because I have a new fear. For the first time, I'm terrified of myself. They say auto-immune diseases are your own body attacking itself. It seems to me like the ultimate self-sabotage. Like giving up in the middle of a race, and I cannot understand why this is happening to me, the one who always strove for the finish line. But now, I'm in such a fix. . . . How do you outlast yourself? How do you fight against yourself and win?

While my mother spends her time researching Crohn's therapies and teaching French to make extra money, I start to sense Dad sliding away. It's subtle at first, the change. Yet the more time that passes, the longer my body rejects treatment, the more I notice it. He still carries me to the living room so I can look out the window. Still says consoling things. But he's losing interest. He was never one to repair something when it malfunctioned; you buy new or move on. I tell myself I'm imagining it, letting my mind run away with me, but I catch him watching me with a strange, distant bewilderment. As if he can't understand what happened to his champion.

"CAN YOU REMEMBER having a traumatic experience in your childhood?" The specialist's brown eyes are sympathetic as he looks at me across his immaculate desk.

My mother and I stare back at him. Maybe the most unexpected side effect of my illness is that Mom has come alive. Her research found this man; her daily vigil in his waiting room helped me jump the four-month wait list. She scraped the hefty fee together and now she sits by my side. Watching her over the last months, I glimpse the woman who, all those years ago, refused to accept defeat.

I should be grateful for her, just as I should be annoyed with my father who is at home on the couch, thinking we are wasting money on something that will pass if I strengthen my mind.

But instead, it's her I'm often irritated with. Why did it take me almost dying for her to realize I'm alive?

"Hmm?" I say, buying time.

"A shocking or traumatic event," the Crohn's specialist repeats, "something that would have stressed you deeply."

Which one? I feel a crazy laugh building inside and can sense them both watching me. I struggle to keep it at a chuckle, slumped in the chair, a pile of bones. "No. No, I'm fine."

He folds his hands and leans forward, frowning. "Cheryl, you weigh ninety-eight pounds when you should be at least one forty, and you had to be wheeled in here, so you're not fine. Tell me what you're feeling."

I nod, gathering myself. "My body doesn't work anymore," I say finally. "I can't do anything."

He looks at me in confusion, and I begin to understand that I don't know how to express my pain—this terrible hurt within. I just don't have the vocabulary. All I seem to know, deep inside, is that if I ask for help I'll be seen as weak, and people will leave me.

I THOUGHT I had succeeded in evading the doctor's questions, but the alternative medication he prescribes me, low dose Naltrexone, is often used to treat soldiers returning from war with post-traumatic stress disorder. Two weeks later, I notice I can lift a glass of water without effort. Then slowly, I'm able to eat small portions of food.

The doctor's advice is clear, disturbingly so. Since there is no cure for Crohn's, the best to hope for is that it could go into remission. I'll need time, perhaps years, to slowly build strength back up, strict medical supervision, and a stress-free environment. I don't tell him all three are impossible.

HOPING THAT SOME link to my past, to the good memories, will help me heal, Mom calls our former storage place in Germany. It's silly, of course. All our belongings are certainly gone by now; we haven't paid the rent for years. But all of a sudden she's doing things of her own accord; its disorienting, and increasingly annoying. It feels like she's blinking awake, fumbling to put things right, when it's already far too late. Mom buys an international calling card, hoping the storage people may have spared our family photos. She gets through. The owner explains that, after a decade of unpaid bills, he's auctioned off all our clothes and books. But, incredibly, he's saved the few photos we had, inside a drawer in his office. "You looked like a nice family," he says, and then mails them to us free of charge.

Sitting alone, crossed-legged on the floor of my bedroom, I tear open the package and look at the beat-up shoebox for a long time. I wonder if I should even touch it. Slowly, taking a breath, I open the lid.

It's full of Fujifilm prints, the envelopes yellowing at the edges. I trace the logo of *Foto-Fabrik*, its Heidelberg address still familiar. The little print shop on the same street where we lived, right down from my favorite bakery. I remember going into the place with Mom, munching on apple bread while she handed over piles of negatives from her camera. Years of memories that we'd never taken the time to print.

Cautiously, I open the first envelope. The colors are startlingly vivid. I guess I was unconsciously expecting the photos to be battered or singed from one of our escapes. But I'm staring down at a little girl, sun-screen smeared across her freckled nose, wearing a too-big baseball cap and a brilliant grin. Every photo album we had was lost or incinerated long ago. This is the first time, as an adult, that I've ever seen myself as a child.

Quickly, I open another envelope, sifting through the pictures, my fingers clumsy and unsteady. My parents on our big couch in South Africa, his beard still long and wild, her smile unstoppable. Dad and me on a blueberry farm, one red bucket each, my little body leaning against his, our lips blue from getting the most bang for our buck. Then suddenly, I am looking at my siblings again, sixteen years ago. The three of us leaping toward the camera, outside summer swimming practice, wearing our team Marlin shirts, back in Vancouver.

The afternoon light outside my window has turned to pink by the time I take out every envelope, stacking them all in front of me. Some papers fall out and I brush them aside. What disturbs me most about the photos—the person I have the most trouble truly remembering—is myself. The structure of my face has remained unchanged, I am obviously the same person as this child, but she seems so far away. Holding my six-year-old self in the palm of my hand, I cringe at the thought of all that is about to happen to her

I close my eyes against the tears. The worst hurt isn't my illness, this pain in my body—it's the feeling that I've failed. In one way or another, they all left me. I tried so hard to earn their love, to be brave, clever, beautiful, fearless enough. And I've fallen short. It crushes me in a way no physical pain ever could. Because it comes from within, from the people who should be biologically programmed to hold me close. Is there something about this girl—I search my own young face—is there something I've been doing to draw all this to me? Chiara, the one I try never to think about. Mom, who drifted away, becoming a responsibility rather than a mother. Frank, who took my love and trust and then did something, again and again, that left me convinced I was forever tainted. And my father. I don't even know how to think of him. Because I love him still. Because he was my hero. But also because the ideals he raised me with, those mantras in India of truth and loyalty, are what I've built my very identity around. Losing my father—or, really, acknowledging that he has lost interest in me—would feel like the death of myself.

I cry silently, my fingers digging into the carpet, the images a jumble in front of me. Our faces intermingled, all the places, all the things we would end up leaving behind. Why was it all necessary? Why did my father drive us all so hard, why did he pit us against each other? He'd said it was because my grandfather and Interpol were chasing us. But was it because he'd stolen all that money, or was it . . . because it's easier to make a family do what you want when they are terrified?

The instant the thought occurs, I flinch, remembering to never question my father's actions. But when I try to comprehend why, all I come up with is that I'm not allowed. That it is disloyal. Confusion overwhelms me so strongly that it takes several minutes before I look closely at the faded pieces of paper scattered on the floor, so ordinary among all the bright colors. I unfold them.

It can't be.

I am holding my New Zealand birth certificate and my certificate of Brazilian citizenship, issued by the embassy. These were supposed to have been lost years ago, impossible to replicate, and the only real proof of my existence. We were all certain they'd been misplaced in one of our hasty escapes. Further down in the box are my parents' fake Brazilian birth certificates.

I wonder if this means we could all get our original Brazilian passports reissued. The first ones Our Friend crafted, the ones with a backstory that can actually hold up. Does this mean we wouldn't have to buy brand new documents? I've never been allowed a say in our passport situation; all I understand is that they are expensive and we need them. But even though I have no idea what to do, I know these worn pieces of paper are valuable.

I go to my mother's door. Lifting my hand, I knock quietly. And then I tell her. Only her.

36: New York City, age 22

Dad wants to jumpstart the process and buy a new passport from Our Friend, just one, as a test. It's been over a decade since they did business with Our Friend—we need to know if she's still got the connections to produce solid documents. He has no idea that I've found our old ones.

On the couch, I nod as he speaks; it seems logical. But after years of using my savings to pay the bills, there's not much money left. I keep it in cash, of course, in a worn copy of my favorite book, *Papillion*. Even though we only dip into the pages for necessities—rent, food and when I need to see a doctor—there are just ten thousand dollars remaining. We counted it a few days ago, and it will have to last us until I can get back on my feet. Spending it all on a gamble seems too risky. . . . I'm still puzzling on how to get us extra cash when Mom, standing quietly by the window, asks a question.

"Which document?"

He turns to her, annoyed. "Don't be stupid. A passport, obviously."

"Yes, but for Bhajan, right? Hers will be the first."

"No. We'll try mine, it's safer that way. We shouldn't expose her."

Watching them, I feel unequipped to have an opinion. I was so young the last time we bought papers, and I've been too busy surviving since then. The complexity of our situation always makes my head ache.

They are staring each other down. "Documents are the priority, with all the increased checks, we can't slip notice much longer," my father says.

"I think doctors are the priority. Even before Bhajan's passport." Mom's holding her ground, but her hands are already fidgeting. Then in a rush, she tells him about what I found mixed in with our old photographs: Our documents. Those things he's obsessed over. And the fact that we may, all of us, be able to walk into a Brazilian embassy and have fresh passports issued from those birth certificates.

He stands, "Give them to me."

She looks up at him, I see how scared she is, and I regret ever finding the papers. I should have told him right away, so he wouldn't be upset. Why did I even keep a secret from him? It seems silly now, like playing with fire.

"I'm holding onto them," she says.

My father and I are so shocked that we are united, staring at this small woman in disbelief.

"When Bhajan has her passport you can have whatever you want. Nothing until then." She turns and goes into her room, locking the door.

I can hardly believe it. She simply ignores him, even when he screams, pounding her door, the wood shaking. Sitting on the couch, I clutch my knees, feeling childlike, everything more frightening and loud because I'm too unwell to even think properly. But the fact that he backs down within a few days surprises me more. He's never done it before.

37: Florida, age 23

IT ALL COMES undone, once and for all, in a little beach town, with a sky so clear it makes you squint, sunburned tourists, and a string of motels scattered along the road an hour north of Miami. It's where people who can't afford Miami Beach come, and after all the medical expenses, it's where we're at. Starlight Motel, suite 301: two bedrooms, a minikitchen, and me living in the middle of their cold war.

The vacation was his idea and just that word, so out of place in our current lives, gave me hope. He was right; it sounded like exactly what I needed. The beach, the sea, and some time to pull myself together. Some time for all of us to let the stress drop away.

But that's not what's happening. Even though he's tried to wear her down, Mom won't give him the documents, even when he threatens, even when he throws her to the motel floor. In secret, she tells me that I can have them anytime, to just ask, but I don't even want to know where she's hidden the papers. I've been on vacation for less than a week when I start, once again, to bleed internally. I'd like to beg my father to give me a chance to recover, just a few months to *breathe*. But I never seem to be able to say the words; no one has ever found a way to stand up to him.

Mom and I are walking together, along the boardwalk, she slowing her steps to match mine, when she stops abruptly. "You have to find an immigration lawyer."

I frown at her in confusion, "Can't I just go to the embassy and get my passport?" The naiveté in my own voice unsettles me—how little I know about what normal people need to be legitimate. To have a free life. I've just followed my parents around the world while they turned borders into visas.

"You need help to get your passport." Mom says.

"But we have to get yours, too."

"I don't matter."

"Jesus, Mom—"

She glances behind us as if checking for a tail, and I realize she is. Checking for him. "Bhajan. You need a lawyer."

It must be past 2 a.m. when I wake from a nightmare, fear weighing heavily on my chest, and then remember it's all real. The streetlight through my window blinds falls in bars across the white sheets.

Why did I never question anything he did? Growing up in a world without rules or sense, I've clung to my father's laws. They were my religion, and I never wanted to challenge them. I needed one thing, only one, to be unchanging. To be true. But now I sit up slowly, pushing aside the sheets; then I'm standing in the semi-dark, moving silently toward my still-unpacked suitcase. Lifting the lid, I search through my clothes until I'm holding *Papillion*. I open it to the familiar page and breathe deeply. *Stay calm.* I rifle through the book, though every page, turning it upside down.

It's gone. All of it.

I open the bedroom door, my hands damp with sweat, and walk carefully into the circle of lamplight he's reading by. Dad lowers his book, eyes assessing me. My voice, when I manage to summon it, is quiet.

"Why did you take my money?"

"I'm keeping it safe," he shrugs. "When I get my passport, maybe you can have it back."

"I don't understand."

His head moves slowly, angling to one side. "Understand what?

"Everything. All of it. . . " Desperately, I try to swallow. "Why are you so cruel to Mom? Why—?"

"Stop now! Be very careful what you say." His expression is like ice, body powerful and tense.

But I've been cautious for so long and now it's all spilling out, the tears mixed with words, my chest heaving. "Nothing was ever good enough, nothing I did ever really seemed enough, nothing any of us did. I try so *hard*, so hard, to make you love me—"

"You're hysterical."

"I'm *not*. Why do you always say that when someone speaks up? When they don't do exactly as you say? You're *wrong*." There it is, the forbidden word. But filled with anguish, I don't care.

"Look at yourself." His mouth twists. "Just look."

I can imagine the picture I make, stick-thin, face red and blotchy, barely able to stand in just an oversize T-shirt. But I'm not ashamed.

"Look at yourself, Dad." I rest my hands on the empty sofa chair, trying to stay upright. He stands, but I continue. "Why does everyone else always have to analyze and correct themselves, but you never do? No one's allowed to look at you."

"Shut up." His voice is a whip in the dim room. "Don't say another word. You're out of your mind, making up wild stories about the past."

"No, she's not."

We both turn. Mom's slight figure is outlined in the doorway of her room. "Don't ever call her crazy."

His face flushes red. "Get out! Shut your door!"

"No." Mom is motionless.

Somehow her presence gives me courage and the anger drops away, until all that's left is the one thing I really want to know. "Do you love me?"

"What are you blabbering about now?"

"I'm not blabbering. I'm not out of my mind."

I am sobbing because I see something in him that breaks my heart: an awful blankness, an absence of any sympathy for this girl, his daughter, begging for his love, for any sign.

"Even after everything, I still love you, Dad. I would run, fight, lie, anything for you both. I don't want to break anything, I want us to work." Letting go of the chair, I feel my hands drop to my side. "All I need to know is, do you love me no matter what?"

It is cold, even in Florida, when you stand in the middle of a room so naked. He frowns as if I should never even have to ask. And I start to breathe again.

"Of course I don't," he says. "It depends on what you do."

WHEN I COME to, my head is ringing from where it hit the wall on the way down. I am acutely aware of every sensation, the tiles cool against my back, my mother cradling my head on her lap. So this is what fainting feels like. I try to move my legs, but like a childhood nightmare, they only pedal slowly, as if underwater.

"Are you trying to kill our daughter?!" I feel the scream vibrate in her body. "Stay away!"

He stops midway across the room, assessing.

Slowly, I struggle to stand. He will never take me seriously lying on the floor, pleading for anything—for a lie.

"Stop this," he says, near me now, and I feel my exhausted head lean automatically against his shoulder.

I can't handle this, we have nowhere to go, I have no one else. Why did I ever come out of my room?

"Forget everything." His voice is strong, strangely calming. "You're dramatizing; of course I love you." The words slip out easily, as if he hasn't had to plan them. "Just forget everything."

TWO DAYS LATER, I go see a lawyer.

Anthony's office could use a coat of paint; books and case files are stacked haphazardly and a fly buzzes in tired circles, settling on my knee. I focus on it. Anything to avoid the way he is looking at me. He stopped taking notes long ago, and now pushes the legal pad to one side, leaning forward. "My God, Cheryl. Do you realize what a difficult situation you are in?"

My fingers press into my thighs. Surely it's not so bad. I have my birth certificate, my certificate of Brazilian citizenship. Can't I just get a real passport now and move on with my life?

"I don't even know where to begin." His eyes fill with sympathy. "You poor girl."

In this little back-street lawyer's office, the only one I can afford, my heart stills. Have I missed something big, while worrying about surviving?

He lays it out. I am illegal in every country. Even though I wasn't born when my parents bought their first fake passports, even though I was a child when they entered the United States illegally, I am an adult now, and at twenty-three, I will be held accountable for it all.

"But I didn't know! I thought . . ." My voice trails off as I realize that I never really thought about my legal situation. It seemed like the least of my problems. Dad always said he was taking care of everything, that I should focus on my career. And I never considered that he might not always be on my side—that I may not want to run forever.

"Okay, let's look at this carefully." Anthony straightens his legal pad, pen in hand.

There are potential traps everywhere. My New Zealand birth certificate is a legally issued document, but my parents' names on it and their Brazilian background are false. If I come forward now, as an adult, and apply for a New Zealand or Brazilian passport, I would knowingly exploit a fake backstory. If I go to the American authorities for help, I'm at risk of arrest or deportation.

"But where would they even deport you to?" He massages his forehead. "You have no base, no home country." Dad always told me he was keeping me safe by keeping me off the grid, but in reality I seem to have no rights and all the responsibility.

My eyes dart around the suffocatingly small office, searching for exits.

"Okay," Anthony lays his hands flat on his desk as if trying to steady his thoughts. "Here's what we'll do. We'll go to the Brazilian embassy in Miami together. My wife is Brazilian, so I speak Portuguese. Maybe she'll even come with us. Then—"

"I don't think I can pay you for all those hours," I blurt.

"Just pay me what you can. Don't even worry about that now." He pushes the thirty-dollar consult fee back to me.

It's strange, isn't it? How clearly you begin to see people when you've got nothing left to give.

THE CAR WINDOWS are wide open, wind teasing my hair from its ponytail. I sit in the backseat, clutching my purse with the certificates, short summer dress revealing the boniness of my legs. Anthony and his wife are driving me to the Brazilian embassy, and the closer we get the more nervous I become. He says it's my only option, to try to get my Brazilian passport, even though my parents aren't really from there. I wanted all the lies to stop, but Anthony says I have to go step by step. I need some form of ID in case I have to move fast. In case—I hardly dare admit it to myself—but in case I need to escape my father.

"You know what annoys me the most?" Anthony raises his voice above the traffic. "You could have had total immunity."

"What?" I lean forward between the seats. With her hands on the wheel, his wife frowns.

"If you had gone to the authorities before your eighteenth birthday, you would have automatically been pardoned and given the right to live and work in America. And you wouldn't even have had to implicate your parents."

I sit back as if pushed.

He turns around. "I bet your father knew it. Your mom probably not, or she was too scared to disobey, but you had the right to be completely legal."

Anthony's wife drops us outside the concrete pillars of the Brazilian Embassy, waving as she drives away.

After hours of waiting—me looking suspiciously out of place, the only blonde in a room of a hundred—my number is finally called and we walk stiffly toward a man in his fifties behind a wall of glass. Anthony gives a heavily edited version of my story in Portuguese while I stay silent.

"Why doesn't she speak Portuguese?" the man asks in accented English.

"Well, she didn't grow up in Brazil."

"Hmm."

I have a feeling this is getting too dangerous. The last photo the Brazilian authorities have of me on file was taken when I was a newborn infant. I could be anyone walking in with this birth certificate.

"Wait here." The man stands.

I track him as he walks into a back office, closing the door. Ordinarily, this would be my cue to blow this joint. My feet want to move, fast, but I force myself to stay. It all has to stop somewhere.

When he returns, he sits down at his desk and looks directly at me for endless seconds. I try not to lower my face under his dark gaze. Abruptly, he switches to English. "I don't know if any of this story is true." He stamps a piece of paper with finality, ending everything. "Take care of the girl," he tells my lawyer, sliding the paper through the opening in the glass and calling the next applicant.

He has approved my passport.

38: Florida, age 24

It's a soft midnight and I sit with my father at a little outdoor beach bar, Jimmy Buffet playing on low. Beyond the boardwalk, the rhythmic sound of waves seem to move in time with my heart. Pulling back and forth, unable to make a decision. I've kept the forbidden lawyer and embassy visit a secret, fearing my father's temper. But despite all that's happened, I don't want to lose him; I can't lose what's left of my family. In the past weeks, as I've waited for my passport to arrive at the lawyer's office, Dad has become unrecognizable, a menace in his eyes that he doesn't bother to hide. Now, watching his profile as he stares out at the dark ocean, I long to reach across the emptiness. Swallowing hard, I touch his hand. "Dad."

Even this, even the way he turns to me, is scary. As if he has anticipated my move, a slight smirk curving his mouth. "I really don't want things to be this way between us," I continue. "All I want is to fix this; how can we do it?"

He regards me blankly for a long moment. "You've got to get serious about your life and succeeding."

"But . . . I am."

"Your mother is holding you back; you've got to leave her."

"Dad, don't—"

"As for your career, you should start paying me a proper percentage and taking my advice. Otherwise you're always going to be a failure."

"But wait," my voice breaks, "I published a book . . . with a major publisher at twenty-one . . ."

He waves a hand dismissively, "That's nothing, Bhajan. You should be much further along by now." Nothing? *Nothing?* All those years, all that work. He leans forward, "Give me thirty percent of your future earnings and let's leave your mother and start over."

My world turns into a still photograph. The waves freeze. What did he say? "What you're asking is insane!" My hands begin to shake, "Can you hear yourself?"

He smiles, his eyes empty, "It's up to you if you want to succeed or not. If you'd like to fail, just keep up this independent act. You'll never be able to write another book, you'll never get healthy without my help."

"Dad, look at me. I *won't* betray my mother. You can't ask that of me."

"Sure you can, you're just being weak. You were always too sentimental and it holds you back."

Abandon my mother with nothing, and give him 30 percent of all my future earnings. So there it is. A cold, hard bargain. A way to earn his approval. Can this be the same man who urged me, when I was just four years old, to never let others lead me? To always, always, think for myself. I stare at the table, unable to put the two images of him together.

Between us the years peel back and I am once again a freckled little girl, white-blonde hair in pigtails, thumb hooked confidently around the buckle of her dungarees. My small hand always in his, as we hurried off on some mission or adventure. The memories are so clear that when I look across at him now, I see how much has changed.

I should be furious, but an overwhelming sadness steals through me, a sinking of my tired heart. For years I've bent and beaten a smiling girl into an automaton programmed on success. I've tried to destroy Harbhajan to make him accept me. Somehow, I think I always suspected it—the price of his love is to become him. The price of his love will be the death of who I am.

But I am not a little girl anymore: I'm as tall as him and looking straight into his vacant eyes. "I went to see a lawyer."

On the table, his fist clenches and I sense the punch coming. Just as I recoil, he checks himself, remembering we're surrounded by people. It's why I picked the beach bar. I have to force myself to keep speaking, the words catching in my throat, "You know what I realized while the lawyer was telling me there's no way out of my situation? I realized, you're the one who put me in this situation. It's too intricate to be an accident. It's too smart. . . . So how can I trust the person who set the trap?" I'm almost hoping for an answer that makes sense. I'm hoping to be wrong.

"Where are you going to go, Bhajan? Sick and with nothing?" And there it is, in his eyes— pure hatred.

All around us, the world continues on as normal, families strolling, couples holding hands, the laughter of young people on the boardwalk, but for me there is nothing left. Because he has broken our code, the one I've always lived by. Our unbreakable outlaw code.

I must have been just like one of those bars of gold he speculated on. He's been waiting for his investment to mature, to turn a profit. Those mantras of trust and loyalty, a ploy, something he knew I'd like to hear. After twenty-four years, I have to admit that his greatest performance—his greatest con—was . . . me.

I stand up and walk through the darkened bar, past a couple swaying to Sinatra on the jukebox, and throw up in the stark bathroom. Keeping myself apart from outsiders, trusting no one, and working tirelessly is how I was raised. But now, there's nobody to ask for help, the money I worked for is gone and I'm too sick to make more. He's won. My hands tremble under the stream of cold water from the tap. I hadn't noticed how thin they've become again, my bones standing out. The hands of an old woman.

Someone bangs on the door, making me flinch. "You done in there?"

Yes, I'm done. I know I have to go back to him.

When I weave through the bar, nearing our table outside, Dad lays some cash down and stands. For a moment we are side by side, and then he strolls out, onto the boardwalk. When he glances back, I'm hesitating, beside two empty glasses. Calmly, deliberately, he turns his back, walking away with the gait of a cocky stranger, knowing I will follow. I stare after him, the air tasting of salt, lights swirling from a children's carousel. Standing almost in a trance, I listen to the surf, the air filling my chest and leaving me. I'm looking out at the black ocean when I feel the tug of something familiar. It's only a memory, of a glow, a dome arching toward the night sky, but it's so vivid that I can almost see it here beyond the crashing waves.

A Golden Temple, floating on dark water, and the feeling I had when I closed my eyes to the rhythm of a chant. All those voices building together. Incense and tabla drums, "Ek ong kar, sat nám." *There is but one God, truth is his name.* For an instant, after all those continents and burned names, I am four years old again. Harbhajan again. The girl who would face anything for their love.

Two decades later, it's not that which keeps me standing. I know I'm unloved. It's his very mantra, the one my father no longer believes in, that stops me from following him. I force myself to stare across the water long after the golden glow has disappeared. Remembering—even though now I'm just some girl outside a bar. Because I choose his principles over him. I choose truth.

39: Florida, age 24

I'VE GOT TO take my mother with me.

When I was thirteen, I ignored the signs of violence building in my father and I'll never do it again. The only option is to act fast.

If I were healthy, maybe we could do it alone, but the girl who always knew where the exits are can't even stay upright for long. The medicine I need has run out, and since taking my savings he refuses to buy more. My mother and I can't go to the authorities, we've got no base, no friends, and $100 left. I try to strip away any emotion and think. In whose interest would it be to help us? At night, I no longer sleep, but examine every angle, coming to terms with all the choices we don't have, until there is only one left.

We are going to ask our worst enemy for help.

I tell my mother the plan. Wouldn't it be nice, after years of hunting someone, if you won? If they came to you, needing you?

It's a dangerous gamble, to go to my grandfather. But he's the only one likely to help us break away, for the satisfaction of proving he was right about my father. For the satisfaction of finding me. I'm going to use myself—the daughter of the man he hates—as bait.

A WEEK LATER, on a bright, windy day, I look out our motel room window, scanning, as children play on the boardwalk. In the pocket of my jean shorts is my new Brazilian passport, picked up yesterday from Anthony's office. We have two small suitcases by the door, and Tigger in his cat carrier. Everything else we've left behind, packing frantically in the time it takes my father to go to the supermarket.

"Let's go." I tell my mother.

"What should we do with this?" Mom hands me a piece of paper.

My father's Brazilian birth certificate, the one Mom has been hiding as insurance. Precious seconds tick by. "We shouldn't give it to him, Bhajan. After all he's done." She stands nervously by the door. "But it's up to you."

She doesn't even know the worst of what he's said, the times he tried to make me abandon her. I hesitate. Without this piece of paper, he has nothing to go back to except his real name. I pick up my bag, heading to the door. At the little table I stop briefly, lift his tea mug, and that's where I leave the birth certificate. He's overlooked a lot of things in life, but never his tea cup.

Hurrying downstairs and onto the boardwalk, I keep glancing behind us, walking on adrenaline, forcing my body to keep going. We stop at a large hotel along the beach to check Mom's email. My grandfather said he would send instructions. I watch the hotel entrance while she sits at the computer terminal and reads. The email, written in Luxembourgish, looks worryingly long.

"What now?" I ask.

"You're not going to like his plan, how he wants to do this. He's calling it a compromise." There is fear in her voice.

As we leave the hotel, I am quiet, focused, and I recognize the friend I can count on: detachment. Part of me is walking, but the other is looking down from above, finding it all rather . . . interesting.

WE STAND ALONG a busy highway, waiting for my grandfather's compromise to arrive. I don't know how I'll face it, but this is the only way he will agree to help. He wants someone he knows to watch us, to make sure we are really leaving, really cutting contact with my father. He is sending someone he thinks he can trust. Cars speed past, and I squint into a fierce sun, dreading the future.

"Your father would never have left that birth certificate for you." Mom is distracted, barely holding herself together. "He would have burned it."

I never take my eyes off the road, because that's the point. I'm not him.

A dark car pulls out of the stream of traffic and stops nearby. The passenger door opens and a woman in baggy jeans steps out. Struggling to keep my face neutral, I watch my sister walk toward me. Chiara stops one pace away. She stares up at the woman-version of the thirteen-year-old she last saw a decade ago. "My God, Bhajan . . ."

PART FOUR

40: On the road / Luxembourg, age 24

CHIARA'S HUSBAND, WALTER, red-faced and confident, is driving as she tells us how they met in the D.C. dive bar where she waitresses and regularly gets into fights—a fact she punctuates by cracking her knuckles. Slumped in the backseat beside Mom and Tigger, I am transfixed. Her evolution from simpering yes-girl to this tattooed, cigarette-puffing, street-talking apparition is very convincing. But I suspect this persona is simply what she has adopted to fit her new life—and, the longer I observe, the more I'm convinced it's to cover up her fear.

I scan Walter's profile. Oh, he's definitely in the dark about Chiara's past. Probably about a lot of things. It's why Chiara is so tense. She probes our mother, alternating between confidential and bullying, as if trying to feel out how much fight is left in her. Chiara wears our mother down, raising her voice, ladling blame for all her current problems, even Walter's years-long unemployment. They live off the money Chiara makes, but mostly off the monthly wire transfer our grandfather sends them. No wonder Chiara is on edge.

Watching Mom wilt, I want to scream. She's been doing so well lately. I just need her to stay strong for a little while longer. To *help* me. Chiara and her husband are driving us to New York City so I can see my doctor one time before flying from there to Luxembourg. It's all my grandfather will allow. In the backseat I glance at Mom and feel an overwhelming exhaustion, unrelated to all the walking I pushed my body through. Unrelated to the constant pain in my gut. It's the weight of responsibility; and I can't remember love without that heaviness. Without the feeling of having to save someone.

"So what have you been doing lately, Bhajan?" Chiara switches tacks, swiveling so she can watch me from the passenger seat. "Working?"

I compose my face. "Nope."

She raises a brow. "So, what, then?"

"Oh," I shrug, "nothing much."

I will never tell these psychos about modeling and my book. The name Cheryl Diamond is the only one they don't know, and they never will. I'm not giving Chiara anything to envy, or my grandfather anything to investigate. That's when they are both at their most dangerous.

"Just living the good life, huh?" Walter's belly jiggles as he laughs.

WE STOP FOR the night somewhere in the Carolinas. It happens as we're unloading our bags in an empty hotel parking lot. Chiara won't stop, berating Mom and unleashing years of anger when we're all too tired to think clearly. "You always thought you were such a *princess*," Chiara hisses, "I don't know why I put up with you." Hefting a bag, she throws it hard against Mom's legs. And there it is—the step too far.

I put myself between Mom and Chiara, emaciated, but taller than either of them. "A princess? A *princess*?" I clench my fists. "Who raised three kids in war zones and across dozens of countries? Are you completely fucking insane?"

"You're the same, the golden child!" she screams. "Always perfect, looking down on everyone! You fucking bitch, how can you defend her? She ruined our lives by marrying your father. *Your* father! You're just like him—"

Her husband is frozen next to the car as I walk forward, pressing in on Chiara. "Don't you dare judge Mom and preach." All I feel is rage. I'm made of it. "Stay the hell away from my mother!"

I pick up my bag and head toward the lights of the hotel. Every part of me is exhausted, and so I sense the whisper of movement too late. Her punch hits the back of my neck. I'm thrown forward, asphalt rough against my face. She lunges for me again, pummeling my back, fists against my spine. I try to push myself up, but my skinny arms give out and I fall flat.

Abruptly, the blows stop, and lying on the ground, I manage to turn. Her husband is staring at Chiara as if she's a stranger, while Mom pulls her away from me. A terrible sadness, real as a weight, makes it a strain for me to sit up. Absurdly, I start to laugh. Because here, with snarling madness on her face and arrogant defiance on mine, is the first time we have ever been honest with each other.

FOUR THOUSAND MILES away, my mother and I walk through an eerily quiet airport, our footsteps echoing. Luxembourg. It's strange to think that after all these years, I'm actually moving *toward* our hunter. He looms so large in my psyche, this force; a malevolent giant, controlling lives, making me fear every shadow. For some reason, I also imagine him in a uniform. I tug on the strap of Tigger's carrier and try to square my shoulders. What if I've gambled too far, what if I'm putting my own mother in danger?

Mom and I exchange a long look. Here goes.

At the exit, a stern-faced couple in their nineties stand ramrod straight, scanning us carefully. My grandparents. For the first time, I look into the eyes of the man I've feared for so long. They are dark, dark, blue, like mine, but unreadable. His face is a study of hard lines but even now I see how handsome he must have been. He's wearing a tweed suit, no uniform. Something like hope flickers in me as I move forward, almost shy.

He is taller than me, formidable even at ninety-four. My grandparents look me up and down, black T-shirt and jeans loose on my bony frame, and I feel something similar to the sensation of a modeling casting. The slow anxiety that somehow I do not measure up. He searches my face, a copy of my father's. Then suddenly, his expression brightens, coming alive.

I smile at him.

"So . . ." He nods with satisfaction. "I have finally caught you."

AFTER THIRTY YEARS, all those continents and countless identities, we are in the same attic in rural Luxembourg from which my mother escaped decades before. Cramped and barely lit by tiny windows in the ceiling. The only difference is, now I'm here.

I learn that in the mornings I'm expected to sit with my grandparents at

the table in the wood-paneled kitchen as they sip their coffee. My grandfather speaks formal English, but my grandmother, who knows only Italian
and French, settles for observing me, straight-backed and impassive, while
I fidget nervously. She is a tiny woman, and I tower over her in my motorcycle boots and New York black, but she wins every interaction with just
one look. The one that reminds me, no matter what—I will always be *his*
daughter.

It shames me, how quickly they've been able to make me feel small, so
far from any place I know, with no one to call, weak and broke. Even if I
had any money, I'd be unable to fly out. My grandfather has notified the
authorities that I'm here on a flimsy Brazilian passport, the daughter of the
man chased by Interpol. The daughter of the man he was right about.

My grandfather shares a particular skill with my father; I realize it on
the third day. It's the ability to look at me and see straight to my weakest
point. "Your sister came back to us a long time ago." He sips his coffee. "She
has been very nice."

I squirm, my mother sits at the table, too, looking drained, and begging me with her eyes to stay silent. Everyone is terrified of his temper, of
him being upset by hearing anything contrary to the way he has decided
things are.

"Your sister is a hard worker, and you will have to learn that. You are
used to not doing anything and having your father support you, Chiara
told us."

I want to run from this small kitchen. Instead, like so often, I feel my
mother's anxiety and, for her, I nod my head.

He watches my face, "You will have to learn to be more like your sister."

TODAY I'M GOING to walk into the Ministry of Justice and give
myself up.

"Not there!" Bopa, as my grandfather has instructed me to call him,
shakes his head forcefully. "Zis door!" He thrusts his cane in front of him
like a conquering general and lurches toward the castlelike building in the

city center, hip replacement be damned. Mom rests her hand on my back
as we walk.

"What does Bopa mean?" I whisper.

She looks surprised. "It's 'grandpa' in Luxembourgish. Like Nonna is
'granny' in Italian."

"Ah." I've just been going along with it for days because they seemed
pretty adamant. Who am I to question anything about names? I stop for a
moment at the bottom of the steps, looking up at the imposing stone.

"Forvards, *forvards*." Bopa points to the door impatiently, obviously
annoyed with me.

This goes against all my training, all my instincts, but I wanted a shot at
something almost everyone is born with: an identity, the right to be alive,
to live somewhere legally. So I'm going to have to do it. I'm going to have
to trust the system.

I stand before the Ministry of Justice's Senior Inspector. It's a cold, clini-
cally neat office, and everyone is speaking over my head in Luxembourgish,
but all I hear are my father's words, *You'll never survive.* Outside the glass-
walled office, the hallway is busy with officials, walking by slowly or staring
openly. Their faces hard. After all the horror stories my grandfather spread
over the past decades, using all his contacts to hunt us down, I am regarded
with suspicion and morbid curiosity. The daughter of a monster.

I try to guess what the inspector is saying to my mother and grandfather. Although everyone who works here is fluent in English, they refuse
to speak it with me, communicating instead in rapid-fire Luxembourgish.
Playing with my life in a language I don't even understand. More people
come out of their offices to gape at me, whispering among themselves.

I try to get the officer's attention. "This all started when I wasn't even
alive, the fake identities, all of it. I'm just trying to put it right—"

He waves a hand, ignoring me. There is no precedent for a case like
mine; by law, I'm entitled to Luxembourgish citizenship, since my mother
was born here—but of course there's a catch. When my father registered
my birth, he used their fake identities. Therefore, legally, I am the daughter

of a Brazilian couple who don't exist, and I have no rights in Luxembourg at all.

As more people are brought in to confer, it becomes clear—my grandfather's promises that this would be easy were probably words meant to get me on a plane. I'm caught in a no-man's land. The visitor visa I have for Europe expires in less than three months. I'm not allowed to go back to America. And now, because I told the truth, they've got me. All the officials, the police, they've seen my face, they've taken my fingerprints. The invisible girl is pinned in a glass-walled office. I can't decide if I want to cry or overturn this bastard's desk, sending the official papers flying. They are holding me accountable for something that happened before I was born.

Finally, the Ministry of Foreign Affairs threatens to have me deported.

Back in the attic, I lie in bed. If it were just the threat of spending the rest of my life as an exile, maybe I could handle it. But now that I have acknowledged to myself all that's happened, it has become impossible to bear. Nightmares stalk my sleep, the same scenes from my childhood playing on repeat until I wake, my chest drenched with sweat. I can never sleep for more than two hours at a time. All these years later, I still feel the loss of my brother, still see Chiara climbing the stairs toward me that night.

I try to push the fury, the fear, away, but it all comes back each time my grandparents bring Chiara up, praising her. Each time, Mom's eyes beg me to swallow the truth. Sleep-deprived and shaky, I struggle to hide my emotions, and Bopa senses the tension. He prods at me, like any good interrogator smelling a lie, and makes me greet Chiara on the phone each time she calls, watching my face with his sharp, assessing eyes. Monitoring everything I say. He suggests that I tell Chiara I miss her, and I know it's not a suggestion at all, but an order.

I know I'm trapped between them; it is Bopa's health insurance that covers my emergency medication, the doctors' visits, and the hospitalization they predict I'll need as my internal bleeding becomes heavier each day. Without this attic, my mother has nowhere to go. And he knows it.

Every time I go out, any trip to the supermarket in the nearby village has to be reviewed by Bopa first, and then recounted in detail when I return so he can try to poke holes in my story. I venture out less and less because the debriefing makes me want to tear my skin off. But I keep trying. One morning I pause, gathering my wits and then descend the stairs on the tips of my toes, shoes and jacket already on, trained by a hundred clean escapes. But Bopa has changed the position of his chair in the den, so there is no way to reach the front door without passing through his line of vision.

"Wait!"

My shoulders slump, hand on the doorknob. So close.

"Where are you going?"

"For a walk."

"Where are you walking to?"

"Just around the fields."

"Who are you meeting?"

"I'm just going for a quick walk." We are facing each other and I step backward, immediately regretting the sign of fear.

"If you are going somewhere else," he says quietly, "I will find out."

He has never gone quite this far before and I stare at him, powerless.

"Your parents tried to get away, but I followed them everywhere, Canada, the Bahamas. They lied, they ran, but I recorded every phone call. I *always* found you." He points over his shoulder into the den, and I see an organized stack of cassette tapes, as tall as a person. A shiver travels through me—it's been here in plain sight all along. The calls with my mother after she left, the ones he promised he wasn't recording. I stare mutely at the tapes. He's proud; I can see it in his smirk. The one that says he's outsmarted us all because he doesn't play by any rules.

"What's the difference?" I ask.

He frowns.

"You said you would take her kids away. They lied to be able to escape. And you lied to try to catch them. So what's the difference between you?"

Even as I say the words, I can hardly believe I didn't think of it before. My grandfather's threats, the inflated Interpol alerts, the letters to local police, all stamped and official, just because he was in the secret police. Just because he could. And my father, all the rules, the impossible standards to live up to, the terrible fear of outsiders he instilled. . . . Were we merely foot-soldiers in a war between two stubborn, paranoid men?

My father must have known we didn't have to run anymore. He'd stolen all the money from his investors, but after he bought new passports when I was nine, we were successfully off the grid, the trail cold. We could have settled down, we could have built a normal life. But my father continued to move, to risk, to isolate us. Maybe he was using the past to control us, or perhaps we had all lived in fear so long that none of us knew how to stop.

But now I know for sure this all started in the minds of two men. They made all the monsters real because of the force of their anger. Because they got Interpol and a young family involved in a power struggle, in their fight to outsmart each other at all costs. My God, they are the same. They were just wearing different masks. The secret agent and the yogi. They created a hell with their vengeance, and we were the pawns. We were the cannon fodder.

With my hand on the doorknob I look at my grandfather. "The truth is, you *never* found us Bopa. You found out where we were after we left; and then you went there, and talked to the cops." I try to keep my voice steady, "And you *never* caught me, Bopa. I told my mother to call you. I could have kept running forever."

He may have all the power, but I want him to remember which one of us, exactly which one of us, was quicker than the devil. Turning the handle, I'm out the door—crossing the fields, until I am far from the house. Over the train tracks, to the border of the next little town. I hurry, needing a distraction, needing to speak to someone. At last, I see my friend standing near the fence in the next field. Motionless, almost as if he's been waiting for me.

"Hey." I lean my elbows on the wooden gate. "How's it going?" The day is windy and stark as usual, clouds pressing down. My boots sink into the mud. Pulling my coat tighter, I decide to just go ahead and tell him. "So, there's going to be a big hearing at court to decide what's going to happen to me . . ." I realize I'm hugging myself, as if that will help. "I feel like the head prosecutor has a grudge against me. You know how bureaucrats can be. Well, maybe not."

The cow looks up at me and chews grass.

41: Luxembourg, age 24

Bopa, an adamant believer in rules, has hired a lawyer for my court hearing. He seems to be having difficulty coming to terms with the fact that the law he upheld so obsessively his whole life is now working against him. He wants me be to be a Luxembourger and stay here forever, but my three-month visitor's visa is fast running out. He keeps expecting them to do as he says and give me a passport. Nine decades on this planet, and he still doesn't know that justice is rarely just.

The public prosecutor and a panel of top lawyers convene at the Cité Judiciaire to review my case. As I climb the steps, Mom reassures me. "This time will be different." We have taken an official DNA test, certifying without doubt that I am her daughter. There is no denying my right to citizenship now.

I sit carefully at the grand table, flanked by my lawyer and my mother. The prosecutor and opposing lawyers continue to communicate over my head in Luxembourgish. At only one moment does the prosecutor speak English. It's at the end, when she turns to where I am frozen in my seat, watching them decide my future. She taps her pen. "So, Harbhajan . . . your whole life has been a lie." She smirks. "How do we know you aren't lying now?" It is in this room, when I've finally told the truth, that I feel most like a criminal.

The prosecutor contends that because of what my parents have done, I am not owed citizenship. A shocked silence descends and I stare at nothing. My lawyer gets to her feet, gathering my files, and says we are going to go to the highest court in the country. We are going to have to try to change Luxembourg law.

From that day on, my case works its way toward the Superior Court of Justice at a snail's pace. Whenever she can, the head prosecutor blocks our petitions, causing even more delays. I start to feel myself drifting, speaking as little as possible, my thoughts becoming more undefined each day.

As the numbness increases, I welcome it. It makes the constant pain in my stomach more tolerable. And because this numbness doesn't hurt, because in fact, it lessens the desperation within, I welcome depression. I pull this unnamed savior around me like a blanket and stay in bed, waiting for the day to go away. For the weeks to turn into months. For my life to finally be over. No one really tries to do anything. Because it's easier this way, isn't it? When I'm silent, it's better for us all.

BOPA IS NOT happy with his soup. It's on the salty side, but he will still eat it, because during the war *they had nothing*. I wouldn't understand because I've never worked, never done anything, but during the war you learned not to be picky, you ate whatever you could find. Because there was nothing, nothing!

Nonna hurries to get him more bread and Mom rubs her forehead, already tired from the language classes she has begun teaching. But in my mind I'm far away, in a blank place where everything is muted.

We are finishing a chicken, which was also unavailable during the war, when he fires at me again. Telling me how good Chiara is, how she has been so helpful, and friendly with them. Across the table I feel my mother tense. I drift even further away, trying not hear as he tells me how Chiara has gone above and beyond for her family. How she even used money he sent to go to New York and search for our missing brother.

My head comes up from where I've been staring at the floor. The surge of anger so strong, it overpowers my general lethargy. I stand abruptly. Putting my plate in the sink, I look at each of them. "She will *never* be my sister."

I'm passing my mother on my way out of the kitchen when she whispers, "Bhajan, please try to stay and be nice."

I lean down until our faces are close. "Really? That's your solution to everything, isn't it?" Methodically, I climb the stairs to the attic, pick up one of the old wooden chairs, and hurl it against the wall with all the strength I have left. It shatters, sending shards across the floor.

Breathing hard, I walk through the door to my bedroom. Beneath the window, a train roars through the night, and I rest my burning forehead against the glass. A low layer of fog blankets the night, drifting past the front steps of orderly houses. They're all too similar; it's eerie.

I open the window wide, air damp and cold against my chest, and lean out.

Oh, no. This street . . . at last I know what it reminds me of.

Little houses made of ticky tacky, little houses all the same.

I'm in the exact place I used to sing about as a child, a smile on my face. Because it seemed impossible then—to end up trapped inside one.

A soft sound makes me turn.

Mom is standing apologetically in the doorway to my room, holding a hot water bottle for me. "Bhajan . . . what can I do?"

"I can't take it any longer, Mom. I can't keep hearing about Chiara."

She steps back. "But I was trying to keep you safe. We need him to pay for your doctors. . . . I was trying to do the right thing—"

"No. You weren't." I've heard her say this many times, but I don't want to ignore reality anymore. "You're lying to yourself, Mom. You've been doing what was easy; you've been pretending. And you still are."

When I see the hurt on her face, I almost want to hold myself back from saying more. But the words rush out, hard and angry. "You being a martyr doesn't help anyone! Just because every day's a horrible struggle doesn't mean we're getting anywhere. Can't you see how hard I fought to stop all this?"

We stare at each other in the dim room.

I know how much she fears her father, what he may do to us, and those moods that shift like mercury. In a flash, I see that she will not stand by my side. She fears him more than she loves me. My shoulders sag. "Then just do one thing for me, Mom. Help me get out of here."

The danger of my illness may be my only chance to escape. After nearly five years of unending pain I no longer believe I'll ever recover. No longer believe anything will save me. All that's left is a desperate need to get away from them. "Anywhere, Mom. Any hospital. Any specialist. Tell Bopa I've got to go. *Please.*"

As if in answer, the Ministry of Foreign Affairs disregards the irrefutable DNA evidence, which proves my right to citizenship, and issues an order to expel me from the country. Quietly, I close the suitcase I never unpacked.

All I can say is, I'll miss the cows.

42: Berlin, age 25

"WHATEVER YOU DO, don't kill the people on your team!"

I try not to sigh. Socializing can be so exhausting. I'm running a fever, have difficulty moving my joints, and still have to rush to the bathroom at least fourteen times a day—so it's hardly a convenient time to mingle. But for some reason, whenever I'm allowed back to my little apartment to rest between hospital treatments, I keep doing this to myself. I keep pushing myself out in the world. It makes no sense. People terrify me, I know they are capable of anything, of things I cannot even imagine, and yet I long to talk to them. The only reason I'm even at this laser tag arena is because someone from an "Internationals in Berlin" group said they needed another warm body to round out tonight's team. I don't even know these people. At this very moment I could be home with an ice pack on my head.

A petite girl in her late twenties appears and plants herself at my side. "I'm Amber. That's my boyfriend, Wormy, the one with the weird hair, it's his birthday, do you know how to work this gun?"

I fiddle with it. "I'm not sure how much help I'll be today, I've got a fever."

She slaps her palm to my forehead. *Spack!* It stings a little. For a delicate thing, doll-like in her prettiness, the girl packs quite some force.

"Yup." Amber nods. "Fever."

Unsure how to respond, I stare, as she sighs regretfully. "I don't have cures for it, sorry. Yesterday I had a headache all day and couldn't do any-thing. I'm so sad Wormy threw away all my sketchy meds from Thailand."

The two of us are teamed up with Johan, a muscled young German who actually used to be in the army. He limbers up while surveying the dark, warehouselike competition field, planning an intricate strategy. Amber and I, guns slung haphazardly, watch the swirly lights on the ceiling with interest.

Johan claps his hands decisively. "We must agree on our team signals now." He takes a few steps back so he can point from his eyes to some imaginary target, then demonstrates a drop and roll.

Amber and I nod our heads gravely.

"Teams to your starting points!" someone yells.

"Yikes," I whisper as we shuffle into the blackness.

Five minutes in, I'm crouched behind a stack of sandbags, disoriented and hoping for reinforcements. I peek over the barrier. Some meters away, Johan is poised like a crouching tiger behind an embankment, forming signals with his free hand. *Look, jump, drop and crawl? Spin?* Panicked eyes wide, I shake my head, uncomprehending.

"Eeeeee!" Amber bursts onto the field from behind a wall, running toward my position, hands covering her head, gun flapping loose. Her vest lights up as she is massacred, and she tips over the sandbags to collapse at my side. "Yo."

"Yo," I say, grinning.

Johan rubs his forehead, then starts signing again, only with more force.

"Look at him." I wipe my dribbly nose. "He's like a power ranger."

She giggles. "He's been waiting for this moment ever since the army, and he's stuck with us. How come you don't have a real accent from anywhere?"

We huddle behind the barrier. "I grew up traveling all the time."

"Really? Me, too."

"Why?" I ask.

We look at each other in silence for a while; she seems to be deciding something.

"So, my dad's Canadian," Amber begins slowly.

"Mine, too." It's out before I really think.

"And my mom's this certifiably crazy Taiwanese baccarat player who took me along to her games all over the place, just kinda left me wandering around in five-star hotels and casinos while she gambled and scammed. So that's my story. What did your dad do?"

I prop myself up on one elbow. "He's a con man."

Lying back on the ground, lights flashing all around, we laugh until it's difficult to breathe and then stare at the ceiling companionably. Another misfit. Maybe there're more of us than I thought.

"Oh no." Abruptly I sit up, my stomach clenching painfully.

"What's wrong?"

"I have to go to the bathroom." How embarrassing; this is why I prefer not to leave my apartment. "I'm sorry," I say, starting to stand. "Me going out will lose us a lot of points. But I'll try to duck behind that wall on the way."

"I'll come with you."

"No, no, it's okay."

But Amber is already hefting her gun awkwardly. "I'll provide, like, the counterfire, or cover fire? Some kinda fire."

We are up, over the barrier. Running for the exit sign, I trip over my shoelace and nearly drop my gun, while Amber waves hers intimidatingly at the air.

"What are you doing!?" Johan pops up from behind a pile of bricks.

"We're goin' to the bathroom!" Amber yells, our vests alight with hits.

"You can't do that!"

"What a bureaucrat," I mutter before hitting my knee on a fake rock and stumbling into the hallway.

In Luxembourg, the Prosecutors Office finally presents its conclusions. They threaten to throw out my case unless I can supply two things that seem impossible to obtain: a certificate from the New Zealand doctor who delivered me, stating that she remembers my parents and my birth, and another certificate confirming that she can positively identify my parents and me in photographs.

Stunned, my lawyer approaches the prosecutor in court after the hearing and points out that legally, there is no better proof than the DNA test we supplied. It's scientific fact. Whereas finding the doctor who delivered me, after all these years, seems impossible. Even if we do, how would a doctor who assisted in thousands of births possibly remember one from over twenty years ago? But by now we know—we know the prosecutor is probably asking for the impossible intentionally.

All I have, the reason I can stay in Europe for a bit longer, is a temporary residence card from the court. It should last until the final ruling. After that, anything could happen to me.

I LOOK AROUND my friend Jazmin's Berlin apartment, observing the scene with curiosity. The wooden table is laid, candles glowing, red napkins folded beside our plates, everything cozy and right. There are quite a few holidays we skipped in my family, and this was one of them.

"So what did you usually do at home for Thanksgiving?" Jaz leans down to check the oven, a riot of beautiful black curls obscuring her face.

"We never had Thanksgiving."

"What? Oh, don't answer." She waves a spatula. "I'll get distracted by a story of you guys climbing the Himalayas or something and forget the turkey."

I help cut tomatoes for the salad. Often I can't trace quite how this happened, this little group. Even with all the months we've spent together by now, I haven't worked up the courage to tell them anything but amusing travel anecdotes from my past. I've been battered and alone for so long that when I feel their arms pull me close, wanting nothing in return—I meet them with disbelief. With the fear of it all being taken away.

"This is going to be the best Danke-giving ever!" Jaz plants a kiss on my cheek as her bell rings.

I haul open the door and Peter strolls past, freeing himself from a tailored suit jacket, coming straight from his high-powered finance job.

"'Sup! I have a prank idea," he whispers to me.

"No, no." Jaz marches into the hall. "I'm not letting you two sit next to each other if you're going to act two years old again."

The doorbell rings again; it's Patrick and Amber, who have run into each other on the stairwell. Patrick hangs his coat neatly; Amber's oversize army jacket falls to the floor as she collapses into a chair.

"Whatta day, man." She exhales heavily. "I was at this coffee shop and I met this communist who told me I'm buying into the system, right? But he was drinking the same coffee! And the guy at the next table was writing, and I said my friend Cheryl writes, what are you writing? So he was working on a letter to Death."

"A letter to who?" I have given up on the tomatoes.

"Death."

Patrick drops his head and sighs.

"Yeah, he said he's been doing it for years, as a way to come to terms with life?"

"Peter, help Cheryl with the salad," Jaz calls from the stove.

"Anyway," Amber leans back, "I want to be clear, those beans weren't fair trade."

As we start to eat it comes upon me, as it sometimes does, an out-of-body feeling that I am in some kind of play—*A Normal Life*—but tonight it may all be coming to an end. So far, every doctor's treatment has failed to help and in one week, I'm being sent to a hospital specializing in Crohn's, hours outside of Berlin. I lay down my fork and knife, hands unsteady, and tell my friends the truth.

For a long moment they are silent, absorbing the news of my illness; then Peter turns his chair at my side so he is facing me. "How bad is it?"

"It's bad." I've been hiding my emaciated body under baggy winter clothes.

"Why didn't you tell us?"

It's such a simple question, but looking at them in the candlelight, I'm speechless. Here, in their presence, the voice in my head seems out of place—the one that says I may lose them. The one that tells me no one wants a malfunctioning girl.

"Well, never mind." Jaz cuts in, watching my expression. "I'll look up natural remedies. There must be some herb—"

"She needs real medicine," Peter says decisively. "This isn't the time for those voodoo people you like."

"It's a *healing* circle—"

"Wait. Where is this hospital?" Patrick needs a solid location in the craziness and pulls out his phone.

"Lauchhammer—a tiny town three hours away." Each time I take a step forward in life, I seem to be thrown back, hundreds of kilometers away, this time from Berlin where I was starting to make a place for myself. Crohn's disease, I've noticed, has a few things in common with my father. Keeping me adrift, away, apart. Just like his voice, I've been taking it everywhere I go.

"Okay." Peter breaks the silence. "We'll come visit! And bring cookies." They all nod. Except Amber.

"I could come," she says.

"Amber, you can't come to the hospital with me if there's nothing wrong with you."

"Who says there's nothing wrong with me?" She is offended. "There are *lots* of things. So I'm thinking . . . when you go in, I can just threaten to slit my wrists if they take you away. That should be enough to land me in the psych ward. And then we could, like, meet for tea in the lounge."

We stare at her in awe.

"Or we could just visit more regularly," Jaz ventures.

I clear my throat, "Well . . . if you do visit, I won't be registered under Cheryl. That's just the name I used for modeling and writing."

"Oh, so . . . wait. What's your real name?"

"It's Harbhajan."

Peter bursts out laughing. "Of course it is. Of course! It wouldn't be anything we've ever heard of before!"

"Is that Indian?" Patrick has put down the map app. It won't help him anymore.

"It's from Sanskrit. Because my parents used to be Sikhs and . . . Anyway, they would just call me Bhajan."

"Bomgah?"

"No, Peter!" My shoulders start to shake helplessly at the absurdity of it all, at the surprise of being able to laugh. "It's *Bhajan*!"

Jaz takes a deep breath, "I thought my Mexican family Thanksgivings were dramatic, but this beats them all."

Peter smiles fondly, lifting his glass. "Cheers to our Bomgah."

FOR MONTHS, I'VE managed to discourage my mother from visiting me, but now she's determined to fly in from Luxembourg in so she can take me to the hospital. And that's when I say something I've only said to her once before. No. The time on my own, or maybe the lightness of my friends, has made me understand: My family is killing me. I'm furious with her, with all of them. My grandparents, the court, my father for never having loved me. But most of all, with myself for being soft enough to fall for it. I can't see any way out, so I want to wipe away my whole past. The whole con. I want to run until I'm so far away no one will ever find me.

On my last night in Berlin, my friends take over an underground wine shop off a quiet cobblestone street, and we sit in a circle with the lights down low and Wu-Tang on high. Together like this, it feels like a forever kind of moment, and we need one. In spring, Amber is going to China, Peter to Africa, and me . . . I don't even know what will be left of me by then. I am too weak, but when they get up to dance, I let myself forget for a moment, because watching them is always like glimpsing what may be.

In a silent midnight they walk me the few blocks home. Snow falls like a whisper all around as we slip down the icy street. They run ahead and circle back to pull me along; our voices echoing off the dark buildings and shadowed doorways as Peter kneels to shape a snowball.

For all of them, this is a night they'll have many more of. But for me, I'll never forget the feeling. Them pulling me along, my woolen hat slipping off, laughing like the kid I never had a chance to be.

43: Lauchhammer Hospital, Germany, at Christmas, age 26

ALL THE WEEKS have run together, and when I look out the window of the intensive care ward, I'm not sure I want to leave. Every time I try to visualize walking out of here, out into the world, I become scared again. It's such a huge, chaotic, unpredictable place—and I'm a skeleton, five foot eleven inches tall and ninety-eight pounds. All I feel is weak. Unable to walk more than a few steps. But worst of all, I no longer trust myself. Here in the hospital, I can't stop from replaying everything that has happened. How can I ever have faith in my instincts, my judgment, when I let myself be deceived for so long? For an entire life.

There is the sound of footsteps in the hallway, and I stare out the window of my room, waiting for the nurse to come in.

"Bhajan?"

My mother is standing in the doorway, wearing a winter coat as big as her, hesitating. Instantly, I'm annoyed. Why can't my family ever leave me in peace? It's been so many months since we've seen each other—since I left Luxembourg—since I asked to be alone. "Bhajan, I know you don't want me here. But . . . if you want to tell your grandfather what went on in our family, I'm with you." She steps into my room. "No more lies."

Slowly, almost as if waiting for permission, she settles on the chair at my bedside. My shock begins to ebb and I study her face, realizing how far she's had to come. Not the flight, the hours on the train, the teaching money she must have saved up for this. But what it must have taken for her to want to stand up to her father, the one person she's always feared most.

"Hi," I say softly. Because here is the woman who, all those years ago, called up Noriega and broke my father out of a Panamanian jail. I only saw glimpses, a hint of her, through the years, but I knew she never really went away. Reaching out, I take her hand. "I missed you, Mom."

We sit in silence, fingers intertwined, her in a puffy jacket, me in penguin pajamas and hooked up to an IV. She looks at me the way she's always been able to, and sees straight through my stoic expression. "What are you worried about?"

I want to be honest with Bopa. I want to write to him. He knows of course that we have left my father. But he does not know how awful it all was. How I miss Frank. How I do not talk to Chiara. How everything fell apart. But what if my grandfather punishes me for my letter? What if he cuts off my health insurance? My chin is trembling. In my mind I run ahead, imagining all kinds of hell. All the things he might do to me.

She unzips her jacket, shrugging it off almost impatiently.

"Bhajan, please listen. Do you realize that you have saved my life? You loved me even when I kept falling flat on my face as a mother, through all those mistakes. . . . So whatever happens with my father, I don't care. We'll figure something out."

"I can't take another hit, Mom. I just can't." My voice breaks.

She takes my hand again, fingers strong, forcing me to pay attention. "Darling, remember one thing. You may feel fragile now, but even when you were in dungarees, you were already bigger than all of us."

I frown at her, my arms marked by a hundred needles.

She leans forward in the chair, with a hint of her naughty smile. "Can I tell you a secret?"

"Oh God." I groan.

"No, no, this one isn't traumatic, I promise!" She holds up her hands. "And it may be a good example. . . . Did you know that your father tried to be an author?"

I'm too surprised to speak.

"Oh, yeah, a few years after we met, he wrote a novel based on his adventures in the gold bullion market."

"What happened?" I try to sit up straighter against the pillows.

"Well, the publishers liked the story and said it was interesting . . . but, like a lot of things he did, it lacked heart."

I have trouble even forming the words, "He never told me he wrote a book."

"Of course not, Bhajan. You finished something at nineteen that he was never able to accomplish."

In the silence, I'm aware of every sound: the nurses cart in the hall, my uneven breathing. I swallow hard. "Is that why he didn't love me?"

Mom hangs her head for a long moment, before looking straight at me. "I should have told you this earlier, but I was so angry with him. . . . Your father *loved* you. As much as someone like him ever could. But you outgrew him, Harbhajan. Simple as that. He's a con man, who gave birth to an idealist. And after a certain point, the two just don't go together anymore."

I start to cry, quietly at first and then my shoulders shake; it feels as if my world, or the way I saw it, is quaking. To a child, your family is the whole universe and they defined my perception of it as a place that couldn't be trusted. A place where I would never be enough. The idea of this story that dominated my life . . . The idea of them, as just four people out of billions, is making my head spin.

"And when you walk out of here, Harbhajan—which you will—you're going to attract people who are so much more worthy. People who know how to love the way you do."

I think of my friends who drove six hours through a snowstorm to sit with me, for an hour, in a hospital cafeteria. Mom leans back and sighs. "I'm not sure what a psychologist would think of what I'm about to say. . . . But as for all the rest, everything that came before—Get over it."

I stare at her, my face reddening.

"Oh, punch me if you want, but I mean it. You're born to live such a big, beautiful, courageous life. Don't waste another second on four small people who weren't part of your tribe. Go be Bhajan—and really, to hell with all the nincompoops."

At first, I can't tell what's happening. But relief fills my chest and it's impossible to stop. Through the tears we laugh, the way we haven't in so many years, or maybe ever. My arm hooked to the IV drip, Mom sprawled in the chair, and that's when it occurs to me . . . that if we can laugh with such abandon, in a hospital room, after all we've survived—then, she and I, we're some kind of invincible.

I FEEL IT, the change in my own body, a few nights later. It's not that welcoming numbness, or the absence of pain. Everything still hurts like hell. This is something else, a tiny flame. A bit of strength. I can feel it, underneath everything else, trying to come back. I don't dare think, or wait. It's the middle of the night but I pull myself up using my metal IV stand for support and, wearing my PJs, start to wheel it toward the door. One of the wheels gets caught on the corner and jams. Rolling my eyes, I kick at it repeatedly with my slipper. I don't have time for this!

Finally, I lurch into the hallway, wheels squeaking alongside me in the empty corridor of Intensive Care. From the nurses station I can hear the soft murmur of voices. Soon, all I'm conscious of is the beating of my heart, which seems like it's going to burst, and my hand, slick with sweat on the metal. Fourteen steps. I lean against the wall to rest. Fourteen steps.

Every day after this, twice a day, I walk. Leaning on the IV at first, until I don't need it anymore. Five steps further each day. Closing my eyes at night, I visualize it. For years I've been comparing my current state to what I was before. An invalid versus the girl who went to the Junior Olympics. But the exact same will is within me. In all those years of training, I learned something—how to work with my body, to be patient, and build strength from scratch. I just have to go slower this time. So I'll start here, exactly where I am. Because in the end, maybe my family was right about one thing: Maybe I am the strong one.

44: Tuscany, age 27

THE TINY SEASIDE town we are living in is quaint in the way only Italy can pull off. Terracotta-colored houses, laundry hung from windows to dry, old men sipping coffee while playing chess outside the café, and us: two tall, foreign-looking girls wobbling across the piazza on their bicycles.

I'm still shaky, hopped up on a cocktail of powerful drugs, but there's never a perfect moment to stop keeping the world at a distance. Soon after I left the hospital, Jazmin and I saw an ad for two English tutors in the Tuscan countryside and, completely ignoring our lack of experience, we applied.

The family, whose kids we teach English to, owns a bungalow hotel in the Tuscan fields outside town, and we have our own little casa. Jaz and I can't believe our luck: the people are lovely, the kids no longer run screaming from us, and our weekends are free. Riding the cheap trains during our two-month stint, we'll be able to explore Sienna, Pisa, and Rome.

Outside the post office, we run our ancient bikes into a wall and stumble off. The lack of real functioning brakes is part of the local charm.

"Do you want me to come in?" Jaz frowns, concerned.

For a while I look up at a little yellow sign, UFFICO POSTALE, the envelope in my hand.

This morning, when I wrote a letter to my grandfather, it was not in anger. I've felt in my own body why anger and vengeance are so dangerous—it ties you forever to the exact people and memories you are trying to escape. When I was furious, battling against the injustice of it all, I made myself dependent on the very ones who hurt me. On them apologizing, on them somehow setting me free. Before everything fell to pieces, my family refused to give up control of me. But ever after, it's me who has been holding on. It's me who has been refusing to let myself be free.

So when I wrote to my grandfather, I tried to do so with an understanding for all that we've been through. For everything we have lost. Five sheets of paper in the end, but so heavy in my pocket.

I touch Jazmin's shoulder. "I'll be right back."

Inside, an elderly lady presses a stamp on the envelope and adds it to a pile of outgoing mail. I feel almost dizzy as Jazmin and I climb back onto our bikes, turn onto the road, and ride through the shade of fragrant pine trees. Slowly I pedal, focusing on each movement, holding tight to the handlebars. Like everything else, it's easier with a friend by my side.

One pastel-colored evening, the family invites us to dinner in the garden. It's chaos, of course: little kids running everywhere, Nonna and Mamma calling instructions from the kitchen that no one listens to, young people gesticulating wildly while talking, the sun-bronzed grandpa, his hands rough from years of working the land, watching it all contentedly.

There is no structure or clear plan of action for the proceedings. Here, everyone seems to topple over each other, kissing cheeks, resting arms across each other's shoulders with no regard for personal space. I should hate this, the intrusion, but something about it pulls at me. I know I'm not part of this family, of their seamless love, but lately just seeing that it exists is reassuring. Whenever I try to remain closed within myself, they plow straight through, teasing and firing questions, never shutting up. And when I'm not annoyed by it, I think it's doing me good.

Dinner is late, naturally, but I'm not waiting impatiently the way I used to. It's been difficult for me to comprehend this thing Italians do, this taking so much time. But sitting at the table, watching life unfold, is a pleasure. Italians seem to know what pleasure is and how to find it right where I never imagined: in simply being with *other people*.

My phone shrills and I pull it from my pocket, checking the screen. Immediately, every muscle tenses. My grandfather. Calling on Skype. Excusing myself from the table, I rush up the pathway, until I am inside the bungalow Jaz and I share. My hands are sweating and I nearly drop the phone. I've been scared many times in my life, but not quite like this. This isn't one of his monthly calls for a status update on my health.

I click ANSWER and watch as his face gradually takes shape. It looks as severe as ever.

Our eyes meet on the screen, and as usual, he wastes no time.

"I have read your letter."

I want to throw the phone away and run. Bopa's face starts to move as if he is about to sneeze. In my state of fear, it takes me awhile to realize what I'm seeing. He's crying. Tears trace down the hard lines of his cheeks. Slowly, he wipes his eyes with his handkerchief and refolds it neatly. When he raises his face, I recognize that look. It's identical to mine when I've made a decision: immovable.

"Thank you," he says. I am so shocked that all I can do is stare at this man. I was prepared for every kind of ugly disaster, but not this. "No one ever tells me anything." He shakes his grizzled head.

That's because you are terrifying! My voice trembles as I ask, "Then why didn't you talk to me nicely?"

"I . . . I do not know how."

My God, he has spent his whole life bullying people into submission while secretly hoping to be challenged. Secretly hoping for a connection, made impossible because he is so feared. How much time we waste in life, sliding around the truth, when the truth is that anyone worth having will never leave you because of it.

"So thank you," he says, "for having the courage."

45: Luxembourg, age 27

TURNS OUT, THERE is a good thing about being born into a family of outlaws—people remember you. In Luxembourg, my mother has been working tirelessly on the nearly hopeless task given to us by the court: tracking down a doctor in New Zealand, whose name we don't know, who delivered me so long ago. After months of research, Mom finds her.

Twenty-seven years later, the obstetrician, who met us only briefly, recalls not only our family and the humming baby who kicked off all her blankets; but she vividly remembers my father's controlling attitude during and after my birth, identifies my parents' pictures, and gives sworn evidence to the Luxembourg court backing up my claims.

Mom calls me with the news as I'm locking the door to our little casa in Tuscany for the last time. Jaz and I stand on an empty train platform, surrounded by the silver leaves of olive groves and chirping crickets. Our idyllic teaching stint has come to an end and Jaz is going back to Berlin, while I'm flying to Luxembourg, in case I'm needed for a hearing. It seems, after all these years, I may still have a chance at my passport. How much hard evidence can they possibly ignore?

"I dunno," Jaz says wistfully as we wait for the airport train, "I feel like you're not going to come back to live in Berlin."

"You think I'm going to stay in Luxembourg?" I rear back in panic.

"God, no!" She touches my shoulder reassuringly. "I mean Italy. This place . . . it suits you."

I've noticed it, too. There is something about this country—the infuriating chaos, afternoons that last forever, and people who look you in the eye to smile—that makes me feel close to something I might call home. It makes me think of Nonna, of her childhood in this sun-drenched place, and whether there is more to her than hardness. Italy is part of my confusing bloodline, and I'm beginning to wonder if instead of running from my roots, I could try to make peace with some of it. I've already picked up enough of the language to have basic conversations, but what if I really learned? What if I learned a language my whole family could communicate in?

What the hell. I've been a lot of things. Perhaps I could be more Italian.

It makes no sense, of course. I should be thinking practically, of a place where I can try to build back some sort of career, of stability and organization. But Berlin never did feel like home, only the people I met there did. And deep down, I know, even though Amber and Peter will leave soon, it doesn't matter. The group of people who pulled me down an icy Berlin street, snow falling all around, will be with me forever.

Jaz heaves on her backpack as our train rumbles into the station, "You know what I think? For once in your life, you should do exactly what you feel like."

I wish it were that simple, but my future is still hanging in the balance. I may have to run again. Through the window of the train, terra-cotta houses and olive groves roll past on repeat. I try to memorize it all, the light and shadow, because the things I love are so often what I have to leave behind.

"I NEVER LIKED taking orders!" Bopa informs me as he sips coffee in the kitchen. "But, I also never liked giving orders."

Doesn't like giving orders? That is the foundation of his very persona. I've only been in Luxembourg a few days and the initial awkwardness between Bopa and me has passed. We will never again speak directly of my letter, but it seems to have lifted a barrier between us. He now regards me with something like anticipation; an elderly bull who has finally found someone stubborn enough to ignore every red flag and stay in the ring.

At the dining table, Bopa lifts his chin nobly, preparing to continue, and I close my eyes for strength. "I never wanted to tell people what to do," he says. "After all, what right do I have?"

On either side of me, Nonna and Mom are silent. Solemnly I nod, trying to line up the right words in Italian. "But you were in the secret police. Giving orders is what they do."

Nonna focuses on me intently. It's the first time she's heard me speaking a language she can understand.

"It was my job!" he declares.

"And you were good at it, right?" I wink.

"Finalmente!" An unfamiliar sound fills the kitchen and we all freeze. Nonna is bent over her plate, back shaking. She is laughing, actually *laughing*. Frankly, I'm still terrified of them both, but I like where this is going. Nonna raises a gnarled fist. "Do you know," she pronounces the words carefully so I can follow, "that when he became a policeman after the war, his mother warned me—"

"She did not warn you!"

"She said—"

Bopa raises his voice, "There is no need for such silliness—"

"Hold on," I interrupt in Italian. "Why don't we let Nonna talk?"

In the brief window of silence, Nonna seizes her moment, "His mother said, watch out—he'll only get worse!" Her green eyes flash.

"How *interesting*." I clasp my hands together. "Tell me more."

THREE DAYS LATER, Bopa has sequestered himself in the study with Tigger, as sixty-nine years of marital rule begin to crumble. I am grasping more Italian daily, but Nonna is picking up my propensity for questioning authority at a much faster rate. Surrounded by the certainty of his Luxembourg Law volumes, Bopa resembles a man under fire.

"Hi." I lean on the doorframe, hands in the pockets of my thrift-store 1920s-style men's trousers.

He harrumphs. "Why must you always be different?"

Walking toward his favorite armchair, I lean down and plant a kiss on his cheek.

"By now," I sigh, "I think it's mostly habit."

We regard each other shyly as I sit across from him on the edge of the couch. I used to hate this man. Watching him now, though, his shoulders still broad, face etched in stone, I see he is scared, always has been, of losing people. The tighter he clung, the more his panic became reality. He's spent a lifetime making his worst nightmares come true. I swallow hard, because I've done something different, yet equally devastating. I tried to hold on to my family, to the people I thought I couldn't bear to lose, by silencing myself. By denying reality. And all I was left with was hating everything. Furious with myself, and with life. But really . . . I think I was scared of everything. So maybe they're the same in the end, hate and fear.

I try for common ground. "The steak you made was good."

"It is from Luxembourg." he says proudly.

I must look surprised, because he chuckles. "Not all in Luxembourg is bad. We have cows here, you know."

"I used to talk to them, on my walks."

"When I was young," he says, "my father had cows."

"Really?"

"Yes, six cows and forty pigs . . . one of which was me."

Spontaneously I chuckle, then settle back on the couch holding one of the pillows.

Bopa looks like he's considering whether or not to say something. "I was given an order once, in Italy during the war . . ." He stares down, frowning, and I wait. "My squadron captured three partisans. My commander told me to take them out into the field; there were fields of tall grass where you could lose yourself. . . . He ordered me to kill them."

My hands have gone cold. "What did you do?"

"I took them into the field. The day was bright, so I told them to lie very still until nightfall and fired three times in the ground."

I feel my heart soften. "Not all rules are meant to be obeyed."

"No." He lifts a finger. "But most of them are. You must learn that."

The stubborn way we hold our heads is so similar.

"You must learn to be *normal*. When your mother ran, she took everything from us. Our grandchildren, everything!"

Not looking for a fight, I tread carefully. "There was more to the story, though."

He clenches his fists, transforming from kindly grandpa into something menacing. "She broke laws, faked passports! Your father is a criminal! They raised you children wild, without education—"

My shoulders square. "Bopa, let's not do this. You said you would take her children away; she felt she had to run."

"She lied about where they were when she called. Always a lie! But I followed the tracks, I have the tapes!" He waves an arm at shelves behind his desk stacked with cassette tapes. "I recorded every lie your mother told!"

"And you lied about it." I'm done playing nice.

"What?"

"She heard the click on the line, but you told her there was no recorder. Why would she tell you the truth when every conversation started with deception?"

"She destroyed everything! She—"

"Stop." I hold up a hand, tired. "Please stop."

"Your mother—"

"Yes, she's my mother. And I won't go against her—not for you or anyone. Never."

He opens his mouth to protest again, and I cut him off. "If we're going to get along, you can't do this. There are a lot of things we don't agree on."

He shakes his head angrily but stays silent. I leave it unsaid—the fact that he and my grandmother have decided to stay in contact with Chiara. The fact that they still send her money. But I'm struggling to accept them needing to hold on, even if it is just to the memory of her as an innocent child. "I'm willing to let it go." I rub my eyes. "Truly. So just let me know if you can, too."

ALL THE EVIDENCE the court asked for, and more, is submitted by my lawyer to the prosecutor. All these years have come down to one final decision. Now all we can do is wait, probably months, while they determine if I will ever be legal.

We're walking out of the lawyer's office in the city center, when my mother pulls me aside and hands me a sheet of paper. The printing in Italian. I am so focused on my court case that I stare at it, confused. "It's the registration for a language school in Rome." She smiles. "You said you wanted to study there, right?"

The words only filter in slowly as I look at her.

I've always loved my mother, but it wasn't until I came here that I began to understand her. To respect the depth of determination it took to run for freedom after being raised in fear. Even now, from a cold attic in her childhood home, a place most people would call defeat, she is steadily rebuilding her life; teaching languages, saving up enough to give me what I thought was out of my reach. For as long as I can remember, ever since I was able to think, I've felt responsible for my mother, for keeping her safe. And now, I don't think I have to anymore.

Nothing is perfect. But my war is ending.

IT'S BARELY DAWN on the day of my flight, and I kiss Tigger's sweet-smelling forehead, tugging my suitcase down the path toward the car where Mom waits. A thick mist is drifting across the lawn, obscuring the grass, when a sound makes me turn. I see Bopa, following me, bathrobe tied over his pajamas. "Pfft, you are still wearing those motorcycle boots, I see." He leans on his cane.

"Still being critical, I see." I cross my arms.

"Ach, the rebel."

"Ooooh, the cop."

We stand alone, in unsteady silence, looking at the houses along the street, little houses all the same. He hesitates, tapping his cane, and then turns to me. "Do you think cops and rebels can be friends?"

Against my will, I picture all the times I dreaded walking up this path. All the times I felt like a reminder of a man they hate. The scar is still so vivid that I want to punish him, want him to know how much it hurt, how desperate and alone I felt, how—then I remember what my mother told me. He's asked her to let him be the one to pay for my lodging while I study.

Bopa stares at his slippers, resisting tears, his face maneuvering for control and then giving up.

"I don't know, Bopa," I say as my tired shoulders drop. "But it wouldn't be the weirdest thing we've ever done."

46: Rome, age 27

IN THE EARLY Roman mornings, still crisp, scented with espresso and baked cornetti, the Pantheon is nearly empty. Gathering my books, I always leave my tiny apartment well before class and find my way here. It's hard to believe that, backpack slung over my shoulder, I'm allowed to stroll into an ancient temple that has stood for two thousand years. As always, I sit in one of the pews under the circular opening of the dome and tilt my head back. The pure light of a new day forms a golden column in the air. Two millennia, first as a pagan temple, then a church, and now I get to close my eyes and feel my heartbeat slow, the way it always does in this place.

Before the church clocks strike nine, I hurry out onto the cobblestones, waving to the guard, and walk past the senate toward school. My favorite classmate, Melissa, is waiting outside, holding her homework sheets against the door as she fills them in guiltily. "Did you finish yours, or were you daydreaming in the Pantheon?"

Smiling, I press my pages next to hers and start copying the answers.

Even as we sit in the classroom, absorbing new words, I can't stop looking at this city. My eyes stray beyond the window, to the carved stone of the building across the street and the bustle of the café beneath us. My magic time, though, will always be around midnight, when the streets are nearly empty and I can hear my footsteps. I like to walk alone. The ancient buildings, bathed in warmth from the flickering streetlamps and unchanged for centuries, seem both mysterious and comforting. Some say Rome is stuck in the past, but for me it feels so good to be somewhere unchanging. Someplace where things last.

I'm about halfway through the first month of school when my doctor in Berlin recommends I go to see Dr. Petrucci, a renowned gastroenterologist. She wants me monitored as I come off the powerful immunosuppressant medication that I take every day. I'm happy to be in Italy for it, because, it will have to be done, like everything here, very slowly. For once, I seem to fit into the rhythm of life.

Dr. Petrucci settles into the leather chair behind his desk and regards me gravely. "Let us talk about the thing with the name of Karma . . . and if it is indeed *presente* all around us?" He always begins our visits this way, with some obscure existential question. Taking his eyes off me for a moment, he picks up a small light bulb with short silver wires still attached, and turns it over in his hands as if it holds the answer. Dr. Petrucci has a favorite drawer in his elegantly carved desk that he opens periodically to extract different playthings: a miniature engraved door knob, a keyhole frame. Apparently they help him in his musings.

In his sixties, tanned and understatedly suave, with a deep sonorous voice, Dr. Petrucci could have become a picture-perfect psychologist rather than a well-known gastroenterologist. He's an odd duck, and rarely gives me any medical advice whatsoever, preferring instead to talk about the meaning of life. But the sessions are comforting, or at least not *uncomforting*. I'm still experimenting with telling my story. To him, to my new friend, Melissa. Getting it off my chest is what I imagine skydiving to be like: terrifying but also addictive.

He rummages in the drawer and pulls out a silver teaspoon, which he holds horizontally in front of his stately nose. "Do you enjoy school here?"

I nod, though for me it's more than just enjoyable. It's a revelation. The chance to learn something for the pleasure of it, something I choose to learn.

"Who is in your class?"

"It's me and three priests." I grin. "One of whom is German. And a Danish girl called Melissa."

He shakes his head sadly.

I'm confused by his response. "But she and I really get along."

"This is most unfortunate." He taps the spoon thoughtfully on his desk,

"I was hoping you would be thrown together with men your age and stop being so closed off. Alas."

"I'm not closed off anymore," I protest. "I've made friends."

"It is not friends I am speaking of. It's men, romance, vulnerability . . . the fact that you always say no, because you still think you are a child."

I stop watching the teaspoon and listen.

"In this one way, you are frozen at nine years old, when your brother got in your bed, when you didn't have a say. But now, you are an adult. You can say no, or you can say yes."

In the chair, I am motionless.

"And yet . . . many writers and artists only reach their true potential in isolation, in despair." He gazes pensively at the ceiling, "Something to consider for next week, no?"

Dr. Petrucci sets his plaything down and we both stare at the abandoned teaspoon.

It always takes me some time to digest his insights, especially since they are so difficult to decipher. More like a challenge than clear advice. So almost every night, I walk through the city, past the restaurants that are closing, toward Piazza di Santa Maria in Trastevere, until I can hear the music. A man in a careworn suit sits on a folding chair in the middle of the square, behind him the church spire reflects the moon. With his head bent over the cello, his hands caress the strings softly, coaxing out a melody. I sit on the steps of the fountain, spellbound, arms wrapped around my knees, and listen to what is almost a lullaby. On these midnights, I don't think it's the loveliness that brings me to tears. It's the fact that somewhere along the way, somewhere during my long fight, I stopped believing in beauty. I stopped believing it could be mine. Here, with the irrefutable evidence laid before me, I finally start to cry.

There is something people rarely tell you about war, and that is how another battle begins when it is over. I thought I was brave when I felt nothing, when I forced myself to be numb, but what's really scary is peacetime. I want so desperately to be normal, or at least some version of it, but the past, these emotions rushing back, are far more confusing and unsettling than numbness ever was. It would be much simpler to keep parts of myself forever locked away. Because to truly feel would mean opening myself up to being hurt again. War is simple. Perhaps it's the aftermath that requires real courage.

WHEN HE RIDES into my life, it's with a black eye, a motorcycle, and the type of smile elderly ladies warn you about. I'm collapsed on a chair, away from the people, at an outdoor party. Sometimes I forget to manage how much I walk during the day and the exhaustion hits me hard. I'm still too weak to stand for long periods, and so I'm forever appearing antisocial or disinterested in humanity.

"Ciao."

I look up and am confronted with . . . my type. Due to my life having been slightly busy, it's only dawned on me recently that dark-haired men who move like athletes and wear incorrigible expressions have a certain effect on me. Pretty soon, he's sitting next to me and we're arguing. "*Three* priests, in one class? I don't know if I believe it."

"Trust me, it's very real," I insist.

"I'm unconvinced."

I lift my chin. I've got three priests, and I can back it up.

"Okay," he looks at me measuringly. "We can resolve this. How about I come pick you up from school tomorrow and we'll see if these guys exist?"

I can think of about a dozen reasons to say no. I mean, the man probably thinks I'm a sweet American girl studying abroad. Poor bastard. But maybe it's Dr. Petrucci and his teaspoon, because I feel myself nod slowly, and say yes.

The next day, I walk down the ancient marble steps inside our school building, Melissa at my side. "I can't believe this is happening." She links her arm excitedly with mine. "Your first date! But whatever you do, *don't* tell him that. We gotta play it cool." Nearing the towering carved wood door, always open to the piazza, we slow down and lower our voices. "Are you going to tell him any crazy stories from your childhood?" Melissa whispers.

"Hell no."

"Yeah, probably best."

Stealthily, Melissa and I keep to the shadows, tiptoeing toward the front door to peek outside. Tomas is actually here, wearing dark jeans and standing in the bright piazza, helmet slung over a muscled arm. Immediately Melissa wilts backward, plastering herself against the wall. "I'm so proud of you," She clasps her hands giddily. "I want to climb him like a tree!"

I'm trying to stifle my laughter when a small scraping sound startles us. Looking over our shoulders, we see the three priests, standing an arm's length away—listening somberly. With great dignity, they go through the door, into the piazza. It's satisfying to see the doubting Tomas turn to watch them. But I stay inside, wavering and feeling awkward. I've got to come up with some sort of strategy before making a move. Experience has taught me to make detailed plans before confronting anything new. I'm mulling over potential disasters and embarrassments in my mind, when Melissa slips behind me, places one hand on the small of my back, and pushes me—hard—out into the light.

TOMAS AND I are leaving a restaurant, walking toward his motorcycle, when I glance up at him curiously. "How did you get the black eye?" It's almost gone, just a shadow.

"I train at grappling and got elbowed."

"So, you lost, then?" I can't resist teasing.

He gives me a long look. "Are you saying you'd give up, just because you got elbowed?"

Speechless, I climb onto the back of his Ducati, and the motorcycle speeds into the night, leaning into a sharp curve around the Colosseum. I laugh, clinging to his leather jacket as he guns the engine, my hair whipping around the helmet. Lights illuminate the arches where gladiators used to fight; I can almost imagine the wheels of ancient chariots churning the gravel track, racing alongside. A tiny street, framed by whispering trees and the scent of orange gardens, climbs a gentle hill, and at the summit, a single lamp stands in the moonlight.

"Where are we?" I fumble to unfasten my helmet.

Click. He undoes the buckle and lifts it from my head. "Follow me, I'll show you."

It's a door. A large, impressive door, but still. "Look through the key-hole." Leaning down, I blink until I realize what I'm seeing. Instead of the inside of a building, it's a perfect cameo view of the shining Vatican dome.

I learn that this is Tomas in a nutshell. I thought he was some sort of street tough, and it turns out he's a neuroscientist. He brings me to a door, and it's the Vatican. I'd thought I had a monopoly on the book not match-ing the cover, but under all our casual bravado, we seem to confuse the hell out of each other.

Beneath the leaves of the orange garden, our feet crunching over the gravel, Tomas stops and pulls me to him. In the long silence, he leans down to kiss me, and any of my lingering swagger fades away. I've spent so many years with my only entertainment consisting of watching my heart rate beep across hospital monitors that it's difficult to process this kind of sen-sory data.

"Are you okay?" He draws back, puzzled.

"Yup, yup." *Act alive!*

We sit on a stone wall high above the lights of the city, his arms around me, teetering on the edge of a freefall. In between kisses, I observe two other couples with an almost intellectual interest, somehow unable to catch up to the moment. I guess this is the first time I've actually wanted to be touched—without someone forcing me—but escaping is all I know. The first rule of a good street-fighter is straightforward—never let anyone get close enough to hurt you. Sitting above the lights of Rome, I fear I just don't know how to be a girl, or become a woman.

THREE WEEKS AFTER we meet, Tomas is leaving. It's an interesting change of pace—someone blowing town before me. "I'm nervous," he says in his direct way, as we pass through the shadow of the Basilica of Santa Maria, a magician in a top hat setting up out front.

"Just look at it like an adventure. Something you can learn from." To me, being hired as a researcher and flying halfway across the world to Singapore doesn't seem like that big an adjustment. I mean, he's choosing to go. No one is even chasing him.

Tomas looks at me sideways, something unreadable flickering across his face. "So when you were growing up, you just kept traveling every-where, but your dad never had a real job?"

"Well, he wanted to see the whole world, and I guess he did. . . . But it wasn't always fun."

"Your dad sounds like a rock star."

"He wasn't." Tomas should hear the warning in my voice.

His smile is a challenge. "He seems like one."

I absolutely refuse to be baited. We cross Viale Trastevere in silence, heading toward the bridge, a heaviness descending on my shoulders. He's just a normal guy; he'll never understand. All the hard years rush back; no one will *ever* understand.

"Was he the one who was so interested in yoga and health food?"

"Yes, I basically grew up on salad."

He starts to laugh, "You grew up *on* salad. Do you really say that in English?"

I glare at him.

"I still think growing up in your family must have been an amazing experience."

I have such an urge to push him off a bridge, and conveniently, we are crossing Ponte Garibaldi, water rushing into the falls below. I quicken my pace, hurrying across, and in a move so quick I don't see it coming, Tomas catches me around the waist, pulling me toward him, forcing me to look in his eyes. His voice comes out quiet. "Why are you angry?"

Funny how I never noticed, but his eyes turn from brown to green in the setting sun. I look away.

"What have I done that makes you not trust me?" He seems so focused on my answer, and as quickly as it came, the anger leaves me.

"Oh, it's not you." I sigh. "It's because of the way I grew up."

He tucks a piece of wind-caught hair behind my ear. "You mean, on salad?"

I start to laugh, and he smiles. "Tell me."

So I do. I tell him some of it, at least. All the times, all the people I had to leave without warning. The way I could never win my father's acceptance no matter how hard I tried. Honestly, my brief stint in jail was the only time I felt part of a structured environment. I tell him of New York, alone and homeless, struggling to survive in an industry of sharks. My vision becomes a blur. I turn away, wiping my cheeks.

"Cher, come here." He's frowning with worry, and then my head is resting on his hard shoulder. The tourists are staring.

"I didn't mean to make you sad, I'm sorry," he murmurs against my cheek.

But I'm filled up with a kind of elation. I just cried. In front of a man I hardly know. Like a normal human. And so we talk, really for the first time. He, too, grew up in a kind of a combat zone. Running wild, no rules, he got into fights outside while his parents battled each other at home. It explains, I guess, the ways in which we're similar.

When we part, I walk along the river, all the way from Trastevere to Piazza del Popolo, thinking. At my apartment door, I pause. It will be interesting. It will be interesting to see if he keeps our date tonight.

Later, when he calls to cancel, I'm not surprised. It's late, his flight is early, but I read through it all to the fact that today was too much. I'm a bit too much.

EVERY MORNING A bent old man pushes a wooden cart of my favorite sunflowers slowly up the street, impervious to the speeding cars. Leaning out my apartment window the next morning, I watch as he sets up on the corner, in his brown cardigan and felt hat, straight off an old-time postcard. When I answer my phone, it's almost on autopilot.

"Can I see you before you go to school? I think I can still make the airport."

Twenty minutes later, Tomas rolls up in the leather Ducati jacket I like and parks his motorcycle beside the riot of sunflowers. I buzz him up. *Oh, Bhajan, at least attempt to act cool.* In the tiny kitchen, I pour green tea into my one lone mug. We are silent for a while. Morning warmth seeps through the shutters into the shaded rooms. By noon it will be scorching.

"I've thought a lot about what you said," he begins, handing me the cup to share.

"Which part?"

"The serious part."

"Ah yes," I cover my nerves with a grin. "The only serious conversation we ever had."

He doesn't smile. "I kept thinking all night. I don't know if there's an expression in English that's really the same. But, mi dispiace."

"You mean, you're sorry?"

"Yes, but it's different. I'm sorry you had to live through that. Mi dispiace veramente."

I look down, because he still only knows a tenth of it. We are sitting on tall kitchen stools, our knees just touching, his hand on my bare leg. He leans in, kissing me, biting my lip lightly. When he breaks away, he takes one of the many pens that litter my counter, flips over the business card from a local gelateria, and starts to write. "I want to stay in touch. We can still talk, will you?"

I wasn't expecting this. In fact, I have been distracted by his muscles moving beneath that white T-shirt. I've been thinking that, for once, I want to remember someone, want his weight to press the memory onto my body. Accidentally, I seem to have brought him to the point where he is behaving too well, spending precious time earnestly writing down various video-call contact details. Maybe it's the fact that he is leaving that gives me courage; the fact that we don't really have enough time to go too far. Or maybe I'm finally starting to understand; not everything real has to be forever. Sometimes two people are meant to meet, but not to last—and that doesn't make it any less important.

Pressing my lips to his stubbled cheek, I say, "Take your shirt off."

He swivels the stool in my direction and raises his dark eyebrows in that challenging way. "Why?"

"Oh, just do it!" I laugh, exasperated.

Smiling, I take his hand. At first I'm leading him to the bedroom, then he spins me around and presses me back onto the white sheets. He pulls his shirt off the way guys do, with one hand and no regard for messing up their hair. For the first time, I reach up happily, feeling every inch of him on me. He sits up, knees on either side of my legs, in just his worn jeans. I want to pull him back, but he is such a picture. Tousled black hair, strong jaw, and the lean body of a fighter, with a long scar running down his chest.

He stays there for a while, memorizing, too, then he's back, kissing my neck, tracing the curves of my face. How strange, to understand, only now, that I've never been touched by someone who actually means it. In this, like everything else, honesty makes all the difference.

47: Luxembourg, age 28

IN LUXEMBOURG, ON February 6, the Superior Court of Justice overrules the prosecutor. The Ministry of Foreign Affairs orders that a *Heimatschein*, a certificate of citizenship, be issued in my name. Months later, it becomes official. I am entitled to full citizenship.

My footsteps echo through the quiet airport in Luxembourg, and I remember the day I arrived here with my mother. The automatic doors of the baggage claim slide open and I see her waiting for me, beyond the gate. We hug each other silently, disbelievingly, and drive to the Ministry. Standing in the office, still too slim but getting stronger, I raise my chin as the camera flashes. There have been a lot of photos taken of my face, but this one is my favorite. It's going into the passport that will be my own. I am no longer a ghost.

IN THE LATE afternoon, we sit in the garden, apples budding on the trees, my grandfather and I. He licks at a Cornetto while I sip my tea, legs thrown over the arm of a wicker chair. Nonna, one year away from her hundredth birthday, is attacking something in the arugula patch with a rake. "So, you are still wearing these hats meant for men," Bopa sighs.

Tilting my fedora back, I reach across and try to snatch away his Cornetto.

"I . . ."

We both jump at the sound of Nonna's voice.

". . . like her hat!" She hurls a weed over her shoulder and returns to the salad patch.

For a long while he looks at me, eyes soft but puzzled. It's ironic, the very things he appreciates most in me are those that would never have been allowed to flourish, let alone be encouraged, if he had raised me. My stubborn optimism, so at odds with his opinions, and the way I've decided to believe in tomorrow, despite it all. Life seems to be a long process of shaking up our convictions. So one day, a twenty-four-year-old walked into his world on skinny legs and threw a chair at everything he believed in. I destroyed his idea of our family, of the justness of the court system and laws he spent his whole life enforcing. But I've learned to respect him, because once I started being honest, he never blamed any of it on me. He paid for a good lawyer, he lurched to the courthouse with his cane, ninety-six years old, nearly every week. While I was in Berlin, while I was in the hospital, he fought for me to have the one thing he'd never given anyone: freedom.

It's never going to be completely okay between us. We still disagree on so much, but perhaps that's family. It's hard to realize they are just people, especially when they don't turn out to be the people you hoped for. It would be easy to waste a lifetime being angry at someone just for being themselves. My grandfather nearly did, and that has been his great lesson to me. So when people ask me about forgiveness, about whether I found peace because I've forgiven my family, I tell them the truth. I never did, or didn't.

Because, in this case, I don't believe forgiveness is mine to give.

During the years when I was so tortured, so sad, it was because I believed everything was about me. That something within myself—something unlovable—was causing people to want to inflict pain on me, to betray or abandon me. But if the universe has a center, I'm not it. The people in my family had deep issues and possible mental illnesses, and I happened to be there. In the crossfire.

With time, I can even see how often they tried their best, how I brought out the most they could give. For as long as they could give it. They didn't set out to destroy the girl they seemed to cherish. But when a person self-destructs, the shrapnel will tear your skin, too, if you're the one standing resolutely by their side.

So I don't forgive them, or not. Because I finally see it had nothing to do with me. It is something I lived through, it is the beginning I was dealt, for better or worse. This will not be my whole story. I have the ability, both scary and liberating, to shape the rest of my life. To create a sequel that is, for once, better than the idea from which it was born.

In a quiet garden, under the shade of an apple tree, the eternal cop and the daughter of a con man lean back and smile at each other.

EPILOGUE: Rome, age 30

I WALK THROUGH my own little apartment, the first I've actually decorated, and out onto the terrace. Resting my hands on the rough stone balustrade, I close my eyes. It's one of those summer evenings, warm with the memory of Roman sun and soon to be sparkling with stars. I look down over the terracotta buildings, over this place that has become a home. The towering pine trees, the *pinetti*, whisper in the wind if you listen close, their branches casting now-familiar shadows on the street. Sometimes it's hard for me to believe it was only a few years ago that I walked out of the hospital on shaky legs. I've never been back.

Of course the doctors can't explain it, and sometimes I still wonder. How I can wake up most days, one leg flung outside the white sheets, opening my eyes to the view of my wooden table and its flower pot on the terrace, and feel no pain. Feel my body strong and young again.

But there's one thing the doctors don't know, something I've only grasped recently myself—I think Crohn's disease saved my life. In reality, I was ill long before I became sick. Long before the outward symptoms appeared. But without the physical pain, I may never have become conscious of how wrong it all was.

I was never meant to be the cold operator I was being molded into by my father. At the time, it seemed like the only way to be, and so I fought against my instincts, against what I knew to be right. I may even have become quite successful at it. But that life, over time, would have been worse than any pain I endured in seven years of hospitalizations. Because our beginning, our first reality, is not our destiny. It's not always who we're meant to become. It's simply other people's idea of who we should be.

Not every day is easy for me now. Health and mental peace is something

I must work for, steadily and—most of the time—patiently. But for once, I don't have to do it by myself. When it's hard, when I have to push through, I have the people I was lucky enough to meet in Berlin, in Rome, and spread across a world I no longer fear. It is ironic that, after a lifetime spent dreading every moving shadow, every knock at the door, I was rescued by the kindness of strangers. They walked with me when I was sure I wanted to be alone, sat beside me as I cried, and taught me to laugh until the darkness became something I could face. My friends. My gang.

If anyone saw me now, climbing up to sit on the wide balustrade, hair loose and uncut, they would see a young woman. But I'm a veteran. I know that hurt and confusion will be inevitable if I am to be truly part of this world, as I learn to be a woman rather than just a warrior. Joining any party so late isn't easy. And there will be moments when sadness overwhelms me.

I can even comprehend now why my father and grandfather tried to control their lives, and those of others, so manically. It's terrifying to live with an open heart—to share it with others and not seek to lock them down. Life is sometimes, both the beauty and the pain, unbearable. It's just too much. And we begin to cast around for a way to hammer some certainty into it. It is tempting to live a life where you never get involved enough to get hurt, where you're always the one to do the leaving. But obsessively seeking to avoid pain, to avoid mistakes, may be one of the most dangerous things we can do. Craving dominance means you'll always be standing still, even if you travel the whole world, forever scared, even if you pretend there is nothing to fear. I watched two men do it for decades.

To be truly alive means to risk, to fall, to have your heart broken, and to acknowledge an inevitable truth. We can't possibly get it all right the first time, we wouldn't even know how. It is our darkest moments that build true compassion. It's failure that gives us courage, and scars that make us someone to remember.

Life will unfold in its own way, in its own time; we have little say in the adventure. We only have power over what we learn from our story, what we decide to make of it. The difference between heaven and hell is simple: It's not what happens to us, it's not what other people do—it's what we choose to hold on to.

FROM MY PERCH, I hear a sound and turn in time to see a flock of parrots, bright green and blue, so unique to Rome, sweep through the pine trees. They fly above my head and I watch them until they are just specks on the horizon, heading toward the ancient Tiber. Sometimes, in these silences, in peace, I'll think back, to the good and the bad. And to one memory in particular—because it's my first. It happened before the brakes failed on our family car. It happened that same Indian morning, just before dawn.

I'm four years old, standing in a mist so deep I can hardly see, up high, where the air is thin and pure. We haven't yet had the first chapati of the day, and I'm wishing Dad would take us on these mysterious odysseys at a normal hour. But I'm happy, surrounded by my family, unafraid of the dark. As the sun begins to climb above the Himalayas, my father's hand rests on my shoulder. Slowly the fog burns away, and all around, the world appears. It was here all along; Pakistan, China, Kashmir, stretching beneath us as far as I can see. More than two decades later, I can still hear his voice, and the promise it held when he knelt beside me. "That's the earth, Harbhajan. It's *yours.*"

For years I replayed my life, without really seeing, only trying to figure out where we went wrong. It hurt so much, and all I wanted was a reason. Even if there were beautiful memories, if it ended badly, the whole of it must be thrown away. It was all a lie. A horrible con. It must have been, because look how it turned out. But what I was about to discard, is a part of who I am. Those moments when I believed anything was possible are my core. My soul.

It may sound odd, but I appreciate my family for the start they gave me. My first seven years were a time when I was adored, cherished, and taught to trust in myself. They showed me the world, and taught me to move with it, they lifted me up on their shoulders so I could see forever. Everything that happened after, the terrible unraveling of them, shook my universe but was never able to erase the foundation they gave me.

I've so much left to understand. But one of the most important, the most priceless, forms of knowledge is something all the hard experiences forced me to discover. At a relatively young age, I know myself. Who I am is not a mystery, or something I must spend my life searching for. It is already here, within. Maybe it always was. And as I build my future, it won't be in revenge, or to show them up. For nothing born from anger will ever be worthwhile. I'll build from joy, from remembering what I knew in my very first memory—that beauty and love is something I deserve.

We were unforgettable, back then, because we belonged to no place— only to each other. Because we were brave, unafraid to challenge fate. In that little car, held together with chicken wire, we had so much to fear, and yet every day we chose to live without it. There was real beauty in us. It was real. It was true.

So no matter how badly things turned out, or how far I go, there will always be a place in my heart for the way we were . . .

On the road to Amritsar, under a sky of endless stars. A gang of five.

FROM MY TERRACE, the sky begins to change colors, rose and gold, so it's hard to tell if the sun is rising or setting. I let my bare feet dangle over the balustrade, hair tangled from the wind, and feel with relief how little has changed. How much I still feel like the girl who stood on the Himalayas and watched the world come to life. The most important things, I think we're sure of them quite early. Then life comes at us, and we get confused, we let ourselves be told that faith is naiveté, that dreams are for children. Often, we are told this because it's easier to mold a person who has lost hope.

The most complicated part of our lives—knowing ourselves—may be very simple. It's remembering who we were, and the way we believed, before anyone tried to strip our faith.

So when I go forward, it will always be toward that little girl in worn-out dungarees. To a mountainside, and the world waking with the morning sun.

On this journey to hell and back again, I've had many a name. But no matter what any passport says . . .

I am, and will forever be, Harbhajan.

ACKNOWLEDGMENTS

WRITING THIS BOOK was a ten-year process, and I would like to thank my agents, Larry Weissman and Sascha Alper from Brooklyn Literary, for reading the first one hundred pages, five years ago, and believing in it with such passion all the way through; and for being such lovely people. My deep gratitude to my amazing editor, Amy Gash, and the team at Algonquin Books for being fearless enough to take a risk on a book that was unlike anything they had ever come across.

Thank you to Elena Chronopoulou in Berlin for transcribing the handwritten pages of my manuscript with such efficiency and encouragement.

Finally, and with my whole heart, I would like to acknowledge a few of the very special people I met during the years I was writing. I wasn't able to include you in the story of this particular book, but you have stood steadfastly by my side and cared for me when I still didn't believe such a thing was possible. I'm mentioning your names in *alphabetical* order to avoid a straight-up gang war breaking out in the friend group.

To Massimo Arlechino for making sure I feel like part of your family and so safe at home in Rome; Thierry Bouffeteau for his dedication in convincing me that tomorrow will be better; Evan Firestone my rock; Jun Ichikawa for the beautiful lessons; Joar Jakobsson, who inspires me creatively and is so strong yet gentle enough to be my voice of reason; Muna Jibril for your wisdom and understanding; Derrick Jones my forever twin; Carolina Korth for flying across oceans when I needed you most; and of course, Varo Venturi for being sweet and crazy in the best possible way.

I know that you do not think of yourselves as heroes, but to me, you always will be.

Bhajan
Rome 2021